Digital Health

*Meeting Patient
and Professional Needs Online*

Digital Health

*Meeting Patient
and Professional Needs Online*

Barrie Gunter
University of Sheffield

LEA

LAWRENCE ERLBAUM ASSOCIATES, PUBLISHERS

2005   Mahwah, New Jersey   London

Copyright © 2005 by Lawrence Erlbaum Associates, Inc.
  All rights reserved. No part of this book may be reproduced in
  any form, by photostat, microform, retrieval system, or any other
  means, without prior written permission of the publisher.

Lawrence Erlbaum Associates, Inc., Publishers
10 Industrial Avenue
Mahwah, New Jersey 07430

Cover design by Kathryn Houghtaling Lacey

Library of Congress Cataloging-in-Publication Data

Gunter, Barrie.
  Digital health : meeting patient and professional needs online /
  Barrie Gunter
       p. cm.
Includes bibliographical references and index.
ISBN 0-8058-5179-8 (c. : alk. paper)
  1. Medical informatics. 2. Medicine—Data processing.
  3. Online data processing.   I. Title.

R858.G865 2005
610'.285—dc22   2004056291
                                                      CIP

Books published by Lawrence Erlbaum Associates are printed on acid-
free paper, and their bindings are chosen for strength and durability.

Printed in the United States of America
10 9 8 7 6 5 4 3 2 1

Contents

Preface   vii

1   Public Services Online   1

2   The Need for Digital Health   19

3   Health and Medicine Online: A Diversity of Applications   37

4   Digital Health on the Web   50

5   Digital Health Via Kiosks   72

6   Digital Health on Television: Early Adoption and Use   90

7   Digital Health on Television: Service Usability
      and User Psychology   112

8   Digital Health: Perceived Benefits and Health Impact   133

9   Digital Health: Public Confidence and Trust in Sources   154

10 The Future Potential of Digital Health   166

References 184

Author Index 213

Subject Index 223

Preface

Computing and telecommunications developments are extending and transforming the ways public services can be delivered to citizens. Technologies such as the PC-based Internet, touch-screen kiosks, video-conferencing, and, latterly, interactive digital television (iDTV) have evoked proposals for applications in governance. Support for governmental applications of information and communication technologies (ICTs) is often driven by pressures to reduce spending by exploiting the continuing fall in ICT costs and increase in their capabilities. This belief has led a growing number of public service agencies around the world to pilot a wide range of innovations in electronic service delivery (Dutton, 1996, 1999).

E-government initiatives are geared toward breaking down a digital divide between the new technology haves and have nots and to enhancing the overall effectiveness with which public services are delivered. Such developments are believed to be beneficial to democracies in an age when citizens have become increasingly politically alienated (Norris, 2001). In the health context, the provision of effective remote access, online information and advice services has been regarded as one solution to reducing the strain on public health services required to cope with an ageing population (Wetle, 2002).

As ICTs become more commonplace, not just in public settings but in private ones (i.e., the home), a growing bottom-up demand from citizens has been observed, especially in developed nations, as more and more people become computer literate (Pew Institute, 2000). One way in which this bottom-up drive to use online technologies for access to public services has been illustrated in the use of the Internet to obtain health and medical information. In the United States, for example, more than half those with Internet access (55%) reportedly used the Web to get health or medical information (Fox & Rainie, 2000). Across Europe, approaching one in four (23%) of Internet users said they had accessed health information online (Eurobarometer, 2000).

In Britain, a significant commitment to the provision of online health information has been witnessed with the launch of National Health Service (NHS) Direct services that have been designed to facilitate wider and more convenient public access to public health services using a range of old and new ICTs, including the telephone, touch-screen kiosks, the Internet, and iDTV. These services have been systematically piloted and evaluated to ensure that valuable lessons are learned as early as possible about their effectiveness and acceptance among the public, patients and health professionals.

Online technologies offer the capacity to communicate interactively and transactively in a variety of modalities—text, audio, and video. They can provide a dynamic communication environment that can, potentially, have a more powerful impact on the recipients of health messages than single modality, mediated presentations (Rimal & Flora, 1998).

Communication networks can also be established with online technologies through which users can interact with each other. Thus, as well as acting as repositories of health content for online consultation, such interpersonal networking can provide more direct support that may be emotional as well as factual. Live interactivity facilitates quicker feedback and a more dynamic responsiveness to users. Thus, online services can operate as mass-communication systems that provide content to large numbers of users and as interpersonal communications systems that cater to the specific needs of individual users (Kreuter, Farrell, Olevitch, & Brennan, 2000).

This book is concerned primarily with the provision and use of online health information services. This analysis of the roll-out of such *digital health* services, however, is considered within the broader context of electronic service provision. The book presents new data from research conducted within the United Kingdom on the use and impact of recent online health service projects. The evidence from this work will be examined alongside research conducted internationally—and especially in the United States—on the provision of online health and medical services, their use, and their impact.

Most of the research to date has focused on the Internet as a delivery platform. This is understandable given the growth in health and medical Web sites around the world. The full potential of digital health provision, however, lies not simply in the establishment of vast online databases that the public and patient groups can consult, but in the provision of remote, synchronous, and asynchronous transactional services through which users can interrogate medical and health professionals directly about personal health issues and the development of online support groups, especially significant for individuals suffering from stigmatised illnesses or health problems (King & Moreggi, 1998).

The emphasis on online provision of health and medical services in government circles stems from a growing need to provide widespread access to such services and to encourage population subgroups not normally in touch with their personal health status to make more effort to engage in preventive medicine and healthier life styles. Not only will this be better for them, it is also hoped that it will reduce long-term health maintenance and medical treatment costs that currently place a major financial burden on public-health services and private citizens in terms of insurance premiums. The effectiveness of online health and medical services, however, cannot be measured in terms of access alone. It also depends upon the ease with which citizens can utilize these services and the appropriateness of different online formats for specific remote transactions.

As the range of platforms on which digital health (and other public) services are supplied widens to include television, considerations of the usability of online services will become paramount. The mindset of users may vary with the platform. PC-based Internet users are accustomed to engaging with the medium in an interactive mode, whereas television viewers are not often disposed to work hard to find the content they desire. The TV is a "lean-back" medium, whereas the Internet is a "lean forward" one. To date, interactivity on digital television systems has been fairly crude and simplistic (e.g., choosing between different camera angles when watching a live sports broadcast), but even so only a minority of subscribers use such interactive functions (Towler, 2002). Hence, formative research is needed alongside the development and roll-out of online health and medical services to ensure that they are user friendly and application appropriate.

In addition to the usability of online health services, there are important issues related to the quality, authority, and reliability of the information they provide. Although online media can convey large quantities of content and provide an infrastructure for two-way transactions between citizens and service providers, consumers need to know how much these services can be trusted. Such issues of content authority and branding have already been considered in relation to the Internet, particularly in relation to news and health information provision. These same issues apply just as much to multichannel, interactive television. Indeed, users might be more likely to believe content they get from the television because television is the most trusted information medium (Gunter, 1987; Towler, 2002).

Finally, can online health services take the strain off health professionals? On the evidence collected so far, the jury would seem to be out on this point. In some ways, access to comprehensive, navigable online health information databases can encourage public and patient proactivity in finding out about health conditions for themselves. Although use of these information sources might displace pestering their doctor for some people, the better informed patient may also be more likely, on some occasions, to challenge his or her doctor's diagnosis.

This book explores these issues through a review of relevant developmental projects and research. In particular it will draw on the lessons of online information and transactional public services that have been rolled out over the past decade in different parts of the developed world, and especially in Europe and North America. Recent British research will allow some direct cross platform comparisons to be made in terms of patterns of use and user reactions between the Internet and iDTV. The lessons learned from the early iDTV applications in Britain will have relevance for other countries that are beginning to consider this medium as a health communications platform.

—Barrie Gunter

Public Services Online

Computing and telecommunications developments are extending and transforming the ways in which services can be delivered to citizens. Technologies such as the PC-based Internet, kiosks, video-conferencing and, latterly, interactive digital television (iDTV), have invoked proposals for applications in governance. Support for governmental applications of information and communication technologies (ICTs) is often driven by pressures to reduce spending by exploiting the continuing fall in ICT costs and increase in their capabilities. This belief has led a growing number of public service agencies around the world to pilot a wide range of innovations in electronic service delivery.

Some observers, however, have noted a growing bottom-up demand for online public-service access from citizens—especially in more developed nations—who are becoming increasingly computer literate (Pew Institute, 2001). One way in which this bottom-up drive to use online technologies for access to public services has been illustrated is in the use of the Internet to obtain health information. In the United States, for instance, more than half of those with Internet access (55%) reportedly used the Web to get health or medical information (Fox & Rainee, 2000). Across Europe, approaching one in four (23%) of Internet users said they had accessed health information online (Eurobarometer, 2000). In Britain, significant commitment to the provision of online health information has been witnessed with the launch of NHS (National Health Service) Direct services that have been designed to facilitate wider and more convenient public access to public health services using a range of old and new technologies that include the telephone, touch-screen kiosks, the Internet and interactive digital television. These services have been systematically piloted and evaluated to ensure that valuable lessons are learned as early as possible about their effectiveness and acceptance among the public, patients, and health professionals. This book is concerned primarily with the provision and use of online health information services. This analysis of the roll-out of such "digital health" services, however, will be considered initially within the broader context of electronic public service provision. Later chapters then focus on issues and concerns linked specifically to the online provision of health information and transactional services.

ONLINE GOVERNMENT AND PUBLIC SERVICES

Historically, there have been many attempts to modernize governments and other public institutions and make them more businesslike (Campbell & Birkhead, 1976). Governments at all levels have proven to be resistant to structural and technological reform. Institutions of governance have evolved through decades of negotiation and bargaining among conflicting groups and interests to balance a variety of relationships within and between governments and citizens. These social institutions are unlikely to be susceptible to change. There are understandable reservations about *e-democracy* whereby citizens take decisions about government by pushing a button or clicking a mouse. Despite the reluctance of many governmental institutions to embrace radical change, many are nevertheless using ICTs to change the way public services are delivered, as well as the ways in which citizens can interact with governments.

As major users of ICTs, government can make a substantial impact on their use and wider acceptance over time. For example, the U.S. General Accounting Office reported in 1997 that the federal government spent $350 million on Internet and related activities over a period of 3 years. The U.S. Telecommunications and Information Infrastructure Assistance Program (TIIAP) of the National Telecommunications and Information Administration (NTIA) provided $79 million in federal funds to support 277 projects over 3 years after its inception in 1994. These included start-up funds for innovative ways of using ICTs to provide better public services, enhance community cohesion and provide readier access to public information. In Europe, meanwhile, the European Commission has also emphasized innovative uses of ICTs in public services as have successive U.K. governments in the 1990s (Bellamy & Taylor, 1998; Hopkins, 1995).

Upon coming to power in 1997, the U.K.'s Labour government made a manifesto commitment that every individual, business and community in society should be enabled to enjoy the benefits of the Internet and e-commerce, as well as easy access to government services (Labour Party, 1997). This endeavor is not simply about getting services online, it is about government itself moving into the electronic era by offering most of its own services online. There has also been a growing concern about increased political alienation among citizens and low voter turnouts in major elections. It is hoped that new digital technologies may provide conveniently available channels through which the people can be politically re-engaged.

In this regard, the U.K. is by no means unique (Norris, 2001). As international evidence has indicated, information technologies can serve many different internal administrative and organisational functions for governments. They are believed to have the potential to enhance communications with citizens and improve the internal coherence and operational efficiency of central government departments, local government organisations, and quasi-autonomous non-governmental bodies. New online media have been identified as playing an increasingly central role in democratic communication in an era of growing public distrust of politicians and alienation from political and governmental processes (Coleman, 2000).

In Britain, the U.K.'s Labour government stipulated the target of bringing all government services online by 2005 (Office of the e-Envoy, 2002). Going online, in this context, included the use of a number of channels of communication. Telephone was seen as continuing to represent one primary route through which the public can gain access to those supplying public services. In addition, newer technological developments such as touch-screen kiosks, the Internet and interactive digital television were also highlighted as being likely to play significant roles.

Central government departments and local government organizations have already made significant progress in establishing Web sites. Even so, there remain significant challenges ahead in terms of equity of access. One of the key objectives of electronic public services is to achieve greater social inclusion and equality of access across different sectors of society. Yet, the people who often face the greatest difficulty in using online services are those who tend to show the greatest dependency on public services—those from economically deprived and older segments of society (Cline & Haynes, 2001; Norris, 2001).

Catching up with the times in the use of ICTs in governance is important if the public are to realize the opportunities afforded by tele-access in enhancing democratic relationships among all actors with society. Technological innovation in governance, however, is a complex undertaking. It entails a serious orientation toward change—particularly in terms of organizational culture (Siegel, 1999)—which is why it needs to be accompanied by careful and open consideration of the full range of opportunities and problems in providing electronic citizen access and digital government.

The spread of ICTs across and within societies is neither even nor universal. An international review of the distribution of online governance revealed a so-called *digital divide* whereby some regions of the world and some sectors of society had adopted online technology—most especially the Internet—more extensively than others (Norris, 2001). Analysis of government Web sites found that they were used in 105 out of 179 countries studied. These sites were situated mostly in western Europe, the Asia-Pacific rim, and North America. Digital diffusion was associated with national economic well-being, investment in *human capital* (i.e., training in use of IT and overall standards of education), and the degree of democratic development. Of these factors, the status of a country's economy was most significant. Controlling for this factor, the human capital factor incorporating the spread of the Internet and its use was the next most important variable in relation to the prominence of online governance (Norris, 2001).

CLOSING THE DIGITAL DIVIDE

The penetration of technologies such as the Internet and iDTV are known to vary within societies as well as between them. Even in developed countries, there are certain sectors of the population who are slower than others to take up new technologies and the services that may flow through them. This phenomenon of variability in the diffusion of technologies within social systems is well-established (e.g., Rogers, 1962, 1995). Individuals vary in the degree to which they are receptive to new ideas (Midgely & Dowling, 1978). Some people adopt new technologies early in their life cycle, while others wait longer before doing so, and yet others will never do so (Rogers, 1995).

The adoption of innovations is associated with demographic characteristics of population subgroups. Early adopters of new technologies tend to be younger, better educated, better off, and male more often than older, poorly educated, financially struggling, and female (Rogers, 1995). Some observers have also pinpointed differences in the psychological make-up of early and late adopters. People differ in their venturesomeness and willingness to try new experiences (Foxall & Bahte, 1991). Some individuals have stronger novelty-seeking motives than others (Hirschman, 1980). Regardless of individual personality and character, however, the adoption of new technology—and this applies especially to computer-related technology—depends upon the much more pragmatic matter of personal resources. In other words, can the individual afford to purchase the technology or pay an ongoing user subscription?

Socioeconomic status has emerged as the one consistent factor linked to computer technology adoption across a series of separate investigations with different populations (Atkin & La Rose, 1994; Dutton, Rogers, & Jun, 1987; Steinfield, Dutton, & Kovaric, 1989). This distinguishing factor between early and late adopters applies not simply to acquisition of the technology per se, but also to the use of online services provided through it (Garramone, Anderson, & Harris, 1986; Rafaeli, 1986). In addition to being better off, individuals with a higher education and with young families have also been found to display greater openness to new technologies and online services (Crispell, 1994; Mitchell, 1994). Thus, a higher discretionary income provides a base-level capability to obtain new technologies, but an open attitude toward innovation and early recognition of its functionality and usefulness further enhance likelihood of take up. Furthermore, once a new technology has been adopted, adoption of other similar technologies or services made available through new technologies may swiftly follow. The functional similarity of technologies can affect new technology expansion. Once consumers have crossed the psychological barrier of committing to a particular technology, it becomes easier to encourage them to adopt other similar technologies subsequently (Jeffres & Atkin, 1996; Lin, 1998).

The use of ICTs to access specific online services also varies across population subgroups within societies. In the online health context, for example, differences were found in use of the Internet for health information across the European Union between men (21%) and women (26%); the over 55s (26%), 40s to 54s (22%), 25s to 39s (26%), and 15s to 24s (15%); and between the lowest income households (28%) and biggest income households (24%). In the United States too, different reported patterns of utilization of online health information between men and women have been found. Women are more likely to seek online health information than are men. Women also worry more than do men about the reliability of online health information. Women were twice as likely as men to search for information for a child, although the sexes were equally likely to search for information for a parent (Fox & Rainie, 2000).

Top-down initiatives have been instigated to ensure that as many people as possible not only get online, but are comfortable and confident about doing so. In the U.K., the Office of the e-Envoy in the Cabinet Office led the drive to get the British population online. It has worked with central government and local government organizations in this respect. Its *U.K. Online* initiative was designed to close the gap between those who have most and least ready access to online services. From the turn of the century, U.K. Online centers were rolled out in local communities across the U.K. that offer free or low-cost access to online technologies and training in their use. These centers help people develop the skills to use the Internet to access information, to send an e-mail using a PC, mobile phone, or iDTV, and to explore the opportunities that new technologies offer. Many of these centers are located in public libraries and with at least 6,000 such centers in place by the end of 2002, an overwhelming proportion of people in the U.K. will have local access to the Internet, even if they are not online at home. The government's aim also is to get virtually all central government services online by 2005.

The U.K. Online citizen portal was initially a key part of the U.K. Online initiative. This was launched by the Prime Minister in September 2000 and provides a single point of entry for comprehensive access to all U.K. government information and services online. The priority in developing the site was easy access and simplicity. The portal's content was organized around the needs of the citizen, to make dealing with government as seamless as possible. Given the scale of government online business, a simple, one-stop entry point is vital. It has been estimated that the U.K. government conducts 5 billion transactions per year with citizens and businesses spread over 20 large departments, 480 local authorities and more than 200 other associated agencies. Together these bodies have more than 2,000 Web sites. For citizens with little or no experience of Web searching and equally limited knowledge of how government is organized, users need all the help they can get. Amidst criticism that it suffered serious shortcomings as a usable and effective portal to multiple government online services, the site has been upgraded and rebranded as *Directgov* (Johnson, 2004).

APPROACHES TO DELIVERING ONLINE PUBLIC SERVICES

The rapid evolution of online technologies has provided a number of different technology solutions to the problem of rolling out widespread access to usable electronic public services. The foundation platform on which most initial online services were developed is the Internet. This has offered a fairly cheap solution in the form of Web sites that have become accessible by steadily growing numbers of people in developed nations such as those in North America and Western Europe. Web sites can be interrogated for information, whereas e-mail offers a facility for more interactive and personalized online communications, albeit asynchronously.

Although, Web site access requires individuals to possess computer equipment with Internet access via a standard telephone line, other technologies such as touch-screen kiosks have been established in public locations to enable those who cannot afford to purchase such items to gain access to online public services. Touch-screen devices are perhaps best known in the context of personal financial transactions with banks. They have also been used in the context of online public service provision including online access to health information services.

Touch-Screen Technology

Electronic kiosks have offered networked technologies with easy-to-use interfaces, such as a keyboard or touch-sensitive screen, and can provide information in a variety of formats including text, audio, and video. Some kiosks are linked to external computer networks to provide wider access to information sources and other services. Kiosks are generally sited in well-used public locations such as shopping malls, libraries, and health clinics (Nicholas, Huntington, Williams, & Chahal, 2001).

Kiosks have offered a diverse range of applications. These applications include direct access to a wide variety of information from local and national government agencies, covering topics like jobs, health, and the environment. In addition to information search facilities, online technology can provide access to transaction services as well as static, off-the electronic-shelf information. An example of this type of service is Info/California, one of the first large-scale public systems to include transactions, such as requests for copies of birth certificates or renewals of driving licences, using electronic security checks to identify individuals. Another illustration of this kind of service is the Tulare Touch Welfare Advisory, also in California that offered consumers advice about welfare claims and payments and also provided videophone links to advisors.

In some cases, online technology has provided access to both public and commercial services. Project Vereda in Spain provided one example of this mix of applications. Its kiosks encompassed facilities for public service information and transaction capabilities—like renewing a driving licence—as well as private sector facilities, such as arranging a private insurance policy or booking a theater ticket with a credit card. Then there have been systems for individual agencies. Singapore Post's "automatic office" kiosk, for example, allowed the public to weigh letters and purchase stamps automatically. Ask Congress (U.S. House of Representatives) used multimedia kiosks to answer commonly asked questions and to obtain public opinion feedback. INFOCID (Portugal) offered online, including kiosk, access to information from government departments (see Taylor, Bellamy, Raab, Dutton, & Peltu, 1996). There has been widespread development and use of kiosks in the U.K. to convey health information to the public and to patients. Research has shown that kiosks attract a different user profile from other platforms, such as the Internet accessed via personal computer from home, and that users search different kinds of content on different technology platforms (Nicholas, Huntington, Williams, & Gunter, 2001).

The Internet

As previously noted, the Internet has been the key vehicle used for the carriage of online public services. Norris (2001) found nearly 14,500 government Web sites around the world, of which nearly 3,000 were national-level government sites. The densest concentrations of government Web sites were found in North America and Western Europe. In each of these regions there were more than 400 government Web sites per nation.

Web sites have been provided by central government departments and by local governments. As well as administrative government departments, Web sites have been established by national parliaments and by political parties (Norris, 2001). In addition, there are private intranets and list serves, developed by special and public interest groups, to disseminate government information relevant to legislation, court rulings, and reports, of interest to their subscribers (see Bellamy & Taylor, 1998; Dutton, Taylor, Bellamy, & Peltu, 1994; Taylor et al., 1996;).

Further analysis revealed that the government departments most likely to be online were science and technology, followed by finance and trade. Health was, in ninth place with 134 government departments online across the globe. Departments used their Web sites primarily for posting information. This tended to include mission statements, details about departmental structure and activities, and official reports and other documents. Interactive services such as e-mail links to key officials were rare (Norris, 2001). Thus, despite pronouncements by some governments (e.g., the U.K.'s) that the Internet will enhance citizens' access to government, the reality is that such access has so far been limited and on governments' own terms.

The Web can be used as a repository for the storage of large amounts of information. This is clearly a function that has been adopted by governments in their electronic government initiatives. This can be counted as a positive development in that citizens in nations where this service has become established now have more access to government information than ever before. As cross-national comparisons have indicated, those countries with greater online technology penetration have more government Web sites (Norris, 2001). The usefulness of the Internet when used simply as an information storage device, however, may vary across different public services. For some services, such as health for example, there is also likely to be a need for online channels to be open that provide synchronous interactivity between citizens and service suppliers. For example, individuals may wish to have instant access to direct and personalized medical advice from a trained professional. This kind of service represents a different kind of online service application from the online library concept that characterizes most government Web sites (Gunter, 2003b; Williams, Nicholas, & Huntington, 2003b).

Web sites have been widely established, but levels of public awareness and use vary. Two government Web sites stand out in Britain—those operated by the Inland Revenue and NHS Direct. MORI research in December 2002 indicated that nearly two thirds of U.K. adults with Internet access (64%) had heard of the Inland Revenue site and just under one in four (23%) claimed to have used it. Somewhat fewer respectively had heard of the NHS Direct site (53%) and had used it (13%). More than half of Internet users (53%) agreed that government Web sites contained useful information, whereas under one in two (45%) said that their local government Web site offered a good alternative to using the telephone when contacting a local authority (MORI, 2002).

Interactive Digital Television

A third platform has emerged in relation to provision of electronic public services. The attraction of television in this context is primarily twofold. First, it is a familiar technology. Second, virtually every household in developed countries possesses at least one TV set. The television has been regarded as a solution to concerns about technology roll-outs, access to services and service usability.

Traditionally, of course, television is a reception-only medium. It is fine for broadcasting information to large numbers of people. Unlike the PC-based Internet, however, television has not permitted viewers to interact with its content or to conduct two-way transactions, except in very limited ways. The emergence of interactive digital television, however, has changed all this. It offers far greater capacity for carrying content and permits genuine interactivity. Such interactivity is, as with the Internet, still dependent upon a wired service. This means that digital broadcast services—whether operating via satellite or terrestrial transmissions—must be accompanied by telephone links into the TV set to permit two-way, real-time communications transactions. Digital television services operating over cable or broadband telephone networks automatically supply the technology infrastructure for interactivity.

So far, there have been only limited experiments in provision of public services via television. In the United States, teleconferencing systems involving two-way interactive television have been used in the health field to bridge distances between health care professional and patients (Fishman, 1997; Jones, 1997). The emergence of digital television in Europe has encouraged the exploration of television as a platform for public service delivery, with countries such as Britain and Finland taking the lead. Once again, the earliest experiments have taken place in the health field (Nicholas, Huntington, Williams, & Gunter, 2003b; Niiranen, Lamminen,

Mattila, Niemi, & Kalli, 2002). In Britain, there will be a government-sponsored National Health Service television channel followed by one devoted to school teachers and education (Keighron, 2003). This book reports findings from research into interactive digital television (iDTV) pilot projects in Britain in the provision of health information and advice. These pilots tested the provision of health information in text and video formats, together with interactive services that enabled users to book appointments with their doctor or other health professionals, maintain their own medical records and obtain real-time health and medical advice and diagnosis customized to their own needs. Evidence emerged from research among users that television can reach people the Internet does not. Interactive digital television services were better at reaching poorer people who would otherwise have been disenfranchised by nonaccess to the Internet because they did not possess PCs at home. Furthermore, patterns of health information use on television differ from those observed on touch-screen kiosks in public locations and on the PC-based Internet at home (Nicholas, Huntington, Williams, & Gunter, 2001, 2003b).

Accessing Information

Online technologies have evolved to contribute to the wider availability of public electronic information. However, the presence of these new technologies per se is not sufficient to ensure that public information gets through to citizens. They must be able to access that information readily. As seen later in this book, access means more than the roll out of reception technology. Even when people have physical access to an online platform such as the Internet or iDTV, they may not always be able to find the information they seek.

Access means more than subscribing to the platform that carries an online service. Users must be able readily to find the service they seek among a multitude of other content channels and services that may also be available on that platform. Furthermore, the agencies providing the information must be able to do so in a cost-effective way. Commercial considerations may come into play here. There are financial incentives to shift valuable information from publicly accessible sites on the Internet, and to charge for users to access such material. As more content flows across the Internet, however, ownership of information will become increasingly difficult to regulate (Bekkers, Koops, & Nouwt, 1996). In the context of online health and medical information, users need to know with whom ownership of and therefore responsibility for content resides. This is because such information, when taken at face value, could have important personal consequences. Concerns about the quality and authenticity of information sources have led to calls for effective content classification and endorsement systems (Gagliardi & Jadad, 2002; Impicciatore, Pandolfini, Casella, & Bonati, 1997; Jadad & Gagliardi, 1998).

The cost effectiveness of online health provision is also paramount among considerations that precede their development and implementation. Cost factors relate not just to the resources needed to underpin online services themselves, but also the spin-off advantages versus disadvantages to regular (face-to-face) health services. One hope is that online health provision will cultivate a climate of self-help and preventive medicine that will take the strain off mainstream health services. Conversely, better-informed citizens may ask more searching questions of their doctors, taking up more of their time during consultations, with additional costs to health providers and their employers.

Online access can be used to improve the responsiveness of government and related public services to citizens. Two-way communications systems can be set up that enable citizens to communicate to elected representatives as well as to receive messages from these individuals. The e-mail facilities available to the U.S. President and British Prime Minister are examples. Despite these initiatives, reviews of government Web sites have indicated that few offer genuine two-way interactive dialogue facilities to citizens (Norris, 2001). In respect of government services, such as taxation, community services, and health, however, it is essential that effective and usable two-way interactive channels are offered that operate in real time. Content retrieval services or asynchronous two-way links may be inadequate in relation to certain types of citizen enquiry. In the health context, for example, although online technologies can enhance the widespread dissemination of health information in text form, they also provide opportunities for remote treatments or advice to be administered. These services can take the form of dialogues with health professionals or conversations with fellow sufferers (Grohol, 1998; King & Moreggi, 1998).

An example of the need for electronic public services to fully utilize the communication potential of the technology arose from an online experiment conducted in California. This experiment began positively but lost popularity when it curtailed its original range of online facilities. The Public Electronic Network (PEN) in Santa Monica, California, was an example of the potential value of online access at the local level. Although early signs indicated that it had improved the responsiveness of government to citizens' needs, the service declined as it became more oriented toward the Web and more focused on simply broadcasting information to the public (Doctor & Dutton, 1998; Hale, 1997). The use of interactive communications technologies simply as another broadcast medium is not only an under-use of the medium, but it runs the risk of disappointing users who have originally been led to believe that full interactivity will be available.

The PEN "electronic city hall" was launched in 1986 as a municipally owned e-mail and computer conferencing system operated, through which the city's resident's could use a home computer or one of 20 terminals in 16 public locations. The service allowed users to retrieve information about city services, complete selected transactions with the city government, and send e-mails to city departments about matters of local concern.

By 1992, PEN had more than 4,500 registered public users and averaged about 400 to 600 users every month. This service stimulated discussion on local public issues, offered access to key opinion leaders, encouraging people who might otherwise shy away from public participation to get involved in local government matters. Use of e-mail and conferencing links subsided in the short term after the service became more Web based and online interactions increased in their incivility (Dutton, 1999).

THE POTENTIAL OF ONLINE PUBLIC SERVICES

The drive toward electronic provision of central and local government services is often stimulated by a technological imperative rather than a clear idea about what the public really want. After the socioeconomic conditions of a country, the penetration of information technology has emerged as the key predictor of e-government developments (Norris, 2001). Although it may be true that many people are interested in these new channels of reaching government and public services, government sometimes has an unrealistic view of the level of this interest and of the competence of citizens to utilize interactive media technologies for transactional purposes.

Online access can create new forms of political dialogue among virtual interest groups and communities of interest linked through ICT networks. Many systems have created opportunities for public dialogue among citizens, with sponsorship from individuals, private, and nonprofit organizations as well as government. Thus, in addition to government-sponsored initiatives, there are many others that have sprung up with private backers. USENET groups on the Internet are one such example of this development that has provided opportunities for discussion of a vast number of topics across the political spectrum.

In determining the potential of online service developments in the public sector, it is important that governments study the uses to which the Internet and other ICT-linked services have been most popularly put. It is well established that e-mail is usually the most significant feature of the Internet for most users. In Britain, in terms of transactions, shopping and business-related activities are the most popular and then education-related activities follow on next (Towler, 2002).

Using the Internet to access the World Wide Web for information on various topics is another prominent form of use. In this context health has been found to emerge consistently as a major topic of enquiry (Eurobarometer, 2000; Fox & Rainie, 2000). A survey of European Union countries found that nearly one in four Europeans (23%) claimed to use the Internet to obtain health information. This tendency varied between countries, however, ranging from a high of around 40% of people making this claim in Denmark and the Netherlands to a low of around 15% in France, Greece, Portugal, and Spain (Eurobarometer, 2000). The same survey revealed that health professionals, such as doctors and pharmacists, were still by far the most important source of health information for Europeans and the longer-established mass media—television, newspaper, and magazines—still outperformed the Internet.

The potential of online service provision has therefore been indicated in the case of health, with the Internet in particular providing a source of vast amounts of static health-related content for interrogation and a channel through which individuals may be able to communicated with others on problems of a more personal nature. At the same time, however, it is clear that online technologies cannot provide a complete substitute for traditional health and medical service delivery.

THE POTENTIAL IMPACT OF ONLINE NETWORKS

Digital technologies can convey vast quantities of information to large numbers of people, much like traditional mass media. In addition, however, the computer-driven nature of these technologies means they comprise other important qualities. Their interactive and multimodal attributes enable them to operate as interpersonal communications channels capable of tailoring their applications to the needs of specific individuals (Skinner & Kreuter, 1997). This facility can be provided by the Internet and, increasingly, by interactive digital television. Users can become message senders as well as receivers. This transactional feature means that online technologies can not only provide larger health information libraries that users can interrogate, but also one-on-one support through live links with health professionals or other lay users.

Studies of use of online or computer-mediated communication systems have observed that the normal courtesies of face-to-face communication often can break down in this electronic environment. When using these communications networks, individuals may become more argumentative, angry, and ruder (Lea, O'Shea, Fung, & Spears, 1992). It is not unusual to experience a rapid escalation of insulting remarks between people when using e-mail (Dyer, Green, Pitts, & Millward, 1995). This phenomenon, which has been termed *flaming* when it happens in the online environment, is more likely to be suppressed or avoided in face-to-face conversations. Interpersonal communication via a computer network, however, is likely to be more open and uninhibited (Kiesler, Siegal, & McGuire, 1984). The normal etiquette of face-to-face conversation may not be applied when communicating via the Internet (Gates, 1995). This phenomenon is revisited later in this book. Its manifestation has been explained in relation to the absence, when communicating via e-mail, of nonverbal cues that add a greater richness to a face-to-face communication experience and that, in turn, may reduce opportunities for misunderstanding what another person means by their remarks (Kiesler et al., 1984; Sproull & Kiesler, 1991).

Proponents of electronic networking in politics have argued that the dilution of such social constraints could have a positive impact on democratic dialogue by empowering individuals who might be too polite or too shy to speak up in front of others at public meetings (e.g., Hiltz & Turoff, 1978).

In a health context, the greater openness and uninhibited quality of communications online could have potentially positive or negative consequences for users—whether patients, carers, or professionals (see Joinson, 1998). Disinhibition effects could encourage patients to disclose more about their symptoms to medical professionals online than they would in face to face meetings. Equally, expectations about online health information and advice could run high with users acting upon incomplete diagnostic information. This last point means that it will be important that online health information and advice are originated from authoritative and trustworthy sources among which concerns about patient well-being are center stage. In this regard, online health services will face the same challenges as do other online public or commercial services. Users will not accept or use online services they cannot trust (Bailey, Gurak, & Konstan, 2003).

ESTABLISHING EFFECTIVE ELECTRONIC PUBLIC FORUMS

A technological determinism has underpinned the rapid roll-out of online public services. Online communications engage users to become active participants not just in the sense of having a greater range of content options to choose from, but also to become content producers and suppliers themselves, just as they would be in face-to-face interactions where they contribute to conversation. The anonymity offered to communicants in the online environment, however, encourages them to be less inhibited than they normally might be in face-to-face encounters. For some individuals, this environment may induce them to be less constrained in the way they behave (Dyer et al., 1995). This phenomenon may lead to unpleasantness. As such there have been calls for the establishment of rules or norms of conduct in relation to online behavior. Although this may be a good idea in principle, in practice it is difficult to see how any system of regulations would be enforced.

With iDTV, another versatile information delivery medium could emerge alongside the PC-based Internet that may in the future permit sophisticated transactions to occur and do so within a transmission environment over which more central regulatory control may be possible. Within an Internet environment, there is need for voluntary controls to be adopted by service providers themselves. For some supporters of the Internet, however, any form of control over the Internet is contrary to its core principles when first established.

In some societies, one major difficulty in establishing controlling policies and practices for online communications via the Internet is the degree to which any regulation of a public electronic forum would be viewed as an infringement of free speech. This principle is protected by law in some countries, such as United States in its first amendment (Doctor & Dutton, 1998). This point has encouraged some governments to leave Internet content regulation to private and non-profit organizations that can censor users without the same legal restraints on violating a citizen's free speech. A second problem is the extent to which participants in electronic communities do not agree among themselves on the norms that should govern dialogue about public affairs. This has already arisen as an issue in connection with electronic news publishing on the Internet where a story published and uploaded in one country contravenes laws of defamation in another country (Gunter, 2003a).

The establishment of agreed norms of conduct are important factors in shaping communication on networks (Collins-Jarvis, 1992; Foulger, 1990; Kiesler et al.,

1984). The novelty of online technology, however, has meant that there is no consensus on what norms, etiquette, or rules apply to the new medium. E-mail, for example, is not exactly analogous to a letter, a telephone, or a conversation. The developing set of conventions and practices—a so-called *Netiquette*—among experienced Internet users indicates such norms could eventually be developed, at least in certain cultural settings. Working against such a consensus is the expanding population of Internet users, which will make the culture of the Internet more heterogeneous than ever.

EQUITABLE ROLL OUT

Unlike the private sector, concerns over equity create major constraints on the role of ICTs in the public sector. Shifts in the technology of political or governmental communication threaten to disenfranchise those who cannot enjoy access to online technologies because of their income, location, physical handicaps, or language skills. Many people will still be unable to utilize electronic government services unless governments themselves take initiatives to provide public access (Norris, 2001). The use of online technologies to achieve delivery of more efficient public services must not be implemented at the cost of inequitable access and utility of those services across different sectors of society. This might be especially likely to occur where online services can only be effectively used by those individuals with the technical competence to do so. The benefits of electronic public-service delivery must be available to all people across the social spectrum. Potentially, this goal is attainable, but consideration must be given to usability as well as to physical access (Dutton, 1999, Gunter, 2003b).

Although the development of new digital communications infrastructures can facilitate access to public services across geographically dispersed populations, not everyone is likely to benefit equally from such technology roll out. Not only will the physical availability of digital technologies vary between urban and rural areas, varying degrees of computer literacy among different segments of society will also affect eventual take-up of these services (Allen & Dillman, 1994; Dutton, 1993; Goddard & Cornford, 1994).

The digital divide that may persist even after government initiatives to promote use of the Internet has already been clearly identified (Norris, 2001). This divide may occur within nations as well as across them. Even developed nations with advanced ICT programs in the public sector still experience variable uptake of online technologies and the services that are conveyed by them. Research among TV households in Britain (representing 98% of the population) has indicated that Internet access varies significantly across age groups, as well as by socioeconomic class. Half or more of people aged under 44 in U.K. TV households reportedly at Internet access at home, compared with around one third among middle-aged individuals (45–64), and 1 in 10 or fewer among the elderly group (over 65 years). More than one half of professional and middle-class TV householders had home Internet access, whereas only one fourth of working-class TV householders did (Towler, 2002). Of course, it is sometimes argued that whereas individuals may lack Internet access at home, they may nevertheless get it at work. The same U.K. survey, however, indicated an even bigger socioeconomic divide here. Whereas one in four professional and middle-class individuals reported having Internet access at work, only 1 in 20 working-class individuals made the same claim (Towler, 2002).

Interactive digital television has been promoted as the emerging mass medium that can overcome the digital divide that characterizes the penetration and use of the Internet. Although most people in developed countries have access to television, in most nations, fewer than one half have yet converted to digital television reception. Although digital television offers interactive facilities, in the U.K., only a minority of digital television subscribers (15%) use these facilities. Those who do use interactive services on digital television do so only in a limited way (Towler, 2002, 2003).

One U.K. research agency has offered a fourfold classification of user engagement with iDTV services. These include the *oblivious* who do not know they have access to interactive services or have no interest in using them. The *curious,* who have explored some interactive services in a limited way but do not use them on a regular basis. The *brave* who use interactive services from time to time but still prefer other communications channels. Finally, the *enthusiastic* who use a variety of interactive services, use them frequently, and like to show others how to use them (Collinge, Gray, & Hall, 2003).

BARRIERS TO INNOVATION IN PUBLIC SERVICES

Inadequate government policies represent a critical factor in the failure of electronic public services to become established. The focus on technology roll-out often results in insufficient attention being directed toward human factors in relation to online service utilization. Are online public services user-friendly? Are they likely to be adopted by everyone, regardless of socioeconomic factors, education, and computer literacy?

Taylor, Bellamy, Raab, Dutton, and Peltu (1996) outlined a number of barriers to the effective development of online public services. Public-service organizations themselves must be prepared to change their corporate self-perceptions and their internal organization upon entering the online world. A failure to standardize online systems across different parts of large government organizations can create confusion among employees and outside users (i.e., citizens) and impede online service establishment. Single gateways that give clearly explained and readily manipulate access to varied online services have greater long-term potential because they encourage a degree of standardization, making locating content in vast government sites easier, and can potentially reach a wider base of user groups.

Some corporate cultures are risk averse. This means they are not comfortable trying new ways of doing business. Public-service organizations frequently fall into this category. Innovations in organizations are frequently pushed by "champions," but they may become demotivated if their own corporate culture is slow to act upon the new opportunities presented to them.

Overcentralization of government is another restricting factor because it can reduce opportunities for innovation at the local government level. Central government can overcome this problem by taking on the role of key innovator and motivator in this context. It can lead the way by developing electronic versions of its own services, by promoting the use of online public services, and taking appropriate steps to ensure that electronic services are user friendly and appropriate for their designated tasks. In Britain, this has happened to some extent, with central government forging ahead with their own online systems and, in some cases, coordinating and sponsoring similar developments at local government levels. Online health information and advice services have been among the most advanced and innovative systems of this kind.

Other factors include limited financial resources for introducing technological innovation and anxieties among staff caused by fears of employment cuts, job reorganization, and geographic redistribution. Suspicions may be aroused that cost savings are the primary driver behind online service development, and that more effective public-service delivery is a secondary factor.

It is essential that online services are not just user friendly but also application appropriate (Gunter, 2003b). The establishment of these services can be slowed down when their applications have been ill-conceived and plans for their implementation have failed to identify as key priorities the kinds of benefits that will occur for users (Gunter, 2003b). Online services, regardless of the platform on which they are provided, must consider a range of human factors associated with the use of interactive technologies through which access to public services might be obtained. The success of online services—public or private—rests on an understanding of user psychology and placement of effective design interfaces (Ratner, 2003). Failure in this respect could mean not only that existing online public services have a slow take-up, but also that a negative climate opinion toward any further introduction of electronic service delivery will develop. Linked to this issue is the reaction of citizens who do not want to be treated purely as customers or clients by public-service organizations, but perhaps wish to be considered as stakeholders in public services that they pay for anyway out of their taxes.

There are other potential difficulties that reside within the providers of online public services that need to be addressed. Although public-service organizations may be encouraged by central government to engage in small-scale pilots in online service delivery, scaling up from these to large operational systems can prove problematic. Once again, there may be resource issues at play here. Full-scale online services require adequate organizational resourcing. This means that staff must be available to maintain the services who have received the training required to do this job. The introduction of electronic systems, however, may also require changes in the corporate working culture because the online world does not operate in the same way as the offline world. Any online service-related developments within an organization must eventually be joined up. Serious problems may occur if different departments, local authorities, levels of government, and private enterprises have installed incompatible technology systems that do not talk to each other.

Within the context of online health-service provision, all of the aforementioned concerns apply. Digital health provision must be accessible to all regardless of demography, geography or technological proficiency. In the case of developments such as NHS Direct (a telephone service) and NHS Direct Online (an Internet service) in the U.K., a mixture of services are planned that will vary in the complexity of remote interactivity users will be called upon to engage in. They may eventually convey an electronic library of health information in text and video formats, online personal medical-records management, patient-to-patient support networks, online appointments-booking facilities, and medical or health professional-to-patient advice and diagnostic services.

There are also a number of strategic matters to be considered. In order to ensure that diverse electronic service delivery capabilities are harnessed effectively to meet overall goals, a coherent public-policy framework toward service delivery needs to be established. Such a framework would set out a clear vision that would provide a focal point for debate and action aimed at ensuring innovative electronic service delivery applications meet social as well as economic goals.

This strategic framework would coordinate telecommunications policies with those of closely related areas, such as regionalism, industrial development, employment, and regulation of the mass media. For example, policies that offer all citizens equitable access to vital facilities are crucial to gaining widespread commitment to online service delivery innovations. The framework would also seek to develop charging policies for online service applications that are anchored in principles that are defensible in the light of public service obligations, including provision for subsidized services. This could include guidelines on how, and under what circumstances, government information and services should be paid for by users. In addition, appropriate legislation and regulations could be developed in areas like editorial control over networked information, public access to information, privacy and data protection, and intellectual property rights (Raab, Bellamy, Taylor, Dutton, & Peltu, 1996). A clear distinction could also be made between the provider of information and communication technology infrastructures and the suppliers of information and services on them (Dutton, 1999).

In Britain, for example, an evolving media and communications sector, driven by technological developments, has caused a rethink of the legislative framework within which the sector operates. Traditional ideas of public service broadcasting are being challenged as mainstream broadcasters find their hitherto dominant market position undermined and eroded by a plethora of new players and a population of media consumers who demand greater choice and control over content reception. One alternative notion is that the public service broadcasting of the future could comprise the transmission of public services, such as online health rather than the transmission of programs of high cultural value as defined by a politico-socio-cultural establishment (Harrison, 2003).

Research in Britain indicated that, by early in the new millennium, penetration of digital television, with interactive facilities, had reached that of the Internet, but in far less time (3 years) and was likely to surpass PC-based online connections (Towler, 2002, 2003). Although much of the attention regarding online public service provision has been directed toward the role played by the Internet, there is a growing recognition that near universal public access to many such online services will ultimately be achieved via television sets rather than personal computers. If this thinking is true, then the successful roll-out of electronic public services will depend upon a different psychological orientation on the part of individuals toward a medium that traditional has not been interactive in nature. Despite its rapid penetration, as already noted in this chapter, only a minority of its subscribers acknowledge using the interactive features of digital television (Towler, 2003). In fact, interactivity was not the primary reason for acquiring digital television. Users were far more interested in expanding their range of television channels and program choices

Use of television as the key delivery platform may also produce different expectations about the provision and performance of online public services than would prevail in the case of their provision via the Internet. One reason for this will be that television already has a firmly established public image in terms of its trustworthiness and credibility and overall quality of content. The more open-ended and uncontrolled nature of the Internet may invite greater tolerance on the part of users in regard to the types of content that might be found there. During the remainder of this book, the provision of online public services within the domain of health is examined in relation to different platforms and formats. The aim of this exercise is to find out how much is known at this stage about what works and what doesn't, what is acceptable to users and what isn't, and to explore how far there is yet to go before digital health becomes a usable and effective reality.

The Need for Digital Health

◇

THE CHANGING POPULATION PROFILE

Many factors influence health information demand and the ways the public would like to have it provided. One of the most important factors driving governments to explore the role that might be played by information and communication technologies in health care is the shifting demographic profile of populations. Most significantly, people are living longer and the proportion of older people in the population is growing. Because it is this age band that demands the greatest amount of health care, this changing demographic has serious implications for the logistics and cost of future healthcare provision.

Sieving (1999) offered an American perspective. First, there has been a changing demographic profile in the general population that has brought the need to consider carefully how to organize healthcare to the fore. Specifically, there has been a marked rise in the elderly population (Walker, 2002). The increase in number and proportion of this older population has led to an increased need for medical information and more time to look for it and digest it.

Second, people are generally better educated and literacy rates are higher. These changes have increased the ability of the population to understand medical information and given people greater confidence to act upon it. Third, there is increased comfort in dealing with new technology with significant proportions of homes possessing personal computers with Internet access and growing numbers with interactive digital television (Klein, Karger, & Sinclair, 2004; Towler, 2003).

Fourth, there is greater demand among the public to be given informed choices. People prefer to have access to a number of information sources and to choose from a range of options in regard to service supply because they do not invariably or automatically trust governments. In Britain, for example, a series of food scares linked to salmonella (Cross, 1989), CJD (Leake, 2000), and genetically modified food (Nuttall, 1999) have generated public scepticism of the government.

The Aging Population

In major industrialized and developing nations, the aging nature of society has become a serious issue (Morrell, 2002; Walker, 2002). This demographic trend is generating greater effort to understand and develop new treatments for illness and chronic conditions. For society, the aging population is presenting a serious challenge in how to manage acute and long-term health care costs. Communicating to an expanding knowledge base about health is regarded as a critical part of developing and adopting strategies for an ageing population (Morrell, Mayhorn, & Bennett, 2002).

The number of people in Britain aged over 80, for example, is likely to treble and the number aged over 90 to double in the first 25 years of the new millennium (Department of Health, 2001b). This presents challenges for the providers of health- and social-care services, directed primarily at supporting older people.

In the United States, the number of persons aged 65 and older has been growing for some time. More worrying still is the fact that the percentage of people at the advanced age of 85 and older—those most at risk for disease and disability—is rising faster than the elderly population as a whole. In 2002, there were 4 million people aged 85 and older, a figure expected to double by 2030 (Wetle, 2002).

Older people experience an increased range of chronic conditions, many of which can affect their independence and ability to look after themselves. Meanwhile, even younger, especially middle-aged people, are increasingly focused on how they will cope in old age. There are financial concerns. But most significantly, people seek information about strategies to maintain good health and prevent disease in older age (Lindberg, 2002). Efforts to improve the general health status of older people have had some success. The United States, for example, has enjoyed a decline in disability rates among the elderly (Manton, Corder, & Stallard, 1997).

In Britain and across Europe, the largest group of users of health services are those aged 65 and older. In 1998 and 1999, this age group accounted for 40% of the NHS budget and 50% of the social services budget. This amounted to over £15 billion. This massive use of the health service by the older population was outlined in the National Service Framework for Older People (NSF; Department of Health, 2001b). The NSF outlined a framework for redirecting health care provision to meet the needs of older people and their carers. Emphasis was placed on independent home-based care wherever possible. The latter point was consistent with the wishes of elderly people indicated by earlier research that reported that 80% preferred to stay in their own homes for as long as possible (Department of Health, 1992). Given a further prediction that there would be insufficient numbers of informal carers available to look after frail older people (usually spouses or other relatives) and that those who did fulfil this role would need more centralised support (Nolan, Grant, Caldock, & Keady, 1994). This prediction is becoming a reality across the western world with older populations wanting to remain active and fully engaged in community life.

In economic terms, it was judged in Britain that funding for the care and treatment needs of older people would be better direct toward a more personalized service based around home and community care. Hence, care in the home is being promoted and an emphasis placed on the provision of information that older people and their carers will have available to them in their homes (Department of Health, 2001b).

It is envisaged that this approach will be further enhanced through the effective deployment of information and communication technology. Care in the home will be facilitated via integrated information systems that provide information for both service users and health professionals about local services available from public, private, and voluntary sectors (Department of Health, 2002).

Beyond the United Kingdom (as well as within it), the need to continue to enhance the improved health status of older people has been widely acknowledged (Morrell, 2002). It is important, for example, that the latest advances in scientific knowledge and medical treatment are effectively communicated to health professionals and responsible citizens. Causes of chronic disability among older people such as osteoporosis, cardiovascular disease, diabetes, vision and hearing loss, and cognitive impairment are becoming better understood. More preventive steps are being developed to reduce health risks—including advice on diet and exercise, and information about preventive health care and screening. More people are showing an awareness of the need to take control of their own lives and to cut down on or cease altogether high-risk behaviors such as smoking and excessive consumption of alcohol. In addition, people are becoming more receptive to information about how to deal with doctors and the health care system (Brown & Williams, 2003).

With the growth in the amount of information being produced and in the public's need to be informed, important questions have been asked about how all this information can be distributed and made accessible to different sectors of society. Although the traditional mass media have provided one set of communication channels that can reach large numbers of people, increased attention is being directed toward the potential of new electronic media, most especially the Internet and interactive digital television.

In Britain, the significant role that ICTs can play in providing an effective and economic solution for the enhancement of health care provision was underlined in another government report commissioned by the Chancellor of the Exchequer (Wanless, 2002). Major new media, including the Internet and digital television were spotlighted as channels through which people can receive more information and advice on the management of their own and their families' health. Such media can be used for health promotion and disease prevention through raising the public's awareness of important health-related issues and the provision of remote, personalized information, advisory, and diagnostic services (Wanless, 2002).

The Promise of Online Health Information

Technology has been deployed in health care since the 1940s (Brownsell, 2000) but tended to be manifest in fairly limited ways (e.g., community alarm systems to call for help). Rapid and significant technology developments have opened the possibility of more sophisticated health care applications. In Britain, technology is now regarded as having a key role to play in health care provision (Department of Health, 2000a, 2000b). A key assumption is that the expense of investing in technology is outweighed by improved care outcomes and in some instances costs may actually be reduced (Brownsell, 2000; Allen, Doolittle, & Boysen, 1999). Despite this anticipation, the application of information and communications technologies does not automatically bring with it a guarantee that cost efficiencies will be made. With ever-growing numbers of older people and increased expectations of health care among the population as a whole, considerable investment will be needed in upgrading care systems (Emery, Heyes, & Cowan, 2002).

Older people are not the only group of significance in the context of provision of enhanced health care services via online mechanisms. Families have an important role to play in health care at home (Nolan et al., 1994). Work undertaken as part of the European Union-funded ACTION (Assisting Carers Using Telematic Interventions) project identified the information needs of carers in carrying out their role (Berthold, 1997; Emery, 2001). Most carers tend to be volunteers and members of the family of those being cared for. Health information can be most effective when held by large numbers of people (Naisbitt & Aburdene, 1990). In this light, online health information systems have been envisaged as one integral part of the solution.

The National Service Framework (NSF) in Britain highlighted the importance of treating older people as individuals and making it possible for them to make choices about their care. The aim of the National Health Service (NHS) in Britain therefore is to facilitate empowerment of patients and, in particular, to help them to be involved in making decisions about their care and treatment (Department of Health, 2000a, 2001a).

Service users, however, will first need to have access to appropriate information that can help them to make decisions affecting care and treatment. The NSF suggested that this will include information about their own health, including assessment and diagnosis, referral, and eligibility criteria for procedures and services. In addition, service users will require access to information regarding the range of local health and social services available including financial allowances and benefits.

For all patients, and especially for older people, information needs to be delivered by the method an individual finds most useful (Department of Health, 2002). Many health care providers, social services, and voluntary bodies produce written material—although this needs to be updated regularly. One of the core principles of the NHS Plan was to provide information services and support to individuals in relation to a range of health care services (Department of Health, 2000b).

Growing use of dedicated telephone support systems has helped people who are isolated at home to obtain health and social care information that may be useful. Pilot studies in Britain (e.g., CareDirect, 2001; NHS Direct, 2001) provide users with the opportunity to explore new ways of obtaining information that can improve the quality of their lives. The advantage that these helplines have over many other forms of provision is that a user can participate in synchronous telephone conversations with health or social care professionals. NHS Direct is now widely accepted by the public and health professionals, but a smaller number of calls are received from older people compared with other population groups (Munro, Nicholl, O'Cathain, Knowles, & Morgan, 2001).

In addition, both service providers and voluntary bodies produced printed material containing information about health and social care that can be sent or handed to the client. This can also be an excellent method of information provision. The main disadvantage of this mode of delivery is the task of keeping data current, as it is necessary to reprint leaflets when the information changes.

Traditional forms of communication will be supported and eventually supplanted by electronic communications systems. The NHS information strategy paper, *Information for Health,* recognized the Internet as an important source of public access to health information (NHS Executive, 1998). In this context, two services have been highlighted: (1) the NHS-hosted online information service for the public (NHS Direct Online) and (2) an online service direct primarily at health and medical professionals, although also available to others, called the National electronic Library for Health (NeLH; Department of Health, 2001a).

The U.K. government also instigated a social care initiative specifically aimed at older people. On October 1, 2001, the Department of Health launched *CAREdirect.* This initiative aimed to provide easy access for older people to information about health and social care. It consisted, in its original form, of a freephone telephone helpline and local help desks. A Web site linked to local authorities has been under development that also provides Internet links to a range of appropriate online resources. These include voluntary and charitable agencies supporting older people, self-help groups and chat rooms all focused on those who are aged over 50.

CATERING FOR HEALTH INFORMATION NEEDS

What health information needs do people have? How have these needs traditionally been catered for? It is important to consider the nature of these needs in the context of how health information in future can best be provided. In Britain, when the National Health Service was set up in 1947, communication with patients was not given a high priority. During the last two decades of the twentieth century, a consumer ethic emerged in health care that was largely inherited from the U.S. Successive governments, during this period, placed a degree of emphasis on providing patients and the public with more information about their health. An early manifestation of this ethic was the NHS telephone helpline, known as the *Health*

Information Service, launched in 1993. In Britain, government policy emphasized the need for giving greater voice and influence to users of the NHS. This approach was embraced in *The Patients' Charter* (Department of Health, 1992) and *Patient Partnership* (NHS Executive, 1996).

With a change in government in 1997 after 18 years, the New Labour administration made a commitment to develop this consumer orientation further and to make full use of new information and communications technologies in doing so. In proposals outlined in a document titled, *The New NHS: Modern, Dependable,* the telephone-helpline concept was developed to include more sophisticated triaging mechanisms conceived in a report from the Chief Medical Officer (*Developing Emerging Services in the Community*) and rebranded as NHS Direct (Department of Health, 1997). This document provided a framework through which NHS organizations would become accountable for the quality of their services and included systems for safeguarding high standards of care (Vickery, 2000). The lay public were considered as important participants in this process, working with health professionals and their managers toward the goal of ensuring that decisions about care were patient focused and reflected the needs and wishes of those receiving health care.

Further impetus to this patient-centered approach was provided by the NHS document *Information for Health* (NHS Executive, 1998). This document set out a strategy for giving U.K. citizens the best health care in the world utilizing various communications technologies. The NHS Direct initiative aimed to provide a range of health information and advice services to patients, public, and professionals in health and medicine via the telephone, PC-Internet, touch-screen kiosks and digital interactive television. The idea was to develop a system through which members of the public and patients could obtain information on a wide range of health topics, seek professional advice or help, interact with other patients, be more informed when dealing with health professionals and better equipped to engage in self-care and to adopt a healthier lifestyle. In addition, there would be spin-off economies for the country's health service and the medical and health professionals working for it (Robinson, Patrick, Eng, & Gustafson, 1998).

Over time, NHS Direct has been developed as the public interface with the NHS, providing health information, advice on self-care, and guidance on the appropriate use of NHS services. From a core service comprising a telephone helpline staffed by qualified NHS nurses, the NHS Direct Online Web site (www.nhsdirect.nhs.uk) was launched in December 1999 to form a gateway to reliable, evidence-based patient information for patients and the public. Munro, Nichol, O'Cathain, and Knowles (2000) monitored the telephone service and found that call rates to the telephone "hotline" were continuing to rise, doubling during the first year of operation. Just under 5-million calls were registered during the first full year of operation.

Subsequently, online health information services were rolled out via a network of touch-screen kiosks located around the country in doctor's surgeries, hospital waiting areas, health centers, pharmacies, and other retail outlets. In addition, the provision of health information and advice services, including two-way interactivity between public and health care professionals and organizations, was piloted on iDTV.

UNDERSTANDING HEALTH INFORMATION NEEDS

Before the Internet and iDTV, health information was disseminated to the public by other available means. For instance, leaflets, posters, videos, and audiotapes have all been used for this purpose in the past—and still are today. The effectiveness of such materials in terms of satisfying public and patient information needs, however, was often unknown. It was not common practice for producers of these materials to pretest them to establish how useful they might be in promoting the public's health knowledge and awareness. In one investigation of this subject, various health information service suppliers such as voluntary organizations, drug companies and NHS trusts were asked about the degree of patient involvement in the production of their information materials. It was found that few had researched patients' information needs before they started (Coulter, Entwistle, & Gilbert, 1999a).

This apparent ignorance of the needs of the public and patients was a significant oversight. A number of studies had indicated that people have a range of health information needs and that these can become especially acute, not surprisingly when they are ill themselves or responsible for caring for those who are not well. Parents struggling to cope with acute illnesses in their young children have stressed the need for a wide variety of information that is both physically accessible and easy to understand. The topics that parents wanted information about included: how to gauge the severity of illness; how doctors assess illness; when to seek advice; how over-the-counter medicines and antibiotics work; the nature of rashes and viral diseases; and learning about other parents' experiences. Furthermore, such individuals turned to mediated information sources such as television, magazines, and medical literature to learn as much as they could about specific illnesses (Kai, 1996). Such research revealed therefore a market for media information about health even before the online world had become established.

Another exploration of patient information needs identified 12 distinct needs through interviews with patients, of which five were classified as being appropriate for mediation via remote forms of communication—offline or online. These five needs comprised: (1) gaining a realistic idea of prognosis, (2) making the most of consultations, (3) learning about available services and sources of help, (4) identifying self-help groups, and (5) preventing further illness (Coulter et al., 1999a).

A study of cancer patients found that they wanted as much information as possible and used television as a source of both general and cancer-specific health information (James, James, Davies, Harvey, & Tweedle, 1999). Digital health information systems would certainly have suited this group. Large volumes of information about health topics can be relayed through the Internet, touch-screen kiosks, and iDTV.

Another investigation of information needs among chronically ill and physically disabled children and adolescent revealed that these covered not just the need for factual medical information, but also emotional reassurance related to ways of coping with the disruption to their lives caused by their illness or disability. The need for emotional and social support underpinned a need for content that provided advice on self-help and also relayed the experiences of fellow sufferers (Beresford, 1999).

In a qualitative study of patients from doctor's surgeries, not related to any particular condition, Williams, Nicholas, and Huntington (2001) identified several information needs among a sample of women aged between 55 and 74 years who were interviewed while waiting in surgery for treatment. These needs included: to take prescribed medication successfully; to understand and provide reassurance about their condition and its severity; to cope with the condition; to understand and provide reassurance about the treatment of the condition; to help make a treatment decision; and to deal with or challenge a doctor.

HEALTH INFORMATION SEARCHING IN CYBERSPACE

It can be more complicated trying to assess the information needs of those not immediately affected by illness. Members of the public may require health information even though they are not themselves suffering from an ailment. Indeed, cultivating a proactive interest in health on the part of the public is an important objective of government and underpins the rapid roll out of online health information services. Taking an interest in health is regarded as a core aspect of wider adoption of preventive measures designed to maintain good health and avoid or, at least, to seek early diagnoses of poor health conditions.

The Internet has emerged already as a source of health information of growing significance. Indeed, health Web sites are among the most popularly visited sites via the Internet. Figures for use of the Internet for health purposes have indicated widespread use, but volume-of-use estimates have not always been consistent. Bowseley (1999) calculated that 40% of all American Internet users had sought health-related information on the Web. A Harris poll found that 98 million Americans had searched the Web for health content (Taylor, 2000). A later study estimated that 70 million Americans had used the Web to get medical or health information (Pew Internet & American Life Project, 2003). An international study by Reuters (2003) reported that on average 53% of Americans used the Internet to search for health information. In contrast to these findings, a U.S. survey by the Gale Group (2003) reported that 62% of respondents said they obtained health information exclusively from their doctor, whereas only a minority (16%) said they sought it from the Internet.

One in three Internet users surveyed across the European Union said they would be interested in online services through which they could ask for a doctor's advice. Three percent said they would be prepared to pay 10 euros a month for such a service (Eurobarometer, 2000). The promise of the Internet in a health context is further supported by statistics confirming increased used of the medium by older people. Across Europe, the biggest users of health information on the Internet were people older than 55 and between 25 and 39 (Eurobarometer, 2000). The latter age group was significantly represented by parents, probably seeking health information on behalf of their children.

Internet survey company Net Value (2002) reported that Internet use by people aged 55 and older in the U.K. has increased by nearly 90% between March 2001 and February 2002. A U.S. study indicated that by the beginning of the millennium, more than 6 in 10 (63%) of people aged 50 to 64 years had used the Internet to find health information (Metcalf, Tanner, & Coulehan, 2001). The same study also suggested that older people look for online health and health care information to help them to maintain their independence, whereas carers sought information about resources that might assist them.

Cyber Dialogue (2000) found that approximately one half of all Internet using health information seekers advised a family member or friend to see a doctor, changed their exercise or eating habits or made a positive decision related to their health treatment. A rather mixed bag of information needs was revealed in these results, with seekers looking for information on behalf of others, to improve their general health or to decide on the next steps they should take with regard to a current condition. Many others joined an illness support group after visiting a disease-specific Web site.

Nicholas, Huntington, and Williams (2001a) found that people used an Internet health site to be better informed and to help change the way they felt about a condition. This was particularly true for those searching on someone else's behalf. This implied that users may have been using information for peace of mind and reassurance. Once again, there were indications that health information needs go beyond purely factual ones. The need for emotional support can often be of paramount importance and may, in the absence of face-to-face meetings, be facilitated by electronic communications links. In particular, access to and participation in online chat for a can supply a welcome source of emotional support as well as an opportunity to share in up-to-date clinical information (Gann, 1998).

Users of online health information services have been found to exhibit a focused and deep interest in information only about their specific condition or disease. They do not regularly surf the Web for general health-related material, but instead visit sites offering specific information. Those individuals who are more actively involved in their diagnosis and treatment decisions are more likely to use the Internet as a resource for information (Boston Consulting Group, 2001; Poensgen & Larsen, 2001). When highly motivated by a specific health condition, online searchers have proved to be resilient and will seek out all the information they can on a specific subject, including that available on sites designed for health and medical professionals (London, 1999). Some professional sites have been found to solicit heavier use by lay consumers than by health care workers (Eysenbach & Diepgen, 1999).

Nonusers and Information Avoiders

Of course, there remain those who eschew new media. Late adopters of information and communications technologies such as the Internet are likely to be disproportionately represented by older people (Morrell, Mayhorn, & Bennett, 2002; Withey, 2003). As an expanding sector of the population, technologies such as the Internet can provide a variety of benefits to older individuals, including improved access to information, enhanced communications capabilities, and increased independence. Research in the U.S. suggested that potential barriers to the uptake of new media by older people include their perceptions that computers are too complicated to use and that they lack the necessary technical skills to use the Internet (Vastag, 2001). However, other observers have noted that while older people may have less experience and encounter more difficulties with computer-mediated communications than younger people, they are nonetheless often willing and able to use computers (Czaja & Lee, 2003).

It is also important, once new users of communications technologies have been acquired, not to lose them. One crucial factor in this regard is new users' degree of satisfaction with services provided through communications technologies. Satisfaction stems from being readily able to access the information being sought, the degree to which that information comprehensively answers the questions users have asked, and the degree of authority and credibility attached to that information (Bray, Lovelock, & Philp, 1995; Heathfield, Pitty, & Hanka, 1998).

There are specific problems associated with particular groups of users of online services. The aging process, for example, is associated with changes in perceptual, cognitive, and motor functions. Visual acuity, contrast sensitivity, color perception, and ability to adapt to lighting changes may decline. Hearing abilities typically decline with age too, resulting in difficulties with high frequencies, understanding speech, and locating the source of sounds (Mead, Lamson, & Rogers, 2002). There are further age-related difficulties that can occur in cognition, affecting attention span, memory capacity and the length of time taken to complete certain mental tasks (Park, 1992). Motor skills may deteriorate affecting hand-eye coordination (Rogers & Fisk, 2000), with knock-on effects on ability to use standard input keys and mouse (Smith, Sharit, & Czaja, 1999).

Similar issues were highlighted in U.K. research into the potential market for digital television. This medium has been envisaged as a platform for delivery of electronic government services in the future. However, even basic-level functions associated with digital television, such as channel selection, use of the electronic program guide and making video recordings, can cause serious problems for people who suffer visual, hearing, dexterity, and cognitive impairments. Such findings have raised important questions about interface designs and service configurations many of which have implications for users in general (Klein, Karger, & Sinclair, 2003).

Thus, although much attention has focused on the spread of the Internet, it is equally important to examine usability factors that may affect longer term commitment to use interactive technologies once access has been obtained (Sears, 2003).

In the medical field, nonuse of health information is not universally regarded as a bad thing. In relation to some conditions, such as cancer, patients' attitudes to information provision and coping strategies can vary. Some people want to know everything, whereas others find that ignorance is better for them (Leydon et al., 2000). It is not invariably the case therefore that information is beneficial to health; sometimes it may represent a barrier to coping. Medical professionals can play an important role as information filters and can control patient uncertainty through selective disclosure of information. With some serious conditions, sufferers may seek out only that information that maintain their hopes. Elsewhere, research has shown that the great majority of cancer patients said they want as much information as possible (James et al., 1999).

In effect, there are different types of patient. There are those who prefer knowing as much as possible and those who avoid being in this position, and for whom no news is good news (Pinder, 1990). There may also be conflicting opinions between health professionals and their patients in respect of the ability of patients to utilize information effectively. Doctors may display little confidence in the ability of their patients to assimilate more than small amounts of health information, let alone to act effectively upon it. Patients, in contrast, may argue that they know how they feel and, with chronic conditions such as asthma, they have a good idea about the conditions that trigger attacks (Jones et al., 2000). In addition to nonuse of information, cases of noncompliance may also occur. Under these circumstances, patients welcome information on their condition, but do not necessarily agree with their doctors' treatment prescriptions (Dervin, Harpring, & Foreman-Wernet, 1999).

Other information needs research has indicated that people often display selective information seeking behaviors. They will consult with sources perceived to be relevant to their needs (Nicholas, 2000). Whether they act upon the advice given can depend upon the authority and credibility they attach to particular sources.

ENSURING SATISFACTION ONLINE

If user satisfaction is the key to capturing their loyalty to new information and communications technologies in the health care sphere, it is vital that online health information systems understand their users' needs and also the wider context in which health information is sought. It has already been noted that individuals can display a variety of health information needs. Need profiles vary across individuals and may shift even for the same individual depending upon his or her particular circumstances. Hence, health information seeking among healthy individuals may differ quite radically in nature from that observed among individuals who are suffering from an illness or disability (Cline & Haynes, 2001; Huntington, Nicholas, & Williams, 2003a).

An understanding of principles and attributes of health information seeking more generally should be seen as fundamental therefore to the design and implementation of online health information systems. Indeed, although the focus has usually been centered on "seeking" information, there are other information-related activities that may be just as profound in their impact upon the use of online health information services. On some occasions, individuals may seek health information, but on others they may seek to avoid it. On certain occasions, individuals may act as health information "providers," whereas on other occasions, they may wish to "appraise" health information (and its sources) or "interpret" it (or have it interpreted for them; Brown & Williams, 2003).

Health information can be used to decrease uncertainty, especially when the individual is faced with an actual or threatened ailment that causes them distress. However, health information sources can be used to achieve the converse effect of increasing uncertainty in order to promote hope and optimism. Thus, if an individual is diagnosed with an illness over which there is disagreement concerning its seriousness, such uncertainty may be preferable to the finality of a single, pessimistic assessment. Yet again, avoidance of information can allow individuals, who suspect or know they have a complaint, to circumvent learning of its true nature, especially where there is a possibility that the news may not be good (Brashers et al., 2000). People avoid diagnostic information that might help them determine the meaning of symptoms. For example, people often delay getting treatment for myocardial infarction despite warning signs (Alonzo & Reynolds, 1998).

A person who is healthy (without signs or symptoms of illness) may avoid information to prevent anxiety if risk awareness calls into question the person's health or potential for disease (Brashers, 2001). Clearly, this last tendency conflicts with government-led projects to utilize online health services in the context of cultivating a more health-conscious society that emphasizes prevention over cure. These features of health information-related behavior may have important implications for the utilization of online health information systems. Information seeking and avoiding may be a balancing act for individuals who need to achieve multiple goals, such as reducing uncertainty, improving or sustaining health, and maintaining optimism.

Information seeking also needs to be studied in the context of networks of interpersonal relationships, such as those embracing family, friends, and health care providers. Health information can service needs beyond the simple instrumental need for factual medical knowledge. Information about health and health care may have a coping function. Individuals who are unwell need social support and emotional reassurance as well as clinical diagnosis. Although online channels may prove to be adequate for the servicing of basic informational needs (i.e., to know the facts of a matter), they may been less satisfactory than interpersonal support channels in the socioemotional sphere. Although, research on computer-mediated communications has indicated that users can successfully develop emotional relationships remotely and that these can be as intense in their own way as face-to-face interactions (Walther, 1996).

For diagnostic purposes, people generally need to see their physician. They need information about the etiology of a disease and their prognosis or treatment options. They may also need to be told what will happen to them or how they will feel in order to understand and make sense of their ailment and the medical treatment normally applied to it (Garvin, Huston, & Baker, 1992). These issues can be effectively dealt with via discussion with the appropriate health professional. In a face-to-face setting, the patient can ask a variety of questions and receive an immediate response and obtain factual information and emotional reassurance at the same time. Although this face-to-face interaction can be modeled in a synchronous (two-way) online communications format (e.g., telephone call or live video link), in situations where the individual is under some distress, remote links are likely to prove less satisfactory than face-to-face interaction.

Another health-related activity might be to seek information to establish risk of illness and ways to prevent it. Once again, lay persons might turn to authoritative professional sources for this information, or they might also rely on family and friends. Although face-to-face interactions might again be sought, with this type of health-related information activity, it is possible to envisage a more significant role for information and communications technologies. Online text or video information systems may prove to be more than satisfactory both for general enquiries and for information seeking of a more personal nature.

Mediated information sources are already utilized by the public for health information. Television programs and magazine and newspaper articles on health topics are widespread and frequently occurring (Johnson, 1997). The World Wide Web now offers an even more substantial resource capable of storing vast quantities of content on a huge range of topics (Borzekowski & Rickert, 2001). In addition, listserves, newsgroups and chat rooms provide information and help with interpreting and appraising it. There is also an important socioemotional function that can be served by these more interactive and interpersonal aspects of the Internet. The significance of emotional support to those suffering from chronic ill health has been established in the offline world (Burleson & Goldsmith, 1998; Dakof & Taylor, 1990). People who benefit from these online support groups include those with stigmatized illnesses (because they might find it difficult to attend a face-to-face group) or people with relatively rare diseases who do not know other people with the illness (Davison, Pennebaker, & Dickinson, 2000).

One major survey of Internet users in the United States in 2000 found that the Web was utilized for health information for general enquiry purposes and to satisfy more specific, personal health concerns. Most users went to health Web sites for research and reference purposes. Few used it to communicate with their care-givers or to buy medicine (Fox & Rainie, 2000). At that time, these findings were interpreted to cast doubt on the potential of the Internet to cater effectively to a wider range of health-care activities online such as filling prescriptions, filing claims, participating in support groups or e-mailing doctors. In fact, in the same survey, 9% of health seekers reportedly communicated with a doctor online, 10% purchased medicine or vitamins online, 10% described a medical condition or problem in order to get advice from a doctor online, and 21% provided their e-mail address to a Web site, whereas 17% provided their name or other personal information.

SELF-HELP ONLINE

Online technologies open up new opportunities for citizens to engage in self-help. This outcome is regarded as a key aspect of consumer empowerment. A communications system that is readily available and through which individuals can connect with others who have similar interests or concerns may prove a valuable source of support. E-mail links can connect users to distant friends and relatives, which allows them to develop and maintain larger social networks. Individuals can use such networks to share health information of benefit to themselves or to others. Although the majority of health information seekers go online to get information about a specific medical problem, many seek such information on behalf of others as much as for themselves (Fox & Rainie, 2000).

E-mail can also provide a direct link to health care providers who can be consulted remotely (Spielberg, 1998). The usefulness and appreciation of this kind of facility may depend on the way it is used. In this respect, there may be some lessons to be learned from health information seeking in the offline world. One factor that affects the usefulness of health information offered by members of a social network is whether the recipient of informational support sought the information or wished to avoid it. Of special significance here is the way the individual may have previously communicated their wishes in this respect. In the world of face-to-face communication, an information avoider may have made their position quite clear to family and friends. In the online world, this may not happen in quite the same way. Advice about everyday problems has been rated by individuals as more respectful and caring when it was delivered in response to a request for advice (Goldsmith, 2000).

There is clear evidence that the Internet and other online health information sources may be used in combination with face-to-face meetings with health professionals. Patients often do not know what questions to ask doctors about their symptoms and their causes. Online health information sources are often consulted before or after visits to the doctor. This pattern has been found with the use of Web sources (Fox & Rainie, 2000) and with iDTV health information services (see chap. 8, this volume). As the next chapter examines in more detail, self-help online can also take the form of networks of patient to patient support groups. Such groups can arise spontaneously among individuals suffering from the same condition, although sometimes they are convened by health professionals. Either way, the Internet can provide a forum for the sharing not simply of clinical information, but also of personal experiences.

Early signs are that there is a market potential for online support group applications. Cyber Dialogue (2000) calculated that one in four health information seekers joined a support group. Online support groups provide an alternative to face-to-face support groups and also supplement professional help. They can allow for shared experiences with other sufferers or victims, no matter how geographically dispersed such individuals might be. The support that can be obtained is emotional as well as clinical, and can have positive benefits for participants

(King & Moreggi, 1998). Users have even been known to rate support groups more highly than professional help on many nonclinical criteria, and even on some clinical ones (Davison, Pennebaker, & Dickerson, 2000).

ONLINE DIAGNOSTICS

Another significant aspect of online health care provision is telemedicine. This comprises medical consultations by text, audio, or video links and provides opportunities for patients to consult with health professionals who they might otherwise have difficulty locating (Mun & Turner, 1999). Such links can be used for patient–professional, professional–professional and patient–patient communications.

E-mail can be used to facilitate rapid remote transfer of medical diagnostic information between health professionals (Della Mea, 1999). A health professional working in one location can seek advice remotely from a consultant situated elsewhere through an Internet link. A number of examples of such remote consultations have already been observed in real life clinical practice. Such remote links between health professionals can use simple text or more complex multimedia formats (incorporating images) to facilitate information transference (Bellon, Van Cleynenbruegel, Delaere, et al., 1995; Buntic et al., 1997; Provost, Kopf, Rabinovitz, et al., 1998; White, Gould, Mills, & Brendish, 1999).

Personal medical information about specific patients can be communicated via e-mail from a remote doctor's surgery to a hospital where a specialist consultant is based (Fredriksen, Pettersen, & Pedersen, 1997). Another arrangement within which telemedicine has been applied is inside a networked health-care system (Branger & Duisterhout, 1995).

The Internet has also been acknowledged as providing an important research tool in the medical field. This application does not simply take the form of using the "Net" to search for information, but also to collect original data from patients and the public via online questioning (Houston & Fiore, 1995).

Online support groups have tended to be associated with particular medical conditions or illnesses. The evidence on their effectiveness is mixed and depends upon how *help* is operationally defined. Benefits can often be psychological as much as physical. This is especially true of illnesses that are fatal and incurable. There are occasions, however, when emotional support is central to the concerns and needs of users. One study of an Internet self-help group for the physically disabled who sought emotional support more than anything else reported that online communication was valued as highly as face-to-face contacts (Finn, 1999).

There is a need also to consider the implications of online health services for patients' relationships with medical and health professionals. Both these parties have specific goals. In a health care encounter, doctors and patients are both seeking and providing information. Doctors need to elicit information from patients about symptoms and potential causes of illnesses, and patients elicit information from doctors about their health status and treatments when ill. Typically, this is an asymmetrical information exchange, with doctors asking the most questions and patients providing most of the information (McNeilis, 2001). The degree to which medical information is exchanged can vary with the type of patient. Doctors have been observed to differentiate between patients on the basis of their personal characteristics and respond to them differently (Beiseeker, 1990; Waitzkin, 1985). Younger and better educated patients may extract more information from doctors because of their communication styles. Less well-informed patients who display poorer abilities to articulate their needs and concerns may experience a poorer information yield from their doctor (Geist & Hardesty, 1990; Street, 1991).

There is further evidence of confusion that might exist between doctor and patient and hence disrupt the quality of information exchanges between them. Doctors may overestimate how much information patients already have about their condition (Guttman, 1993). Patients and health professionals may have different ideas about what kinds of information are needed in a particular diagnostic situation (Hines, Babrow, Badzek, & Moss, 2001). In addition, health professionals may have difficulty explaining things in a way that is clearly understood by patients (Bogardus, Holmboe, & Jekel, 1999).

There have been other signs that patients with access to online health information may place health professionals under greater stress by confronting them with a barrage of information about health conditions and treatments. Health professionals are either called upon to interpret complex online health content for patients or to explain discrepancies between the advice they provide and that found on the Internet or via some other online source (Eng & Gustafson, 1999; Lamp & Howard, 1999).

Eysenbach and Diepgen (1998) explored the attitude and reaction of physicians and other medical information providers toward unsolicited e-mail from patients, by e-mailing them information requests about fictitious acute medical problems. Half the medical professionals who were contacted replied. Some of these refused to give advice without personal contact; others recommended that the patient see a physician, and still others actually gave the correct diagnosis in their reply. Although no incorrect diagnoses were given, and most respondents (93%) recommended face-to-face contact, the researchers nevertheless concluded that approaches to handling unsolicited e-mail were so varied that formalized standards for physician response to such patient e-mails were needed.

The provision of readily accessible health information via online sources could change the doctor-patient relationship. As discussed later in this book (chap. 7, this volume), users of health information services on digital interactive television have reported consulting these services before and after visits to their doctor. They were regarded as useful from the perspective of informing them about their condition such that they could ask more searching questions of the doctors. Thus, not only were these services perceived as useful information sources in their own right, they had an additional functionality in enhancing the quality of information exchange between patient and doctor.

Research has shown that social support, doctor–patient relationships and the management of patients' uncertainty about health must all be considered within a wider social and cultural context (Goldsmith, 2001; Goodwin & Plaza, 2000). Cross-cultural factors can add further complications to the way health information seeking is carried out (Baldwin & Hunt, 2002; Goldsmith, 2001). In some cultures, such as the family-centered societies of the Chinese, Vietnamese, and Ethiopian cultures, the responsibilities for information control and decision making are often assumed by family members rather than by individual patients (Beyene, 1992; Kaufert, Putsch, & Lavallee, 1999). When individuals from these kinds of cultures are involved in health care interactions in countries such as Britain and the United States, information exchanges can involve a complex set of communications involving health care providers, patients, patients' families, and sometimes, interpreters (Kaufert & Putsch, 1997; Kaufert et al., 1999). In developing online health information and advice services, therefore, it cannot be assumed that specific online formats will prove to be equally effective across different cultural groups.

CONCLUSION

Changing population profiles and the rapid development of communications technologies have together encouraged governments to explore the role that online communications might play in future provision of health care. The Internet has quickly emerged as a major source of health information. Most Internet users have visited health and medicine Web sites. Increasingly, the interactive capability of the Internet has been utilized by groups with specific medical conditions, not simply to obtain information, but also to gain emotional support.

The appeal of the Internet as a health information source is based on a number of factors. It provides a convenient information source that is readily available around the clock. It offers a larger quantity of information on a more diverse range of health topics than any other single information source. It also provides an anonymous enquiry source through which users can get information without having to talk to anyone about it. This last feature is especially important when trying to obtain information on sensitive health topics (Fox & Rainie, 2000).

The continuing appeal of the Internet as an information source will probably depend upon the degree to which certain standards are maintained. This point probably also applies to other online health information services. There are two particular areas of concern that are mentioned by most users of medical Web sites: violation of privacy and accuracy of information. Health information seekers are anxious to have their privacy protected. American research has shown that approximately 9 in 10 online health information seekers (89%) were concerned that a health-related Web site might sell or give away information about what they did online. Well more than 8 out of 10 (85%) were concerned that their insurance company might raise their rates because of health sites they had visited. More than one half of health Web site users (52%) were even concerned about their employer finding out about the sites they had visited. More than 6 in 10 (63%) were also uncertain about putting medical records online for fear that the information might be interrogated by other people (Fox & Rainie, 2000).

The accuracy of online health information is another source of concern. Health information consumers can access health information online from known, authoritative sources as well as from sources of unknown credentials. More than 8 in 10 online health information seekers (86%) were concerned about getting health information from an unreliable source. More than one half (58%) said they checked to see who was providing the information. For the most part, though, health information seekers were slightly more likely to find Internet health information credible (52%) than not (Fox & Rainie, 2000).

Despite concerns about information authenticity and reliability on Web sites, there is growing recognition that the Internet can provide a valuable platform not just for general medical information retrieval, but also for two-way health-related transactions. Patients can contact other patients or health professionals remotely, and professionals can seek guidance from other professionals regardless of their locations. There still needs to be careful consideration given to the most effective ways to use these various telemedicine applications. If users become more self-sufficient in relation to taking care of themselves as a consequence of utilizing online health information, this would be deemed a highly positive outcome. If the additional information or advice received online contradicts that being offered to users face to face by their own doctor, however, time consuming (and therefore expensive) complications might arise if patients decide to reject what their doctor tells them or occupy their doctor's time explaining these contradictions. Experience through trial and error and knowledge growth through systematic research, however, should both contribute to the development of effective telemedicine.

Online health information is also being rolled out on interactive digital television platforms. As a medium, digital television has already caught or even surpassed the Internet in terms of household penetration in some countries, such as the U.K. As an interactive medium, however, it still lags behind the Internet. The early adopters of iDTV are also more likely to experiment with its interactive facilities, but they represent only a minority of the population (Klein et al., 2003). Thus, a market for such online services will take a number of years to become established. As seen in later chapters, the uptake of online health services in interactive media environments will depend not simply on physical roll-out, but also on the ease with which such services can be used and the effectiveness with which they can meet users' needs and expectations.

Chapter 3

Health and Medicine Online:
A Diversity of Applications

The online manifestation of medical and health services can be considered under two broad headings: (1) databases from which information can be downloaded by users and (2) transactional services through which users interrogate medical and health professionals about personal health issues. Early transactional services operated via telephone links. These are now being enhanced or superseded by new electronic communications formats operating via the Internet. In due course, further technological developments, as outlined later in this book, will involve interactive digital television as a primary information source and communications medium for health applications. The rapid growth of computer-mediated communication systems, including the Internet and World Wide Web and interactive digital television, has opened up possibilities for the public and, more especially, patients to become better informed about health issues and to take more responsibility for health care decisions. Many online information services were originally developed primarily for medical and health professionals, although attract as many if not more lay users (Lindberg, 2002).

The increased involvement of new information technologies in health matters may also introduce changes in the nature of health care provision (Impicciatore et al., 1997). Transactional services allow members of the public to engage with medical and health professionals online via text (e-mail), audio (telephone), and video links to obtain customized information and remote elementary diagnoses. These services are generally subsumed under the heading of *telemedicine*. Even with the development of early online health data and information sources, it was not always easy for users to access the information they needed. As information search systems have developed, however, health content on the Web has become more accessible (Bower, 1996).

The opening up of health information availability to patients as well as professionals has important implications for the future roles played in health care by health professionals and members of the public when they become patients. New information and communication technologies can deliver vast quantities of general medical and health-related information that can potentially be consulted by anyone, and they can offer more personalized communication channels between health professionals and patients for advisory and even some diagnostic purposes. Such developments beg questions about the nature of future doctor–patient relationships (Cline & Haynes, 2001; Friedman & Wyatt, 1997; Pallen, 1995).

PROVISION OF HEALTH INFORMATION ONLINE: THE NHS DIRECT EXPERIENCE

Online access to health information has been provided for some years via a number of technologies. As chapter 1 (this volume) indicated, there have been many experiments with electronic public service provision since the 1980s, utilizing kiosks with keyboards or touch-screens and telephone links. Behind all these initiatives lies the presumption that the very act of providing people with information leads to a better health outcome. This might entail giving people better access to a wider array of health information than before. Or it might embrace channels through which patients and health professionals can engage in a dialogue.

Patients do attach much authority and credibility to the information they receive from their doctors. Written information, for example, can increase patient compliance with their general practitioner's instructions (Arthur, 1995; Ley, 1982). Information leaflets have also been found to contribute to better health outcomes (Greenfield, Kaplan, & Ware, 1985; Mazzuca, 1982). Using electronic forms of communication to target information to particular groups has been an important goal of the United Kingdom's National Health Service (NHS).

Reflecting the development of a consumer ethic in health care in the 1980s and 1990s, there emerged a concept of the "informed patient." Within this context, the U.K. government placed emphasis on providing patients and the public with more information about their health. An early manifestation of this phenomenon was a national telephone helpline operated by the NHS, known as the Health Information Service.

NHS Direct is a 24-hour telephone advice line staffed by nurses. It was established to provide easier and faster information for people about health, illness, and the NHS so that they are better able to care for themselves and their families (Department of Health, 1997). It was conceived as a gateway to the National Health Service. It was a service designed to give the public health advice and information at the user's convenience. It was also envisaged to act as an encouragement for people to undertake self-care (George, 2002). The first three sites were started in March 1998 in Lancashire, Milton Keynes, and Northumbria in England. By 2002, the service covered all of England. It was not the first telephone health service in the world, but it promised to be the best. It was initially set up to provide clinical advice, health information, and referral to other NHS services via the telephone. Later, it was set to become the hub of out-of-hours care (Department of Health, 2000a).

NHS Direct was presented in a positive light, but not everything about it was good. In addition to difficulty with meeting call handling targets, there had been no visible effect on demand for NHS services overall (Munro, Nichol, O'Cathain, & Knowles, 2000). The hoped for reduction in demand for other NHS services might be achieved by the proposed integration of NHS Direct with other out-of-hours general practice cooperatives and ambulance services. Where such integration has taken place, demand for general practice consultation was observed to fall, especially for telephone consultation (Department of Health, 2000a).

Despite shortcomings, customer satisfaction with NHS Direct was high. A survey of more than 700 callers indicated that three fourths (76%) found the nurses' advice very helpful and most of the remainder (20%) finding it quite helpful. Of all these people, two thirds (66%) were reassured by the information and advice they had received (O'Cathain, Munro, Nicholls & Knowles, 2000). Other evidence indicated, however, that the people who used this telephone helpline service were the same ones who used other health services. The helpline was underused by older people, ethnic minorities, and other disadvantaged groups. Rather than reach people who were currently being "failed" by the health system, NHS Direct might instead have discovered previously unexpressed demand among the worried and largely well middle classes (George, 2002).

Whether NHS Direct has been a cost-saving service is less clear. Early research indicated that many callers were directed to other health services such as accident and emergency services (21%) or their own doctor (20%) immediately. Many others were told to contact their local doctor within 24 hours (13%) or at the nearest opportunity (12%), whereas a small number (1%) were diverted to the emergency services at the moment of calling (O'Cathain et al., 2000). The National Audit Office (an independent body in the U.K. that scrutinizes public spending on behalf of Parliament) published its report on NHS Direct in England. This report suggested that half the £90 million annual cost of NHS Direct had been offset by encouraging more appropriate use of NHS services. Cost savings were calculated according to other health service contracts avoided. These were determined on the basis of caller's stated future actions rather than on actual data, however, rendering these calculations somewhat speculative (The Comptroller and Auditor General, 2002).

COMPUTER-MEDIATED APPLICATIONS AND HEALTH

Although much of this book concerns the online provision of health information databases for lay users interrogation and the online availability of direct communications links with health professionals and with support groups, that are built upon networked platforms such as the Internet and interactive digital television, early applications of ICTs to health provision comprised the use of stand-alone computers or limited, dedicated computer networks available only to specific subscriber groups or small-scale community samples (Kreuter, Farrell, Olevitch, & Brennan, 2000; Morrell, 2002; Ratner, 2003; Street, Gold, & Manning, 1997). Before turning to the use of recently established and still developing networked communications technologies in the health context, it will be helpful to review some of the earlier experiments with computer-mediated technology and health communication.

Even before the Internet became widely established, computer-mediated communications were used in health promotion applications. Health promotion often entails the individual making personal choices about his or her health. A computer system can create a virtual environment in which different options can be represented or different solutions displayed in respect of specific health enquiries or problems. It can offer a rich informational setting and versatile search protocols enabling users to find exactly what they need to know (Manning, 1997).

Controlled studies have been conducted using desk-top computers loaded with health-related software programs. The interactive nature of computer technology can engage users more than might be true of reading printed information or even viewing instructional videos (Skinner & Kreuter, 1997). Computer programs can offer such a wide array of search or problem-solving options, that solutions can be tailored to fit the needs of individual users. In contrast, fixed print or video materials provide only single sets of options for any users. The ability to tailor messages to individual users may also increase the likelihood, in the case of health promotion communications, that attitude or behavior change will follow exposure (Skinner, Siegfried, Kegeler, & Strecher, 1993).

Direct comparisons between interactive, computer-mediated health materials and printed or video materials have consistently (although not invariably) indicated that interactivity creates greater involvement and stronger desired effects. Curry, Warner, and Grothaus (1990) tested the effects of computer-tailored feedback and financial incentives along with a self-help booklet designed to help smokers quit. Adult smokers were randomly assigned to different conditions in which they received: a self-help booklet about quitting smoking; the self-help booklet plus computer-tailored motivational feedback; the booklet plus a financial incentive; and the booklet, computer-tailored feedback and a financial incentive. The results showed that tailored feedback produced significant advantages over the self-help booklet alone. The presence of computer-tailored feedback enhanced rates of quitting smoking at 3-month and 12-month intervals after exposure to the treatment program.

Further research with smokers confirmed the potential of computer-mediated health promotions to produce desired results. Prochaska, DiClemente, Velicer, and Rossi (1993) assigned adult smokers to conditions in which they were given a self-help booklet geared to their stage of readiness to quit smoking; self-help booklets for their own stage of readiness plus booklets linked to later stages in the quit smoking cycle; self-help booklets plus computer-tailored output; or booklets, computer output and telephone counseling sessions. The highest long-term rates of quitting occurred for smokers who received booklets and computer-tailored material.

Further evidence has emerged of the potency of tailored-made materials as compared with nontailored materials in helping individuals with health issues. This applies not just to quitting smoking, but also to encouraging people to take more exercise or to attend screening sessions linked to cholesterol and cancer checks (Brennan, Kreuter, Caburnay, & Wilshire, 1998; Kreuter, Oswald, Bull, & Clark, 2000). The importance of tailoring health promotion messages applies equally to the production of printed materials. However, it opens up opportunities for the use of computer-mediated materials. Computer-tailored programs can be rolled out to large numbers of users. There is greater flexibility in the production of many different tailored versions of a communications package targeted at the needs of specific user groups. Furthermore, computer-mediated programs have interactive facilities that can allow for closer relationships between users and providers (Kreuter et al., 2000).

Computer networks have been developed to provide topic-related health information and social support for specific target groups. Although some projects have used stand-alone computers to which selected users are given access, others have created networked links between computers to enable users in geographically dispersed locations to access information and to communicate with each other. These systems are non-Internet networks but, in many respects, work in a similar fashion. They permit online interrogation of health information, access to chat rooms and bulletin boards, and links to health professionals. Such computer-mediated systems have been developed for young people in relation, for example, to body awareness (Brennan & Fink, 1997) and for carers of the elderly (Brennan, Moore, & Smythe, 1995). The carers program comprised a computer network that provided information, communication services, and decision-making advice. Social support was also facilitated via online peer group contacts. Hence, users could retrieve information online from a topic database and consult with their peers about problems and issues they faced (Brennan et al., 1995).

The application of computer-mediated communication to breast cancer education has yielded some positive results. However, the benefits of computer-based presentations have not been universally endorsed (Street & Manning, 1997). In this context, multimedia programs were developed for women newly diagnosed with cancer and to get women more generally to seek out screening for early detection. In a controlled test of the efficacy of these multimedia packages, women with breast cancer were randomly allocated to two conditions, one of which comprised receiving relevant information in brochure format and the other in a multimedia computer program. Women's knowledge about breast cancer grew significantly in both conditions, but overall the better performance was produced by the multimedia program.

In a second investigation, comparisons were made between a multimedia computer program with text, graphics, music and animation, a video presentation, and text-based information about breast cancer. The participants were young college women. On comparison of pre-exposure and postexposure tests, knowledge growth was found to have occurred in all three conditions, with no major differences between them. The multimedia presentation, however, was rated as less boring than the other two conditions, although more frustrating to use. Less involved participants, in fact, found the brochure and video easier to understand than the multimedia presentation (Street & Manning, 1997).

This evidence indicates that it is essential to build user-friendly information technology tools and to test their usability among all categories of potential user. In addition, it is important to understand when and why different individuals might wish to utilize online or computer-mediated information environments. Multimedia programs need to be interesting and easy to use. If they are not, they will fail, despite their novelty.

Some researchers have taken a step-by-step approach in building computer-mediated health education tools, starting on a small scale and focusing on just a few health issues, before engaging in a managed growth process in which the online system is gradually expanded. The Comprehensive Health Enhancement Support System (CHESS) is illustrative of this approach (Hawkins et al., 1997). CHESS comprises a number of modules that each deal with specific health issues, such as breast cancer, HIV, and alcoholism. Under each module heading, a variety of information is provided that is both medical and non-medical in nature. As well as providing factual, clinical information, some content is designed to offer emotional support to users. Links to other sources of help are also included, such as professional help and voluntary support groups or networks.

The design of CHESS was informed by formative research that attempted to find out what people need to know about specific health issues and in what formats do they wish the information to be delivered? To establish a network environment, signed-up users were provided with computers (if they did not already possess one) and these machines were linked into a dedicated network through which they could extract information from centralized database and make contact with other users. Thus system was found to bring particular benefits to those who were socially and economically disadvantaged. Users reported positive effects that were emotional as well as health related.

There was interest in the impact of CHESS upon the use of other health services. In a study conducted with individuals who were HIV positive, no evidence emerged that use of CHESS reduced outpatient visits to health clinics, but CHESS users were found to make more telephone calls than did controls to health service providers. Despite this, CHESS users reported spending significantly less time with health service providers during visits. Doctors also reported that CHESS users could be distinguished from nonusers because they tended to be better informed and had more searching questions to ask about their own condition and its treatment (Hawkins et al., 1997).

Another application of interactive media in the health education context has been to use interactive video games with health themes to raise health awareness among children and teenagers. Video games designed for this purpose can help players to learn about self-care and improve health-related knowledge. Such games offer opportunities for repetition and rehearsal of specific health messages because players usually have to play a number of times before they master each game. The interactive nature of these games also draws the players into the action on screen and creates an environment in which young people—who may generally be unresponsive to health messages of other kinds—are encouraged to show an interest in health matters (Lieberman, 1997).

Lieberman described a number of "health hero" video games: Rex Ronan, experimental surgeon who featured in a game dealing with the detrimental effects of smoking; Captain Novolin, a self-management game demonstrating the relation between food, insulin, and blood sugar control; Parky and Marlon, two elephant friends involved in a game designed to provide information about diabetes and nutrition; and Bronkie the Bronchiasaurus, aimed at 8- to 14-year-olds with asthma.

Each of these games had a clearly developed narrative and presented engaging and challenging trials that players must negotiate successfully if they were to get to the end. The games encouraged the players to think for themselves about specific health topics and to make action choices within the games that reflect decisions they may have to make in life. A growth in competence at playing the game can lead the player to feel a sense of achievement. The format also represents a way of engaging the attention of young people in health matters that retains their interest (Lieberman, 1995; Lierberman & Brown, 1995).

The aim of these video games is not simply to impart knowledge but also certain skills needed to implement know-how in practical situations. Hence youngsters can feel empowered and confident to deal with certain health matters themselves. This might be vitally important to youngsters with diabetes or asthma, who may need to know how to cope with their condition for themselves on occasions when there is no one else around to do this for them.

The maintenance of good health behaviors can also depend on the amount of social support provided to the individual (Peterson & Stunkard, 1989). Video games with health themes can encourage interaction with family and friends. If children like to talk to others more often about specific health issues, they may be more likely to seek outside help and support (Lieberman & Brown, 1995).

With the development of the Internet, new possibilities are opened up for the provision of games online that might require players to search other online databases for essential information relevant to playing a particular game. Online video games might also be used as conduits through which contact can be made with relevant support groups (Lieberman, 1997).

TELEHEALTH AND TELEMEDICINE

Telehealth or *telemedicine* is the use of electronic and communication technology to accomplish health care over distance. Telecommunications have supported health care for decades. They have been explored as ways of delivering health care more economically to patients who are geographically dispersed. Telehealth or telemedicine is designed to ensure that health-related services reach sections of society who may be unable to access direct care (Bashur, 1997).

Telehealth can be delivered in a number of formats via a number of technologies. Although this book is concerned primarily with the use of newer digital technologies in this context, there are older technologies—that pre-date the Internet—that have been used, including the telephone, fax, and video-conferencing. Information can be relayed in text, audio and video formats, and communications can be one-way or two-way, in real-time or asynchronous. Telecommunications have emerged especially within the context of professional psychological and therapeutic services.

Telehealth has been used, in some form, for more than 40 years. According to Turner (2003): "interactive-video (ITV)-mediated psychiatry was introduced in the late 1950s. By 1975, there were 17 ITV-mediated telemedicine programs in the United States" (p. 519). Some initial clinical success was reported for these applications, but many proved to be economically unviable. Nonetheless, telemedicine programs continued to grow in the U.S. during the 1980s and 1990s (Chen, Turner, & Crawford, 1996).

During the 1990s, advances in technology, consumer needs and pressures on traditional health services have encouraged the expansion of telemedicine programs in many other parts of the world (Allen, 1998/1999; Nickelson, 1998). In the developed world, most especially, governments have recognized the potential of telemedicine to provide solutions to more cost effective delivery of health care, to promote preventive medicine and healthier lifestyles, and to reach those population subgroups that are often socially excluded. Technological developments have meant that increasingly sophisticated communications formats can be adopted that have expanded the range of options open to health professionals when exchanging intelligence between themselves and when providing advice and diagnostic consultations to their patients. For certain types of health-related advice and consultation it is not necessary for clinician and patient to be in the same room. In addition, transfer of diagnostic data or patient medical histories can occur instantaneously between medical professionals situated hundreds or even thousands of miles apart, hence speeding up the diagnostic process and increasing the efficiency with which patients are treated.

ONLINE HEALTH APPLICATIONS

The provision of online or *tele*-health services can take on different forms as well as be carried over different channels. The earlier part of this chapter examined computer-mediated applications that could be provided on site through direct face-to-face interaction with technology, software, and content. The most significant advances in the use of computer-mediated communication to convey health services will occur when such technology is used to carry services to remote user groups. Thus, citizens and patients will be able to avail themselves of a variety of health information services, medical diagnostic services, and other support services without needing to leave home. These services will be provided to them either over the Internet linked to a home desk-top computer or over their television sets.

There are several broad types of application that have already emerged in this context. These include

- general health information in text or video formats;
- health information in text, audio, or video on specialist health topics or concerned with specific medical conditions;
- access to support groups, including fellow sufferers; and
- communication access to health professionals, for online diagnosis or therapy.

In addition there are online services for health professionals that include access to databases, links to other health professionals, and training services.

Online Health Information

As chapter 2 has already shown, there has been a significant growth in use of the Internet and other online services for health information. The information available on the Internet is provided by Web sites targeted at lay consumers and at professionals.

Some online information services are like encyclopedias and can be interrogated by anyone. They may provide information about medical conditions and treatments, sources of treatment, the performance of health authorities and their outlets, names of experts, and links to other information sources. This type of service may be generalized in nature in that the same information is available to everyone. Some online information services may also offer a more personalized service whereby the visitor can make contact with an expert at the site and engage in a dialogue that elicits a tailor-made response for the individual user (Jerome, DeLeon, James, Folen, Earles, & Gedney, 2000).

Online systems can be used as medical information repositories containing general health information or personal medical records. In addition, they can provide communication networks through which patients and medical or health professionals can talk or correspond with one another. Video, audio, and text links can be facilitated via electronic, computer-mediated communication systems enabling one-to-one, one- to-many, or group interactions. In the health context, this means that patients can consult directly with health professionals to obtain general or specific advice and information. It also means that patients can contact other patients to establish support groups who share the same health problems.

Patients Helping Other Patients

The Internet has witnessed the establishment of a large number of online support groups linked to health matters. These groups are often referred to as *self-help* groups. This description can be misleading, however, and some researchers prefer to use the term *mutual aid groups* (King & Moreggi, 1998).

These online networks can offer a substitute for face-to-face meetings. This can prove invaluable to individuals who need help and who are unable to attend meetings in person because of geographical distance from the meeting place or because of physical incapacity. Or sometimes, individuals who need help may be reluctant to meet in person with others because their condition is a source of embarrassment to them and online communications channels enable them to retain a degree of anonymity (King & Moreggi, 1998).

Such online groups may exchange clinical information about their condition and its treatment. Equally, they may seek emotional comfort from the exchange of personal experiences with fellow sufferers (Moursand, 1997). Hence, these networks are often concerned with the provision of psychological support online for the sufferers of particular illnesses. Such groups can be found for various forms of cancer, heart disease, neurological problems, and psychological illnesses. They can be found a great source of emotional support (Ferguson, 1996, 2000). Indeed, real-time, online chat forums can sometimes mimic the feel of regular therapy sessions with health professionals (Grohol, 1998).

The critical characteristic of online support groups is that patients suffering from a chronic disease can seek and receive help from other patients with the same condition. Such support networks therefore provide a different function from online health professionals. Online patient helpers do not necessarily have professional, medical knowledge related to specific conditions, but they can provide unique insights as fellow sufferers and are probably able to identify with other sufferers far more accurately than a medical professional ever could. Online patient-helpers may be able to share the benefit of their own experience with a particular health condition and offer a form of support that professional health care providers are unqualified to give.

Mutual aid groups were estimated in the United States to have attracted 8 to 10 million users only a couple of years after the their initial appearance on the Internet (Kessler, Mickelson, & Zhao, 1997). The biggest groups of this kind tended to comprise individuals with substance abuse problems. One advantage of these networks is that help is available around the clock.

Online networks held particular appeal for individuals who suffered health problems that prevented them from physically getting around or who, because of the remoteness of their location, could not readily attend face to face sessions with health professionals (Madara & White, 1997). These online links were also useful for carers who were unable to leave those in their care and could not transport them very easily (King & Moreggi, 1998). Online support groups were also valued by users who suffered from a socially stigmatized problem (Walther & Boyd, 1997).

Although online support networks serve as valuable information sources, they have been observed to provide direct therapy that can have powerful effects on some participants—sometimes even aiding recovery (King, 1994; King & Moreggi, 1998). Online networks can provide individuals who are suffering from specific conditions or illnesses with emotional support and reassurance. The anonymity of Internet communications, for example, can encourage self-disclosure (Joinson, 1998) and promotes participation even by those who would normally feel uncomfortable in face-to-face contexts (King, 1995; Sproull & Kiesler, 1995). Where differences between people, that would be obvious in face-to-face interactions, might inhibit or limit communication exchanges, on the Internet a level playing field is created because individual differences are hidden (Wellman, 1996).

Evidence has emerged that participation in online support groups can be rewarding and beneficial (Suler, 1996; Young & Rogers, 1998). The Internet can provide a convenient source of social contact and can create a sense of community even among strangers who have never met one another before. Sometimes, individuals can experience a stronger degree of connectedness in computer-mediated environments than when meeting in person (Nickerson, 1994).

Communicating With Health Professionals

Some of the online support patients now seek must be provided by medical and health professionals. Members of the public and patients may be able to be self-sufficient in their search for health information for purposes of self-diagnosis or assistance to others, but there ultimately will come a point at which only professional help will suffice. A big question for the suppliers of professional health and medical services, however, concerns the extent to which online technologies can be utilized to assist with their patient contacts.

Health professionals can potentially offer patients advice and information online, provide online consultations, and, in a limited way offer online therapy (American Psychological Association, Board of Professional Affairs, 1996; Ball, Scott, McLaren, & Watson, 1993; Hufford, Gleuckauf, & Webb, 1999; Jerome, 1999; Stamm, 1998). The therapeutic advantages of online consultations were initially perceived to derive from the anonymity of this remote communications environment in which patients would open up more to the therapist (Joinson, 1998). Communicating over an Internet link might also give rise to more forthright disclosures, especially among patients suffering from medical conditions that caused them embarrassment (Grohol, 1998).

Ample evidence has emerged that with the growth of the Internet and other online technologies, such as interactive digital television and mobile communications, increasing numbers of people are prepared to use online sources for their health information. Indeed, large numbers of Internet users now regard the Web as a primary information source for health. By 2000, a U.S. opinion poll estimated that 98 million adults had used the World Wide Web to find health information, having increased by 81% over the previous 2 years (Ferguson, 2000). The same research found that women were more likely to have sought health information on the Internet than were men. Further, health Web site visitors tended to be older than the average Internet user. It also found that virtually all online health site users stated that they would like to be able to contact their doctor by e-mail.

Ferguson (2000) also reported that many American doctors had indicated that their patients talk to them about health information they have found on the Internet and ask them for recommendations about the best health Web sites to visit. There is a growing expectation among patients that online services will become available, not just in the wider sense of further growth of health Web sites on the Internet, but more specifically in relation the development of online communications links to local clinics and health care centers and hospitals and doctors surgeries. Later in this book, further evidence is presented from pilot studies that tested the efficacy of interactive digital television as a platform for the provision of online health services that indicated the use of such online services to obtain information prior to going to see the doctor.

Such developments have many implications—some good and others more problematic. Although online connections may prove to offer added convenience to patients and health and medical professionals in certain respects, they may also generate workload for professionals. Patients may find the idea of being able to e-mail their doctor with a question about a personal medical problem an appealing type of service. For doctors, however, such a service means they have to budget into their everyday schedule some time for responding to these messages. Although the openness of information provision on the Internet is largely to be welcomed, doctors may have concerns about patients acting upon online advice that is not attributed to authoritative sources or not accredited by respectable medical bodies. Being faced with patients to disagree with their doctor's advice because they have read something different on the Internet is also a source of confusion and potential disruption for everyone concerned.

Some online health-related services provided communication links for health professionals through which specialist information transfer can take place, such as patient records, treatment options, and the latest clinical evidence (Dakins, 1997). The electronic transfer of patient records or the latest clinical research in to diagnosis and treatment among professionals working in geographically remote locations can facilitate greater mutual support networks among medical practitioners.

CONCLUSION

The evidence examined in this chapter indicates promise and potential for the provision of a variety of health-related information, advice and diagnostic services remotely through online platforms. The Internet has featured prominently in early experiments in provision of remote health reference information and therapeutic support. In the longer term, however, television may become equally significant as its interactive capabilities become more developed and more familiar to viewers. In the next few chapters, research is presented that provides evidence concerning the efficacy of the Internet, touch-screen kiosks, and digital interactive television as delivery platforms for online health services.

It is clear that online technologies can provide a variety of local and remote health and medical services, some of which do not involve any direct interaction between patients and medical practitioners. Already there is some evidence that users can obtain a degree of satisfaction from online health services (Baer et al., 1995; Blackmon, Kaak, & Ranseen, 1997; Clarke, 1997; Zarate et al., 1997). Such services can also bring cost benefits to health service provision (Trott & Blignault, 1998).

Research on the spread of digital technologies both within and across nations has indicated gaps between the "haves" and "have-nots" in respect of online technology and service access (Norris, 2001). As seen later in this book, however, the use of enhanced forms of established technologies such as television may overcome the access problem to some extent. Certainly, the use of health information services on interactive digital television has exhibited a different demographic profile from use of such services on the Internet (Nicholas, Huntington, Williams, & Gunter, 2001). Although the lower socioeconomic classes may exhibit lower levels of Internet access than the higher socioeconomic classes, this may not be true for iDTV.

Early forms of online communication have centered on the use of text messaging or retrieval of text content. This may suffice as an effective communications format for certain forms of health enquiry of a general informational nature. They may be less sensitive to and effective at coping with more personalized enquiries that demand direct advice regarding diagnosis and treatment. The spread of video or audio channels to enhance text messaging may improve the position in relation to more personalized services. These formats allow for richer social presence than text communication (Walther, 1996). As more people go online and acquire broadband connections and PCs with built-in video technology, the capacity for provision of more personalized online therapy will grow. More research will be needed into the effectiveness of different online communications environments in providing different types of health and medical service.

Chapter 4

Digital Health on the Web

The Internet has emerged as a major source of health information. It can provide swift access to large quantities of information that would previously have required huge effort on the part of individuals to find. Not only does the World Wide Web represent a repository of health knowledge of unparalleled proportions, it also provides users with a communication channel through which they can contact other people for information exchange (Rice & Katz, 2001).

Edmonds (2003) listed more than 100 key sites covering health matters, fitness and exercise, alternative medicine and therapies, and specific medical conditions. Many hundreds of other sites were not listed because they failed to achieve sufficient standards in terms of their design, usability, and information quality. Many more sites and portals that provided access to numerous other sites were listed by Kennedy (2002) for whom the Internet was labeled as an unrivaled medical library in terms of the quantity of information it offers.

The Internet offers a ready-made information search facility open to anyone who has access to the appropriate user technology. Many health information suppliers have taken advantage of this facility. For example, Stanford University's Hire Wire Library of Science and Medicine (www.hirewire.stanford.edu) provides access to the electronic versions of more than 300 scientific journals. Meanwhile, the Integrated Handheld and Web-based Service (www.bmj.com/handheld), published by Unbound Medicine and the BMJ Publishing Group in Britain, offers users access to the *British Medical Journal* and other specialist journals on portable as well as fixed location devices. Then, the U.K. Health News Digest (www.bmj.com/uknews) provides a free daily digest of healthcare articles for general practitioners, summarizes medical articles appearing in the national daily press, and provides links to newspaper Web sites (Delamothe, 2002).

In the United States, the National Library of Medicine (NLM) initiative with the Setting Priorities for Retirement Years (SPRY) Foundation has been designed to open up access of authoritative medical information to the general public, with special reference to older people and disadvantaged sectors of society (Lindberg, 2002). NLM has also explored making MEDLINE, a database primarily used by health care professionals, more accessible to the public. In 1997, then U.S. Vice-President Al Gore launched the first free search facility for MEDLINE, which generated a significant public response. A more comprehensive service was opened up in 1998 called MEDLINE*plus* which contributed health information in other languages than English. It contained medical dictionaries, a medical encyclopedia, information about prescription drugs, directories of hospitals and health professionals, links to organizations, links to libraries, and information about new experimental treatments and clinical trials for serious or life-threatening diseases or conditions.

The provision of health information on the Internet has been presumed to have the potential to benefit patients and health professionals (Duffy, Wimbush, Reece, & Eadie, 2003). It can provide access to large amounts of health information and represent a communication channel through which public and professionals can engage in a dialogue about health matters. Evidence has emerged that members of the public are increasingly turning to this type of communications link as a valued health information source (Nicholas, Huntington, Gunter, Russell, & Withey, 2003; Nicholas, Huntington, Williams, & Gunter, 2003b). Not only can this information source satisfy personal curiosity about health issues, it may have a functional quality in helping patients in their dealings with their doctors (Howard, Rainie, & Jones, 2001; Nicholas, Huntington, Williams, & Gunter, 2001d).

A report in *The Times* newspaper in the U.K. indicated that families were using the Internet to demand different treatment from doctors because they believed it was better informed. In most cases they reported that their doctors had been surprised by their access to medical information but had taken them more seriously in consequence and ultimately agreed to their requests (Rumbelow, 1999). Another report claimed that the computer would take over GPs' gatekeeper role by 2020 (Stirling, 2001).

Despite the growth of health information Web sites, user research has been sparse. Although this is starting to change, there is still much that needs to be learned about the appropriation and utility of online health information by professionals and public. The apparent use of online information about health in the context of doctors' visits is an interesting development. Research has shown that written information from the doctor is accorded considerable status and authority by patents (Arthur, 1995). Yet, early indications have suggested that people use online health information sources to equip themselves for a more fruitful dialogue with their doctor about their personal health condition. This certainly has been indicated by research conducted with users of online health content broadcast on interactive digital television (see chap. 6, this volume). This phenomenon suggests that doctors are no longer regarded as the only authoritative source of health information available to patients.

Online health information consumers may not only seek content on health conditions, but also information about health professionals. Performance data on hospitals or care organizations may be available over the Internet (Williams, 1999a). Hence, information consumers can shop around online and identify the best providers of health care or treatment (Coile & Howe, 1999; Williams, 1999a).

Of course, online health information may take a cautious line and advise users who remain perplexed about their personal health status even after having consulted a Web site, to contact their doctor for the final word on the matter. Ultimately, in the case of a real health problem of a physical nature, effective diagnosis and treatment can only be administered face to face. There is an additional question of great importance concerning the Internet as an information resource and that centers on the credibility and accuracy of the information it provides.

Although the guiding principle of the Internet is that it provides information for all and access for all information suppliers, it also represents a potential drawback. In the absence of editorial controls over content—with everyone potentially able to become a publisher online—there are no guarantees of information authenticity, authority, or credibility. In the case of health and medical information, and given the uses to which such information might be put by the public or health professionals, this could cause problems especially when the information is of dubious validity (Bower, 1996; Cline & Haynes, 2001).

The need to have confidence in the quality of health information provided online is reinforced by the numbers of people who use health Web sites. Myriad statistics have confirmed a pattern of ever-increasing consumption of electronic health information (Cline & Haynes, 2001). Some observers have noted that health Web sites are accessed more than any other category apart from pornography (Bowseley, 1999). In the United States, by the close of the twentieth century, it was claimed that 22 million adults used the Internet annually to consult health-related sites (Grossman, 1999). If a health site exists, people will find it. Even with a specialised subject such as dermatology, intended for medical practitioners, lay consumers were found to access it more than did professional healthcare workers (Eysenbach, Sen, & Diepgen, 1999).

INFORMATION QUALITY CONTROL

The prospect of empowering patients or members of the public is one thing, but it is important to ensure that the content with which they are being supplied is reliable. With the rapid growth of health-related Web sites, originated from various locations around the world, it is important that users can have confidence in the authority of the information and the credentials of the source. The World Wide Web does indeed present a major opportunity to supply large quantities of information to very large numbers of people. The absence of editorial controls over content, however, has given rise to concerns about the quality of the information provided.

There have been calls for systematic assessment of online health information and for the development of normative standards that such sites should seek to attain. Furthermore, a system of labelling should be developed that can inform health information consumers about the quality of the content being offered by a particular site (Delamothe, 2000; Jadad, 1999).

One key development is that patients and public are being encouraged to become more active in taking decisions about health care. Social policy initiatives have attempted to encourage people to become more self-sufficient in health care and not to rely purely on health professionals at the point at which their health falls apart (Kahn, 1997; Street & Rimal, 1997; Wetle, 2002).

A greater emphasis on prevention of ill-health than cure means that the individual must be better informed about health matters. Part of this process is the roll-out of more health information to the public that individuals can readily access and understand. Online technologies have a crucial role to play in this context. As the numbers of health sources grows, however, users of this content must have confidence in the information being provided. Health professionals will not always have the time to provide guidance (Department of Health, 2002). In that case, some alternative system must be put in place that enables health information consumers to judge the value and validity of information supplied by different online sources. It is important to know whether information is accurate and up to date. Online sources cannot provide treatment, but they may be able to advise health information consumers about the signs to look for that indicate whether treatment may be needed (Charnock, Shepperd, Gann, & Needham, 1999).

If the public and patients are to respond to governments' encouragement to utilize online health information advice services as part of drive toward the adoption of an ethos of preventive medicine and self-help health care, it is imperative that such a resource provides accurate and trustworthy information. The credentials of information sources must be explicit given that there is evidence that users of on-line information sources often fail to pay much attention to information sources or source authority issues. Many seem to adopt the position that if information is on a digital platform, then it must be legitimate (Williams, Nicholas, Huntington, & McClean, 2002). Determining source credibility is further complicated by the fact that so many different parties may be involved with online information sources. One British study gave the example of a touch-screen kiosk operated and produced by one company, presenting content written by another supplier and located in a retail outlet operated by a third party. Under these circumstances, it was difficult for consumers to judge where authority or responsibility for the health information actually resided. For many consumers, the supermarket had a responsibility in this context, although it did not play any part in content production (Williams, Nicholas, Huntington, & Gunter, 2002b).

A number of strategies have been suggested for ensuring public access to high-quality health information. Among the ideas that have been floated are the provision of kite marks or seal of approval and the development of databases of information that have been quality assured (Health on the Net Foundation, 2001). Kite marks are often based on checklists of desirable attributes, however, that have not themselves been approved or standardized.

Despite the concerns surrounding the quality of health information on the Internet, the reasons for establishing a kite-marking system must be clear (Delamothe, 2000). Health information can be accessed through other media, but these have not received the same kind of attention as the Internet although the public may often be exposed to misleading or inaccurate information from a variety of sources (Payne, Large, Jarrett, & Turner, 2000; Slaytor & Ward, 1998).

Health information on the Internet can vary widely from personal accounts of illnesses and patient discussion groups to peer reviewed journal articles and clinical decision support tools. It is difficult to produce a single quality standard that can effectively cover such a disparate array of content. Furthermore, not everyone who uses Internet health information has the same criteria for quality. As some writers have observed: "Patients and caregivers may want simple explanations and reassurance, whereas healthcare professionals may want data from clinical trials" (Purcell, Wilson, & Delamothe, 2002, p. 324).

Online health information can be classified in terms of topic, format, and intended audience. Quality criteria will vary with the nature of the content and the type of use for which it is intended. Medical knowledge that is intended for professional users will be judged according to different criteria from the personal accounts of health problems provided by lay persons in Internet chat rooms. Information that is aimed at the public or patients must be written in a style that is easy for such users to understand. Although clarity of exposition is important for any group of users, medical professionals will understand and expect to find technical terms being used in content designed for their user group.

With online information, the quality of the content is not the only factor of importance to the user. Electronic information resources must be designed to facilitate ease of navigation around their content. The interfaces that enable access to online health content must be easy to use. This aspect of online health Web sites must also be taken into account when judging their overall quality (Purcell et al., 2002).

The thorough screening of databases demands considerable resources. It requires skilled personnel who are qualified to make professional judgements about content (Shepperd & Charnock, 2002).

Some writers have argued that a degree of responsibility should be placed on the publishers of health information and the providers of databases or bibliographies to highlight the strengths and weaknesses of health-related publications. Thus, health content should be accompanied by caveats that clarify whether the information provided meets certain criteria or falls short of doing so (Shepperd & Charnock, 2002).

Government-based health information providers in Britain have an advantage over most other sources as they carry an assurance of validity. Both NHS Direct (a national telephone helpline) and Care Direct (an Internet service aimed at the elderly) are Department of Health initiatives that use researched, clinical decision-support system algorithms to produce quality-assured information. Although the Internet continues to grow exponentially, there is no satisfactory way of preventing poor Web sites emerging, however. The lack of standardization in quality assurance of online health information remains a serious problem.

Addressing Quality Control Concerns

In response to this concern about health information on the Internet, a number of studies have that attempted to assess Web content quality (Jadad & Gagliardi, 1998; McClung, Murray, & Heitlinger, 1998; O'Mahoney, 1999; Shon, Marshall, & Mussen, 1999; Soot, Moneta, & Edwards, 1999). Kiley (2000) warned against biased information on the Web. Coulter and colleagues (1999a, 1999b) pointed out that even "official" information published by government bodies can be of dubious quality. Of interest are both the issue of the quality and appropriateness of information provided by official health information providers and that found elsewhere.

On the issue of quality, Coulter's (Coulter et al., 1999a, 1999b) research indicated a multitude of problems. Much of the information was inaccurate and out of date, technical terms were not explained, and few materials provided adequate information about treatment risks and side effects. These results were regarded as worrying given the rate at which government-backed health content was being pumped out. In Britain, such online information has been conceived as playing a key role in reducing the load on doctors' surgeries and patients' clinics by providing valuable self-help materials (NHS Executive, 1998).

Some writers have argued that there is a need to establish standards of accountability for Internet health content to advise and guide its consumers. Such standards might include disclosure of authorship, ownership and currency of information (Silberg, Lundberg, & Musacchio, 1997). These accountability criteria have been endorsed elsewhere as representing the basis of a system to classify the quality of health Web site content (Jadad & Gagliardi, 1998; O'Mahoney, 1999; Shon et al., 1999). Although this system has been regarded as useful in principle, there have been few empirical tests conducted to find out how effectively it works in practice and to establish the quality of health information that has become widely available on the Web (Griffiths & Christensen, 2000). In early instances in which quality tests were carried out, methodologies were simplistic and judgements were subjective (Davison & Pennebaker, 1997; Impicciatore et al., 1997; McClung et al., 1998; Soot et al., 1999).

Regardless of the methodology applied, a consensus has emerged that health care information provided on the Web should not be accepted at face value. There were serious questions that could be raised about the quality of information provided. This was illustrated in one survey of sites that contained information about managing fever in a child at home (Impicciatore et al., 1997). Relevant information found on these sites was evaluated in terms of accuracy, comprehensiveness, and overall quality. Web site information was judged against the recommendations of a specific medical textbook on the subject. It was found that few Web sites provided complete and accurate information on managing child fever. Recommendations varied between sites, and some sites offered much more detailed advice than others. The authors concluded that there was an urgent need to introduce systematic checks on the quality of health information provided on Web sites.

Griffiths and Christensen (2000) reviewed the quality of Web-based information on treatment of depression. They examined 21 frequently accessed Web sites on this subject and assessed each one in terms of site characteristics, content quality, and accountability standards.

Site characteristics included identification of the purpose, scope, ownership, country of origin of the site, and any involvement of a drug company, professional editorial board, or health professional with the site. The content quality was judged on two main dimensions: (1) in terms of information about best practice via "a 43-item rating scale developed from the evidence based guidelines on clinical practice for treating depression published by the Agency for Health Care Policy and Research (AHCPR)" in the U.S. (Griffiths & Christensen, 2000, p. 1512); and (2) a 17-item scale designed to assess recommendations about treatment. The authors also provided a single overall, subjective quality score out of 10. Accountability was assessed via Silberg et al.'s (1997) 9-point scale for judging criteria of authorship (authors' names, credentials, affiliations), attribution (sources or references mentioned), disclosure (ownership and sponsorship of site), and currency (whether the site has been modified, how often and how recently).

The study found that although the sites analyzed largely contained useful information, there were question marks about information quality as assessed according to the stipulated criteria. Sites generally scored poorly in terms of the Silberg criteria and seldom provided scientific evidence for advice or claims presented. Although a slim majority of sites provided information about authors and their credentials, far fewer clearly identified their owners or sponsors. The authors of the study concluded that the quality of information was poor on Web sites containing information about the treatment of depression. However, they also questioned the value of their quality criteria and argued that a more comprehensive system of Web site content assessment and classification is needed.

Has Quality Improved Over Time?

Gagliardi and Jadad (2002) updated their earlier work from 1998 that examined 47 rating instruments appearing on Web sites offering health information. Of these, "14 described how they were developed, five provided instructions for use, and none reported inter-observer reliability or construct validity of the measurements" (p. 569). The authors revisited all rating instrument sites from their original study to ascertain if they were still operating. New rating instruments were also identified. Over a 5-year period, the authors identified 98 evaluative instruments that were available to assess the quality of Web sites. Many of the rating instruments identified in their original study were no longer available 5 years later. Out of 51 new rating instruments found, very few (five) provided information that could be used to determine their veracity and effectiveness. The authors concluded that instruments that could be used to evaluate the quality of health Web sites were themselves often inadequately defined or provided details about themselves that were insufficient to establish their independence and credentials.

Meric et al. (2002) conducted a study to determine the characteristics of popular breast cancer-related Web sites, and whether more popular sites were of higher quality. They used Google to generate a list of Web sites about breast cancer. Google ranked sites by measures of link popularity—the number of links to a site from other sites. The authors focused on the top 200 sites returned in response to the query "breast cancer" (p. 577). These sites "were divided into 'more popular' and 'less popular' sub-groups by three different measures: Google rank, number of links reported independently by Google, and by Alta Vista (another search engine)" (p. 577).

The more popular sites could be distinguished from the less popular ones in that they contained more about current and past medical research and sources of advice and help for breast cancer sufferers. According to Meric et al. (2002), "more popular sites, by number of linking sites, were also more likely to provide updates on other breast cancer research, information on legislature and advocacy, and a message board service." (p. 577) Many breast cancer Web sites, however, did not comply with American Medical Association benchmarks, although there were signs of some improvement in this respect over the previous few years.

In following up an earlier study by Impicciatore et al. (1997), Pandolfini and Bonati (2002) reidentified 19 out of 41 sites that had been evaluated in the original study. Among these sites, the quality of health information was judged to have shown some signs of improvement.

Kunst, Groot, Latthe, and Khan (2002) evaluated the source credibility and information accuracy of 121 Web sites that provided information on five common health topics: chronic obstructive pulmonary disease, ankle sprain, emergency contraception, menorrhagia, and female sterilization. These sites were identified by using major search engines (AltaVista, Excite, Hotbot, Infoseek, Lycos, Northern Light, Webcrawler). Credibility was based on naming of sources and their affiliation and provision of relevant medical evidence for the advice given. Whether sources were named was the main credibility criterion. Credibility features, however, were only modestly correlated with accuracy of information as judged against rigorous, peer-reviewed and published guidelines for each health topic. Apparently credible sites may not necessarily provide more accurate information.

Standardizing Quality Assessment

Clearly, agreed ways of guaranteeing the quality of Internet information are very important. Wrongly diagnosed ailments could have fatal consequences. It is no surprise therefore that a number of health bodies and information providers have attempted to formulate policy statements, guidelines, and principles regarding Web-based health information.

One quality system identified a list of 10 criteria for evaluating the information quality of health Web sites that included assessment of the accuracy and reliability of site content, site layout and design, disclosure of site originators or sponsors, frequency with which content is updated, the authority and reputation of any identified content sources, ease of use of site, ease of accessibility of site, links to other sites, attribution of evidential sources to reinforce content, and indication of intended audience (Kim, Eng, Deering, & Maxfield, 1999).

The Health on the Net Foundation (2001) has become established as a respected and nonprofit-making guide to medical information on the Internet. There are eight principles that make up the HONF code of conduct for prospective medical and health Web site authors: the authority of information sources, identification of sources, evidential reinforcement of medical information, ability to contact site contributors, identification of sponsorship, identification of sponsorship sources, indication that site content is not intended to replace direct medical advice from practitioners, and confidentiality in respect of any personal information offered by users.

Similar guidelines to those of the HONF were established by the British Healthcare Internet Association (BHIA). Although there is considerable overlap between these two sets of guidelines, there are three BHIA recommendations that do not have HONF equivalents. First, the BHIA states that it is important to distinguish information aimed at lay readers from that provided for professionals. Second, notes of caution should be presented to lay readers in respect of medical conditions for which they should really seek professional advice. Third, sites should respect copyright and intellectual property rights of content producers from whom they derive content.

These various principles that are directed to Web site producers also inform potential users. In order to identify sites to users that have been quality approved, the HONF has used its code of conduct principles to grant the right to organizations whose sites meet the appropriate criteria to display their logo as a quality assurance mark.

A further example is DISCERN. This is a checklist for consumers and professionals which is unusual in having been developed and evaluated for reliability and validity through a research project (Charnock et al., 1999). This entailed detailed discussions with the stakeholders involved. It is a tool to evaluate health resources, specifically about treatment options. Although it can be used to evaluate information on Web sites, it was initially developed (by Charnock & Shepperd, 1997) for print materials. It consists of key questions that ask about information sources, statement of site objectives, referencing of content and clarity of medical descriptions, plus an overall quality rating.

Unfortunately, not all quality ratings are as authoritative as those of HONF and DISCERN. Concern has been expressed about the quality of quality ratings bodies themselves. Many ratings systems provide less than adequate information about their assessment criteria or the credentials of the people making the assessments (Hernandez-Borges et al., 1999; Jadad & Gagliardi, 1998). One solution that has been suggested is to use Internet statistics about consumption and use of sites, objective data on numbers of links offered to other sites, site information about latest date of content updating (if given at all), and official data on site authors' own research and publications. Each health Web site would then primarily be judged against these indicators (Hernandez-Borges et al., 1999).

The validity of health information can vary greatly across Web sites and in relation to different diseases and populations. Given the global nature of information origination and distribution, any effective system of health content quality control must exist at an international level. A European project recommended the accreditation of health care related software, telemedicine, and Internet sites (Rigby, Forstrom, Roberts, & Wyatt, 2001). Here, a mechanism for software accreditation was suggested that was similar to the making of electrical goods, along with suggestions for national regulatory bodies for telemedicine and a European certification of integrity scheme for Web sites.

CONSUMER UPTAKE AND OPINIONS

As already noted, health information is one of the most frequently sought-after topics on the Internet. According to Bowseley (1999), "more than 40% of all Internet users have sought health-related information, making it second only to pornography in popularity" (p. 5). A Harris poll found that 98 million adults in the U.S. had used the Web to find health information, an increase of 81% from 2 years earlier, during which time the number of Internet users who had never looked for health information had declined from 29% to 14% (Harris Interactive, 2000).

In a later study, the Pew Internet & American Life Project found that 70 million American adults had used the Web to get health or medical information (from looking for disease information to downloading fat-free recipes; Pew Internet and American Life Project, 2003). Another major survey from the United States corroborated these findings in reporting that more than one in two Americans (53%) claimed to have used the Internet to search for health information (Reuters, 2003).

Further evidence indicated that lay users find and visit even sites designed primarily for health professionals (Cline & Haynes, 2001). In the U.S., opening up the National Library of Medicine's Web site led to millions of searches every week from the general public (cited in Cline & Haynes, 2001). Such interest in specialist sites may encourage Web site designers to reconfigure or rewrite their sites to render them more user-friendly to nonprofessional visitors. In fact, such is the demand for online health information among the lay public, they may become heavier users of sites designed specifically for health professionals than the latter are themselves (Eysenbach & Diepgen, 1999).

In Europe, research has shown that nearly one in four Europeans (23%) used the Internet to obtain health information (Eurobarometer, 2000). There are marked variations in this behavior across countries, however. In Denmark and the Netherlands around 40% of people reportedly used the Internet for health information, whereas in Greece, Spain, Portugal, and France usage was at 15% or lower. Health professionals, such as doctors and pharmacists, were at this time still the most important sources of health information for Europeans and the traditional media—television, newspapers, and magazines—still outperformed the Internet. Other key findings indicated that medical and health organizations achieved the highest trust rating on health issues, whereas businesses and political parties received the lowest.

In the United Kingdom, a survey of Internet users found that 90% claimed to have visited a Web site for health information and/or medical treatment in the previous 12 months. More than 70% had reportedly visited a Web site for health or medical information or advice at least 10 times during that time. Nearly one half of these respondents (49%) said they had visited the National Health Service (NHS) Web site, whereas more than one in five (22%) said they had visited a pharmaceutical company Web site (Brown & Smith, 2003).

Despite this growing population of users, research into Internet sites with health or medical content has almost exclusively centered on evaluating the quality of information provided and how this can be assured, rather than on the needs and attitudes of users. The certification of medical information in terms of the authority and credibility of its sources is, of course, a very important issue. However, it is equally important to have a clear understanding of users' needs. The growing impetus on auditing the performance of public services has meant that official health organizations must become increasingly accountable to their customers—the patients. Systems must be in place to safeguard high standards of health care and medical treatment. Achievement of these goals is not simply a matter for health professionals. It is increasingly regarded as a partnership involving professionals and patients (Gann, 1998).

Interests and Needs of Internet Health Consumers

Online health service users have accessed health Web sites for a variety of reasons. Research in the U.S. indicated that usage has ranged from those who were looking for specific disease-related information to those down-loading fat-free recipes. Most people looked for medical information about a specific condition rather than for information about healthy lifestyles or health care services, and a great many sought information on behalf of family and friends as well as for themselves. The self-perceived impact of this information was also quite striking. Nearly one half (48%) said that the advice they found on the Web had improved the way they took care of themselves and more than one half (55%) claimed that the Internet had improved the way they accessed health information (Fox & Rainie, 2000).

The same survey indicated that among adults who had gone online for health information, an overwhelming majority said they the last time they went online they found the information they were looking for (92%), learned something new (81%), and claimed that the information they found improved the way they took care of their health. Most Internet users (94%) found it easy to find the health information they were looking for (Fox & Rainie, 2000). The vast majority of those seeking information for themselves found what they were looking for and nearly one half said that it affected their decisions about diet and exercise, treatments, and about future uptake of health care services.

A study with European health consumers found that users tended to have a focused and deep interest in information only about their specific condition or disease. They did not regularly surf the Internet for general health-related material.

Instead, they sought out sites offering specific information and showed little interest in using the Web to obtain general health-related information or products. Those who were more actively involved in their diagnoses and treatment decisions were more likely to use the Internet as a resource for information (Boston Consulting Group, 2001; Poensgen & Larsen, 2001).

In Britain, Nicholas, Huntington, Williams, and Blackburn (2001) found that most people did not come to the health Web site established by the Department of Health (www.surgerydoor.com) for information on a specific illness or medical condition. Instead, they were generally more interested in information on general well-being or information to help them remain healthy.

Internet and Use of Health Professionals

Concerns have allegedly been expressed by doctors about their patients second-guessing their professional advice with Internet information (Ferguson, 2002). Systematic research on Internet health site users, however, has indicated that relatively few tend to admit that this information resulted in any disagreement with a health professional with whom it was discussed (Fox & Rainie, 2000). Most users of online health information tend to report that they did not use this information instead of visiting the doctor (Fox & Rainie, 2000). The majority went online to gather further intelligence. Online information therefore serves as an adjunct to the doctor–patient relationship. Cyberdialogue (2000), for example, found that as a result of using the Internet, around one half of all health information seekers advised a family member to see a doctor, changed their exercise or eating habits, or made a positive decision related top their health treatment. Many others visited an illness support group after visiting a disease-specific Web site.

In another survey of more than 4,700 people, 40% said they had used the Internet and more than 9 in 10 (94%) of these individuals said that the information found did not affect the number of times they visited a doctor (Baker, Wagner, Singer, Bundorf, & Jama, 2003). In contrast, Kalichman, Benotsch, Weinhardt, Austin, Luke, and Cherry (2003) found evidence that Internet health-related information did have health benefits for people living with HIV/AIDS. This suggests that for special interest groups, defined by specific health conditions, the Internet can represent a valued information source that they take seriously.

Indeed, the distrust that many doctors have expressed about the quality of health information provided on the Internet is shared by patients. In the United States, the great majority of Internet users (82%) have expressed concern about the reliability of online health information sources (Ferguson, 2000). Experienced users and health professionals who access health Web sites tend to make a point of visiting a number of different sites. Furthermore, they access more sophisticated online and offline sources of authoritative health knowledge that can assist in interpreting complex medical information. Indeed, experienced lay users have, to some extent, constructed their own informal peer review networks to enable them to judge the quality of online health information (Ferguson, 2002).

ACCESS ACROSS DEMOGRAPHIC GROUPS

Not all sections of the population enjoy access to the Internet and the online information it can supply. Some people may not have easy access to information technology. Others may experience difficulty with computers. The elderly, poor, and less well-educated may be especially unlikely to utilize online health information. Even among the major demographic groups, there may be variations in patterns of use. Significantly, not all research has indicated significant differences in use of health Web sites by age or other demographic groups, or indeed in relation to whether respondents indicated they had recently experienced serious health problems themselves (Brown & Smith, 2003).

Women may be generally more likely than men to seek online health information. Research by the Pew Institute found that more than 6 in 10 women with Internet access (63%) had sought health information, versus fewer than one in two (46%) men. On a typical day, 59% of searches were carried out by women. Women, and especially mothers, frequently adopted the role of health care advocate for their children and other family members (Fox & Rainie, 2000).

Health information seekers were predominantly of middle years (30 to 64 years) rather than from younger or older age groups. The longer someone had Internet access, the more likely it was that they had looked for health information. Site loyalty was also noted. More than 4 in 10 users (42%), once they had found a useful site, were likely to bookmark it for future reference.

The Internet health organization, Health on the Net Foundation (2001), found that the vast majority of Internet health information seekers searched for medical literature (83%), with two out of three (67%) looking for descriptions of diseases and nearly 4 in 10 (38%) looking for clinical trial information.

Elderly people are much less likely than younger age groups to use the Internet. One of the reasons for nonuse of information technology among older people is connected in part with the health status. Cognitive ability, response time, and attention span can all be adversely affected by age, making it difficult to navigate around Web sites and retrieve appropriate information (Marwick, 1999). It is also common for people to lose their manual dexterity with age making it difficult to use keyboards or mice (Hoot & Hayslip, 1983). In addition, the elderly suffer from declining vision, which makes computer use difficult. Despite these problems, research has shown that older people can take to information technology, particularly if it is relevant to their own personal needs (Mead, Lamson, & Rogers, 2002).

Another barrier to online health information uptake is poverty. Despite government initiatives to reach even the most deprived people with information technology service, by placing reception equipment in libraries, hospitals, and retail outlets, there are many reasons to doubt the speedy take-up of information and communication technologies by the economically disadvantaged.

One particular group in this category is that of ethnic minorities. Both the medical profession (Atri, Falshaw, Livingstone, & Robson, 1996) and government (Acheson, 1998) have observed that ethnic minorities are more likely to be unemployed, to be poorer, and to live in poor conditions. Research has shown that non-Whites make up a very small population—perhaps as low as 10%—of Internet users (GVU, 1998). Ethnic minorities are at a disadvantage educationally because of low information technology take-up (Attwell, 1999; Chisholm, Carey, & Hernandez, 1999). Under these conditions, it is to be expected that they may not avail themselves of opportunities for access to health information from electronic sources.

Another problem confronting ethnic minorities is language. Poor command of English language is not restricted to immigrant groups. Even native English speakers may have poorly developed vocabularies. In Britain, NHS Direct (a telephone helpline service) has been faced with problems of public misunderstanding of medical terminology. One study found that 7 in 10 (70%) laypeople were unable correctly to identify the meaning of the word *unconscious* in behavioral terms, believing that an individual in that condition could still walk around (Harrison & Cooke, 2000).

Graber, Roller, and Kaeble (1999) surveyed Internet sites to assess the readability of medical information on the Web that was targeted at nonexpert populations. Text from 50 health Web sites was rated for readability using the Flesch reading score and Flesch-Kinkaid reading level. Most information was found to be written at tenth-grade level—a level that was higher than that likely to be understood by most of the expected reader population.

GOVERNMENT SPONSORED INITIATIVES IN BRITAIN

The U.K. Government has been set on using digital information platforms to expand provision of health information to the general public. The policy document *Information for Health,* for example, reinforced the notion that giving the public access to the right information at the right time was a crucial aspect of modern public health care (NHS Executive, 1998). This policy commitment resulted in a massive initiative known as *NHS Direct.* This comprises a number of information services including two Web sites (NHS Direct Online, www.nhsdirect.nhs.uk, and the National Electronic Library for Health, www.nelh.nhs.uk), a telephone hotline, and touch-screen kiosks to achieve the goals of informing patients. It is also hoped that these new online services will go some way toward alleviating the pressure on an overburdened state-run National Health Service.

NHS Direct Online

Electronic health information and advice services in Britain have been rolled out on the Internet under the general brand of NHS Direct Online. The purpose of this service is to provide the public (rather than medical and health professionals) with access to reliable information and advice about aspects of health and medical care. This includes advice for those facing a surgical operation, attempting to give up smoking or simply desirous of leading a healthier lifestyle. The site also features a health consumer magazine and latest health news. This development represents part of a wider e-government initiative. NHS Direct online therefore represents a rich source of health-related content for consultation and acts as a gateway to a wide range of other health information and advice sources (Gann & Sadler, 2001).

As we have seen in chapter 3 (this volume), the U.K.'s Department of Health has been concerned to ensure that ICTs are implemented and used effectively. As part of this process, detailed evaluation studies were commissioned to measure the penetration, utilization and impact of these services from their onset. Three platforms have been used so far: the Internet, touch-screen kiosks, and interactive digital television (iDTV). The use and impact of kiosks and iDTV are explored in later chapters. To begin with, however, research into the effectiveness of the Internet as a health information platform will be examined.

The Department of Health began the roll-out of largely text-based electronic information services in 1999 in partnership with a leading consumer health-information company, Intouch with Health. In addition to deploying kiosks in different locations around the United Kingdom, this company established a Web site called Surgery Door (www.surgerydoor.co.uk). The Web site information was evaluated in terms of real-time use and user opinions. This research was designed to produce a broad understanding of the way people might use this type of information and of their perceptions of such services.

The NHS Direct Online site offered a number of menu items for users to choose from on the homepage. The search facility on the site is directly related to the modular structure of the content. The structure is hierarchical offering a number of main modules on the homepage and submenus within these main modules that are linked to further, separately headed information sections. The main modules comprised:

- NHS Direct Healthcare Guide (ways of treating common symptoms at home);
- Health Living (how to maintain a healthy lifestyle);
- Conditions and Treatment (offering links to thousands of quality-assessed sources of information and advice);
- Health Features (a monthly magazine with links to external sites); Feedback (an e-mail facility whereby users could comment on the site);
- "Listen Here" Audio Clips on a variety of topics; About NHS Direct (information about the site);
- NHS A–Z (a database of information about NHS services); and
- The homepage also offered a section on Frequently Asked Questions and links to U.K. Online and Care Direct, two further online public services-related sites.

User research was undertaken utilizing digital logs that measured real-time visits to the SurgeryDoor site (Nicholas, Huntington, & Williams, 2001a, 2001b). The log files comprised machine-generated records of user activity. The precise information collected depended on the software and how the server was configured. Nonetheless, Web site log files yielded data on numbers of site visits, which health topics were selected, and length of time users spent at the site or consuming specific parts of its content.

The Web files used in this research provided an IP (Internet Protocol) number that could not identify a specific individual, but could identify the personal computer through which the site visit was made. In some user environments, the IP address might refer to a group of users. In that case, reference to cookies (unique PC identifiers increasingly installed as a default on PCs) could provide another method for distinguishing users. The Web logs were configured to identify page use. The methodology also incorporated a default procedure for determining session lengths, taking into account the failure of many users to log off from the Web immediately after they have finished using it. Under this protocol 30 minutes of inactivity signaled the end of a Web visit session (Zawitz, 1999).

Several metrics were generated from the Web log files. These included: number of pages viewed, number of user sessions, length of user session, page view time, number of pages viewed in a session, and topic viewed.

Mean page view time for the Internet health site was 69 seconds. In considering this figure, Nicholas et al. also explained that downloading time, the density of information being accessed, and caching would all contribute to viewing time.

Looking at session view times, an Internet session end signal was recorded if the user remained on a page for longer than 300 seconds. On average, a Web site session lasted a little less than 10 minutes. The average number of session per hour for the Internet was about 51.

In an attempt to make more meaningful statements about the extent to which people used a system, users were classified according to whether they reached only menu (navigation) pages or whether they penetrated as far as a page with actual information (nonnavigation) content. For actual use to have occurred, the information seeker has to navigate beyond the collection of initial menu screens and reach the actual information pages. This type of classification is especially important in menu-based systems where the user has to navigate through a number of menu screens to arrive at an information page.

Users recording a single page download were classified as not penetrating to an information page. At the time of the research, content pages were single HTML pages containing information on a number of topics with a menu of internal links at the top of the page. There were up to two high menu levels. In addition, there were a variety of links from the opening page that went directly to an information page. Depending on how users entered the Web site it was highly likely that they would have cached a multiple-topic information page and a menu page by downloading just two pages. Caching entails files being downloaded to the user's PC. Further reading of pages on that file are then not recorded in the Web log files held on the server. The user could then read about related topics by accessing the cached information and menu pages. During this access the server would not record any more hits or page downloads. This means that the page view statistics, based on Web log files, may have underestimated total use of the online health content being examined (Nicholas et al., 2001b).

User Opinions About Online Health Information

Nicholas, Huntington, Williams, and Blackburn (2001) conducted a parallel survey of users' opinions about the SurgeryDoor Web site. A questionnaire was posted on the Web site. This was targeted at 2,700 subscribers to the site's newsletter, and 1,068 users responded. The survey sought to find out why the site was visited and whether the health information obtained from it had had any outcome.

A clear majority of respondents (80%) were female. Nearly one half of respondents (49%) were aged between 35 and 54 years. Few respondents (0.5%) were aged over 75 years. Most respondents reported that they had arrived at the site either via a search engine (30%) or having read about it (29%).

Asked about their health information sources, it was clear that the doctor was the most popular primary information source (just more than 50%), with leaflets (38%) being the second most often mentioned main information source. When asked about secondary information sources, however, the Internet (named by 26%) was second after the doctor (named by 28%).

Turning to reasons for visiting the SurgeryDoor site, three out of four respondents said they did not visit the site with a particular illness or medical condition in mind. Indeed, a significant proportion of users (45%) claimed to get advice about keeping fit and healthy. Far fewer visited the site because of current illness (15%) or a long-standing complaint (10%). Indeed, many respondents (48%) said they visited the site to get information on behalf of someone else.

The survey was also interested in finding out about health outcomes for users of this health Web site. Several questions probed this. Respondents were asked if the information they had found on the site had helped them in dealing with their doctor. They were asked if they felt better informed as a result of using the site. Then, had the information found on the Internet changed the way they felt about their condition? Finally, had their condition improved as a result of finding information on the Internet?

Just less than one half of users (47%) felt that the information they had found had helped in their dealings with the doctor, with nearly one in four (24%) saying it had helped them a lot in this respect. However, 4 in 10 (40%) did not answer this question at all. More than 8 in 10 (84%) said they felt better informed having used this health Web site. One half (50%) said that visiting the SurgeryDoor site had changed the way they felt about their condition, although here again, many respondents (38%) did not answer (Nicholas, Huntington, Williams, & Blackburn, 2001).

Nicholas and his colleagues were heartened by these findings. Despite the high nonresponse rates to some of the questions, the findings offered promising insights into the potential health outcomes of online health information. This interpretation of the results was strengthened by more than one in three respondents (36%) who claimed that their condition had improved after having visited the site. Even here, however, a further qualification is needed. The perception of improved health condition contingent on visiting the site was reported by users who searched on behalf of someone else rather than among those searching for themselves. Nearly one in two respondents (47%) who had searched the site on behalf of someone else said that the information had helped a lot in changing the way they thought about their condition. Users were more likely to report that the site had been of no help tot hem when they were currently suffering from or had a long-term illness.

Regular Internet users and regular users of the SurgeryDoor site held more positive views about the helpfulness of the site in various health outcome terms. For instance, more than 9 in 10 (91%) of users who visited the site every day said the information had changed what they thought about their condition, compared with just more than 7 in 10 (73%) people who visited monthly.

Respondents were also asked if they ever used information found on this site as an alternative to seeing the doctor. Was the information they found sufficient to meet their health query and substitute for a visit to the doctor? Nearly all respondents (98%) answered this question, and of these, just over one in four (27%) said that Web information had replaced a visit to the doctor. In the context of the self-help goals of such online health information services this was clearly an important finding. This type of use of the Web was particularly strong among those with more significantly developed health interests, those who had a current complaint, but not a long-term one, and those who attached more quality and authority to the information on the site (Nicholas, Huntington, Williams, & Blackburn, 2001).

In a subsequent publication, Nicholas, Huntington, Williams, and Jordan (2002) presented results from a further survey of NHS Direct Online users. The sample on this occasion comprised 3,374 site users who replied to an online questionnaire over a 13-month period.

An overwhelming majority of respondents were from the U.K. (95%). This contrasted with the geographical profile of users as indicated by computer logs that had indicated that up to 49% of NHS Direct Online visitors came via Internet service providers based in the U.S. There was a fairly even balance of male (48.8%) and female (51.2%) users as indicated by online survey responses. More than one half of respondent users (53%) were aged 25 to 44 years, with one in five (20%) aged younger than 25 and one in four (27%) aged older than 44 years.

Most users said they had accessed the NHS Direct Online site from home (64%), with the next most likely location being at work (28%). Users found out about the site from a number of different sources, including a search engine, a link, or from publicity or press reports about it. An online information sources was most significant in this context, followed by the press and other media. This suggested that users of NHS Direct Online were, to a large extent, already familiar with the Internet and World Wide Web.

Many users (43%) visited just one section, although significant proportions of users visited two (23%) or three or more sections (33%). The most popularly visited section concerned Conditions and Treatment, followed by About NHS Direct and then NHS A–Z. When asked what improvements they would make to the site, the most frequent request (35%) was for an e-mail health enquiry service. Another popular request (21%) was for more local information. More than one in five visitors to the site (22%) said they had telephoned the NHS Direct help-line in the past. More than one half these respondents (57%) were women.

The site was not generally found easy to navigate around. The search system was criticized as was the availability of desired content. Respondents commented on being unable to find the topic-specific information they sought. There were also problems with understanding what to expect in the way of content under specific general headings. One example of this was the section labeled *Healthcare Guide*. It is not at all clear from this heading alone what kinds of topics lie behind it (Nicholas, Huntington, Williams, & Jordan, 2002).

In a further study, Williams, Nicholas, Huntington, and McLean (2002) interviewed 20 health Web site users about their online experiences. These individuals were given information retrieval tasks to perform that ranged from searching for specific content to in-depth probing of a site. The results showed that users were unhappy with the large amount of text on each page and found it difficult to read lengthy content. They also experienced site navigation problems, although acknowledged that the content itself was well produced. Commercial features, such as brand promotions, were not well received. Many participants regarded these features as inappropriate for a health information Web site and believed that it affected the authority of the information. Content producers were recommended to reduce the number and location of content entries and the quantity of textual material per page.

The opinions online health Web site users voice about online health services may be predictive of levels of use. British research found that when users exhibited poor opinions about site attributes such as ease of navigation and speed of response, for example, this could signal a wider dissatisfaction with the Web site and was associated with fewer site visits (Huntington, Nicholas, & Williams, 2003b). Need profiles can, in turn, provide good indicators of specific content areas within a health Web site that users choose to visit. Users who say they visit health Web sites to keep up to date were found to rate medical news and medical research update sections highly. Users who exhibited an interest in alternative medicine rated content on natural health remedies and complementary medicine most highly. Users interested in keeping fit, rated content of general health and diet topics most highly (Huntington et al., 2003b).

ONLINE HEALTH CARE PROVISION FOR THE ELDERLY

A parallel project was undertaken to explore the provision of online health information to older people in Britain. The CarePlus Project was sponsored by the NHS Executive Trust Information Taskforce to investigate where older people find out about local services, where voluntary carers and health and social care professionals get their information from. The objective was to set up a one-stop information service on the Internet targeting older people and carers in four communities in the east midlands region of England. Information was edited and quality assured centrally, put into a database and published on the Internet (www.careplus.info). The system was then evaluated by older people, voluntary carers, and professionals who had used it (Emery, Cowan, Eaglestone, Heyes, Proctor, & Willis, 2002).

A multimethod approach was adopted for the evaluation exercise that combined focus groups, telephone interviews, and an online self-completion questionnaire survey. Two focus groups with users were conducted at each of the four pilot sites, one when the pilot had been established and another after the Web site had gone live. Telephone depth interviews were conducted at three out of the four sites with 24 interviewees at each location. Finally, 60 online questionnaire responses were analyzed.

Initial focus groups revealed that older people experienced fear and anxiety over using information technology—an emotional response driven significantly by a lack of knowledge. There were other more practical reasons for not using computer-mediated communications that included the expense of purchasing one's own equipment and lack of ready access to it anywhere else. Older people were found to display varied attitudes toward different forms of health-related communication, mostly preferring to be informed by word of mouth or on paper, while feeling less enamored with the telephone and not very comfortable at all with computer-mediated communication. Notwithstanding their communications channel preferences, older people indicated that they needed information on a range of health and personal matters, including respite care, medical conditions, legal issues, citizens advice, catteries and kennels, hearing aid battery supplies, and transportation.

Telephone interviews with older people and health care professionals who had used the Web site confirmed many of the findings of the focus groups. Although users had experienced initial anxieties about using information technology, older people who had experimented could recognize the potential of the Internet. There was also an acknowledgment, however, that training and support in its use was needed. The online survey went further and explored users' opinions about the ease of use of the health information Web site. The content of the CarePlus site was thought to conform to the information needs of its target users, although some concerns were expressed about ease of use. Nonetheless, it was seen as fulfilling a potential need and as an appropriate way to store and relay information.

In sum, the CarePlus research revealed that older people can be reached by a Web-based health information service. Although they express initial reservations and worries about the technology, Internet use can be cultivated among the elderly. This kind of online service must be readily accessible and easy to use, and deliver the type of content older people most value and need. Initial training and support must be provided, however, if many older people are to be coaxed into using online services (Emery et al., 2002).

CONCLUSIONS

Health information on the Internet has flourished within the space of just a few years. Individuals with access to the World Wide Web can find huge quantities of health-related content from a wide range of sources. The search for health information is one of the main reasons why Internet users go online. The provision of health information online has been identified by governments as having the potential to support overstretched public health services. Although health Web sites cannot provide treatment, they can offer advice. In turn, they may encourage a climate of self-help among citizens meaning that they might take more preventive measures than previously, or adopt healthier lifestyles. In addition, they may consult the Web rather than seeing their doctor, simply for health information.

The ease with which health information can be published on the Internet, however, does call into question the quality of the information to be found there. Although some information suppliers may be reputable individuals or organizations whose primary motivation is to help people, some health Web sites may have a different purpose, linked more to self-promotion of the supplier or the supplier's business than to helping others. As this chapter has discussed, concerns have been publicly voiced in health and medical journals about the quality of health information and advice on the Web. Attempts have been made to develop and implement quality standards and systems for signaling whether the information on a health site derives from a reputable or suitably qualified source. Some of these quality control guidelines have been aimed at kite-marking health Web sites in general (Gagliardi & Jadad, 2002; Kunst et al., 2002; Silberg et al., 1997), whereas others have focused on sites providing information on specific conditions or illnesses (Griffiths & Christensen, 2000). There is room for further work to be done before a standard set of recommendations and guidelines materializes, although some progress is being made (Health on the Net Foundation, 2001; Kim et al., 1999).

The importance of ensuring that the Internet conveys credible, trustworthy, and high quality information is underlined by the extent to which it is used as a health information source. Significant numbers of people in the developed world turn to the Internet for this reason (Brown & Smith, 2003; Eurobarometer, 2000; Pew Institute, 2003). However, it also clear that many of these seekers of health Web sites, visit sites run by pharmaceutical corporations for which such sites represent one source of promotion for their products (Brown & Smith, 2003).

The Internet has emerged as a valuable alternative source of health information to health professionals. Many users of online health information have acknowledged that it acts as a substitute for raising enquiries with their doctor (Fox & Rainie, 2002). Questions about the reliability of health information on the Web has led to recommendations that online information consumers should visit a number of health Web sites. In fact many experienced Web users do just that. Furthermore, they may even establish their own online networks among other Internet users and exchange intelligence about the quality of online health content (Ferguson, 2002).

Such developments may pass some people by. Older people may be less likely to consult health Web sites not just because they use the Internet less than do younger people, but also because they trust their doctors first and foremost. Understanding the use of the Internet as a health information source, however, requires detailed study of patterns of health Web site use. This ideally should include real-time analysis of Web behavior and user reaction measurement. Such research has indicated that people will use the Internet to locate a variety of different kinds of health information (Nicholas, Huntington, Williams, & Jordan, 2002). Some users, however, do experience problems with health Web sites that content producers and site designers need to know about (Williams, Nicholas, Huntington, & McLean, 2002). Online health information systems aimed at the elderly need to be carefully constructed to ensure that the user group at which they are targeted are not discouraged by accessibility problems and lack of relevance to their needs (Emery et al., 2002).

The Internet has become established as a major health information source and has promise as a support mechanism for public health services. The objective that underpins online health services is that of health consumer empowerment. For this objective to be achieved, studies that have begun to understand how individuals use health Web sites and the problems they experience with them need to continue.

Digital Health Via Kiosks

◇

One of the key technologies to have been deployed in connection with the roll-out of online health information and advice services is the kiosk. Just as information content in text and image formats can be supplied via personal computers on the Internet, similar content can be presented in similar formats via publicly located technologies.

Although the Internet offers considerable scope for pushing out large quantities of health-related information to patients and the general public, access to the Internet is not universal. Internet penetration has grown rapidly within the space of under a decade, but even in countries such as the U.S. and U.K. significant proportions of the population are still without Internet access. This "digital divide" is a critical factor that vitiates the aims of governments to create a world of electronic public services. What is especially significant about this divide is that the digital have-nots tend to be predominantly those people who need the greatest help in terms of their health.

One solution to this problem has been the establishment of public access points to electronic information networks through touch-screen kiosks or personal computers in locations such as libraries, shops, cyber cafes, and health centers. (Eng et al., 1998). Kiosks can provide accessible health information in large quantities for patients and other members of the public who do not have Internet access at home. Even this solution is not universally effective because some people may be physically unable to get to specific locations—even when close by—or once there may be self-conscious about using the technology.

The latest versions of this technology employ a touch-screen format whereby users can access large banks of information via menu items shown on screen by physically touching the screen itself (Jones, 2003). In Britain, the government has sponsored a roll-out of hundreds of such kiosks in a variety of public locations, including health centers and doctors' surgeries, hospitals, public libraries, and even supermarkets. The private sector has been quick to recognize the potential of this new development. One company, InTouch, had installed nearly 170 kiosks in different locations using content supplied by the Department of Health, medical charities and other health organizations by 2002 (InTouch with Health, 2002).

Another system, the Wellpoint Interactive Health Centres, has been rolled out in pharmacies across the United Kingdom providing information on more than 500 ailments and offering tests for blood pressure, heart rate, and body mass index (Greener, 2002). Further kiosks have been sited across more than 180 locations under the NHS Direct banner, representing part of the British government's plans to provide around-the-clock access to health services (Action Multimedia, 2003).

The speed with which kiosks have been installed around the United Kingdom heralds an era of unprecedented health information dissemination that warrants investigation in terms of its use, reception, effectiveness, and impact (Nicholas, Huntington, & Williams, 2001b). As with wider online health information systems, kiosks are intended not simply to give the public and patients in general access to a richer one-stop source of health advice, but also more especially to reach particular groups within society who may be most in need of such help. Indeed, it is hoped that kiosks may reach those sections of society who are not linked to the Internet.

Despite the speed of kiosk roll-out in doctors' surgeries, hospitals, supermarkets, and shopping malls, and even in railway stations (Nicholas et al., 2001b), relatively little research had been conducted on their usability and application effectiveness. Yet, kiosks were set up to generate user data in real time in the form of digital logs. Such logs could be analyzed to yield information about how often these machines were used, how many different people used them, the type of health content accessed, and the length of time spent online. Supplementary user questions, administered off-line through interviews and self-completion questionnaires or online via electronic questions on screen, could be used to provide further details about users, such as their sex and age, and reasons for seeking health information. Demographic information was particularly important given that online technologies were designed to give better information access to specific subgroups within the population who were recognized as having special needs.

HISTORY

The first touch-screen health information system operated through a kiosk-type device was Healthpoint. This was developed by a research team at Glasgow University (Jones, MacLachlan, & Bell, 1990; Jones, Navin, & Murray, 1993).

The first prototype system was developed in 1988/1989. It used a keyboard where nine colored keys represented menu items. The devices were placed in the waiting area of a health center (Jones et al., 1990). Information was included on drugs, contraception, AIDS, and other topics. There were also lists of local facilities and help groups. In an initial evaluation, 35 people were interviewed about the use of the kiosk, almost all of whom were positive about the system. Only two individuals (6%) thought Healthpoint was not easy to use. A clear majority of 32 out of 35 (91%) were in favor of retaining the facility on a more permanent basis.

In a questionnaire survey of 151 users of the health center, about one in three (34%) said they used Healthpoint. Use was not related to sex, age, neighborhood type or length of time spent in the waiting room. More than 6 in 10 (63%) said they used the kiosk out of curiosity, between 3 and 4 out of 10 (37%) sought specific information, and most of those (95%) said they found the information they were looking for.

The first touch-screen version of Healthpoint was launched in 1991. Twenty-five terminals were situated in a variety of places in Clydebank, including a chemist, health center, library, and public house. Ten machines were formally evaluated. A random telephone survey that was conducted 5 months after installation showed that under one in five of the sample (17%) had used at least one of the terminals. Direct monitoring of the machines is use revealed that the most accessed pages were for smoking, AIDS, alcohol, women's health, and sex (Jones et al., 1993). A Spanish version of the system was also developed (Jones et al., 2000).

Pearson et al. (1999) outlined a number of factors that may influence the accessibility of information systems for the general public: authenticity of content, ease of use and navigation around the service, location of sought-after content, situated at convenient location and available at convenient times, and available for use at no charge.

They reported on accessibility of two similar touch-screen computer systems used in a randomized trial in Scotland by patients with cancer. Use, repeat use, and ease of use were related to demographics, level of anxiety, prior computer experience, attitudes, and information need. One in five (19%) agreed that using the computer made them feel a little anxious, but one half (50%) said they were looking forward to it. Most respondents had either no prior computer experience (55%) or only limited experience (39%). A majority (78%) said they found the system easy to use.

Research has been conducted on the use of touch-sensitive video monitor for entering health-related quality of life and found that virtually all users said the technology was easy to use (Buxton, White, & Osoba, 1999). Another study examined the effectiveness of a touch-screen system with an information leaflet for providing women with information on prenatal tests (Graham et al., 2000). This represents a matter for informed choice by patients and is an area in which there have been many technical and medical advances that have advanced the number of conditions for which screening is available. The researchers were also interested in examining the effect on patients' decision making as measured by their understanding and take-up of tests, patients' satisfaction with the information provided and its effects on their anxiety levels. More than 1,000 women were recruited and more than 800 continued until the end of the study. These participants were randomly divided into intervention and control groups. Both groups were given the information leaflet, whereas the intervention group also had access to the touch-screen system.

Similar percentages of women in both groups read the leaflet (57% in the intervention group; 61% in the control group). The women's understanding of the available tests improved significantly for both groups but did not differ significantly between groups. Although, other commentators have referred to the limitations of the questionnaire-based knowledge measures used by this study (see Williams, Parker, Stoddard, Bomken, & Prabhu, 2000). Nonetheless, satisfaction was high for both information systems, with an overwhelming majority (more than 90%) of both groups saying they would recommend the leaflet and touch-screen system. The touch-screen group did exhibit some signs of enhanced impact. Participants in this group exhibited reduced anxiety levels and greater take-up of an anomaly test, as compared to the control group.

Nicholas, Williams, and Huntington (2000b) provided some preliminary data on use of touch-screen kiosks for health information in a small-scale study that formed part of a larger program of research. This investigation reported on the use of kiosks in different locations around England. They reported low use of kiosks by older people. Fewer than one in five users (18%) were aged older than 55 years. The authors commented that use of new information technologies of this sort may be linked to generations. Older people trust doctors as a primary source of health information and therefore feel less comfortable using IT sources. Children, although generally less concerned with health matters than their elders, were more likely than older people to use these kiosks. More than one in five (22%) of all users logged by Nicholas and his colleagues were aged younger than 15. However, it was not clear whether they used kiosks seriously or simply to pass the time while waiting to be seen in the doctor's surgery.

In this survey of 70 kiosks sites, Nicholas, Williams, and Huntington (2000) also examined the types of content users explored and noted a few gender differences. Males were more likely than females to look up information on abnormal heart rhythm and brain tumors, while females were more likely than males to look up pages concerned with migraine. Another finding concerned the extent to which kiosks were used by health professionals. Kiosks were thought to be an excellent medium by which nurses could keep informed, particularly on issues such as the latest vaccinations information. The health staff interviewed for this study observed that patients were becoming more knowledgeable about conditions as a result of reading about it on kiosks. There was no suggestion, however, that this either benefited or undermined the work of health professionals.

A position has been reached where touch-screen technology is used for a range of interactive and non-interactive applications in the health context and the use of this technology has expanded worldwide (Boudioni, 2003).

METHODOLOGICAL ISSUES

Information and communication technologies do not only provide opportunities to achieve wider public information access for the population at large, they also incorporate the technical capabilities to record real-time usage. Although there are many different researchable issues connected to the use of ICTs, the extent to which specific applications are used, by whom, and for what purposes are central considerations. In research on health information provided via the Web, a number of key measures of access and use have already been identified. These have included: user numbers, pages viewed, number of search sessions undertaken, length of time per search session, and length of time viewing individual pages of content (see chap. 4, this volume). With respect to kiosks, however, two further measures have been identified. These comprise the number of prints made and kiosk capacity. The "prints made" measure refers to the number of pages viewed that the user also prints off in hard copy. Kiosk capacity refers to a measure of the number of pages viewed by the user during a single search session.

Although kiosks can yield log files similar to those of the Web and other online services that comprise plain text records of use transactions that are automatically logged by the system, much early research still depended heavily on offline measurement methods even for measuring basic levels of use. The first study of medical kiosk use in the U.K., for example, estimated use via self-completion questionnaire responses and did not utilize log data (Jones et al., 1990). A later investigation did analyze logs, but produced discrepant findings with log data apparently revealing 65 search episodes, and a video taken of users showing that the system was used by 116 people (Navin, Jones, Kohil, & Crawford, 1996). As Nicholas, Williams, and Huntington (2001b) explained: "The discrepancy was due to users taking over the kiosk before the session was timed out, thus appearing on the log file as a continuation of the previous searcher and so both underestimating user numbers and, consequently, overestimating session length" (p. 62). Later studies began to introduce more regular use of log data to measure amount of kiosk use, but still experienced methodological problems that were never effectively explained (e.g., Jones et al., 1999).

The metrics used on kiosk logs have been largely derived from techniques used to analyze Internet log files (Stout, 1997; Williams, 1999a) and online public access catalogue (OPAC) log files (Nicholas, 1996). Key measures include the number of visitors, number of pages viewed, page view time, number of pages per session, and session time. Although a variety of metrics therefore exist through which to represent and paint a portrait of kiosk use, difficulties have been experienced with the validity of some of the time-based variables such as session and page view time. The restriction of reporting to aggregate use measures has been found to omit much of what goes on in relation to kiosk use behavior (Nicholas & Huntington, 1999). A closer focus on what is printed off and the amount of time spent online at a kiosk can often be very revealing. Such measures can indicate which information is of most relevance or importance to individual users. It can also show the extent to which users are prepared to spend time searching for the information they want. Furthermore, given that this particular ICT tends to located public places where the user may face competition for kiosk time for other users, this will also have a bearing on the average length of time users are able to spend online at kiosks.

There are usability issues connected with kiosks. Information systems on these machines tend to be menu-driven. This means that the user must navigate a number of menu screens before they find the information page they need. Hence, simple measures of pages or screen viewed or amount of time engaged in this activity, may be less revealing about the amount of information accessed and consumed than about the time effort needed to find the information being sought. Thus, to be more meaningful, measures of kiosk use need to be sensitive to the hierarchical nature of content organization and acknowledge that not every page viewed is an information page. Instead, some pages viewed may simply be part of the route leading to the eventual page being sought (Nicholas, Williams, & Huntington, 2001).

CHILDREN'S USE OF KIOSKS

Douglas, Jones, and Navin (1995) undertook two studies with children. In the first, pupils at a catholic school in Glasgow were invited to look at a Healthpoint touch-screen kiosk and produce stories for news topics, which they later developed using a computer-based presentation package. Topics the children suggested tended to be oriented around the general themes of sex and eating, and included stories on teenage pregnancies, rape, abortion, anorexia, and bulimia. Some of these ideas were not originally included on Healthpoint and were later incorporated as a direct result of this exercise. Thus, pupils saw their ideas rapidly being disseminated in the wider community.

In a second study, three selected schools were given terminals and pupils and staff were interviewed about their experiences using them. Two Catholic schools participating requested censoring of the information. The whole section on sex was removed (this dealt with contraception and sexually transmitted diseases). In feedback questionnaires and group discussions, girls tended to complain that the system should have been more private. In general, the pupils wanted more information than that offered (e.g., drug-related information).

Williams, Huntington, and Nicholas (2000a) reported a study of single kiosk in a heath center in the south of England. Logs of real-time use were collected and were supplemented by observational evidence. Users aged under 15 were most interested in travel pages, especially boys. Girls exhibited more interest in pages on healthy living. These findings were borne out by log data and direct field observation of use of the kiosk. In a larger study, the same authors, as previously indicated, reported that more than one in five kiosks users were aged under 15, although it was not clear whether their use was serious or simply playful (Nicholas, Williams, & Huntington, 2000).

DIGITAL VERSUS PAPER SOURCES

Graham et al. (2000) looked at effectiveness of touch screen system with an information leaflet for providing women with information on prenatal tests. Two factors led to choice of this subject. First, it is an area in which informed choice for patients has long been applied and second, medical advances have meant that the number of conditions for which screening is available is ever growing.

The principal measure used here was the effect on patients' decision making as measured by their understanding and take-up of the tests. Other outcomes included their satisfaction with information provision and their anxiety levels. Their understanding of content was measured by pre-, during-, and post-test questionnaires and their mood states by the Spielberger state-trait anxiety inventory.

The sample was obtained from women attending antenatal clinics at Aberdeen maternity Hospital. In all, 1,050 consenting women began the experiment, with 875 continuing until the end. Participants were randomly allocated to intervention and control groups.

Results showed that similar numbers of women from both groups read the leaflet fully (57% intervention group, 61% control group) and 12% of both groups glanced at it. In all, 91% of intervention group indicated that they had used the touch-screen at least once. Understanding of tests improved for both groups during the project, but no difference between touch-screen and leaflets informing participants. Of five tests offered only one was undertaken by a significantly different number of women from the intervention group: 97% versus 87%.

The authors suggested that the use of video clips to show what can be gained from such a scan might have helped reassure women and increased their desire for this investigation. Overall satisfaction with both media forms—leaflet and kiosk—was high. Anxiety levels reduced for the touch-screen group, but were unchanged for the leaflet group. The researchers concluded that there was no additional benefit of touch-screen over leaflet. But some differences had been observed, despite this conclusion. One test was taken up more frequently by the touch-screen group. Nonetheless, the cost attached to the touch screen system (£25k) meant that it was expensive.

Jones et al. (1999) undertook their own comparative study of information delivery systems. They compared the use and effect of three information sources for cancer patients: a personalized computer-based information system, a general computer system, and booklets. The authors argued that cancer patients usually want as much information as possible. Their sample comprised patients suffering from breast, cervical, prostrate, and laryngeal cancer. In all, 525 participants were divided into the three intervention groups. Computer logging recorded real-time use of computerized systems.

Average time per computer session was 12 minutes (with a range from one to 44 minutes). Nearly 3 in 10 patients (29%) used the computer a second time during a 3-month follow-up. Of those who had access to the personal and general information, two thirds went to the personal information section. Booklet information was described purely in terms of home use. More use was reported of hard copy material at home compared with computer information and booklets were described as more attractive than computer printouts. Exposure to any of the material produced no significant changes in patients' depression scores or mental adjustment scores across experiment.

Velikova et al. (1999) compared a touch-screen system to complete a Quality of Life questionnaire, and also a Hospital Anxiety and Depression Scale, with paper-based equivalents. One hundred forty-nine cancer patients took part and completed questionnaires in both formats. Fifty-two percent of patients preferred the touch-screen, 24% the paper version, and 24% had no preference. Patients found the touch-screen easy to use. There was near equivalence in scores for the paper and touch-screen versions.

USE BY HEALTH PROFESSIONALS AND LAYPEOPLE

Touch-screen kiosks can provide access to large quantities of health and medical information at different levels of complexity. Such information can be fond useful by the public and professionals alike. Patyk, Gaynor, Kelly, and Ott (1998) looked at how touch-screen systems could be used in patient education. They measured the attitudes and perceptions of medical staff and lay people on the effectiveness of a multimedia computerized package operated by a touch-screen system—the Brain Injury Resource Center (BIRC). This is a multimedia CD-ROM learning center offering 23 hours of educational information on traumatic brain injury. The system supplies basic information, defines medical terms, and allows users to see and hear real patients and their families tell about their brain injury experiences. The BIRC rests on its own base, can be viewed easily from either a standing or sitting position, and is wheelchair accessible.

Data were gathered from a written survey of 31 health care professionals and a 30-minute interview of patients with brain injury and their families. Both questionnaires and interviews covered the same ground: the usefulness of the information, the effectiveness of the teaching methodology, and the most appropriate time frame within the care process for implementation. Both the medical staff and patient participants viewed the BIRC for at least 15 minutes, although most spent more than the required viewing time. The content used most widely included frequently asked questions, information about brain damage, and treatment and rehabilitation information. The content was highly rated by most users who found the text information useful, well presented, and easy to digest.

In the patient interviews, the wealth of information, readability, glossary, and the presentation of real-life cases were all praised. Interviewees said that the touch-screen methodology, format and instructions made it very user-friendly and easy to follow. Such positive responses emerged even among users who reported that they were not computer literate.

The benefits of BIRC were perceived differently by the health care professionals and patients and families. Patients generally believed that the provision of background information was a real benefit, whereas only around one third of health care professionals agreed. Both groups believed that the system stimulated questions and reinforced information obtained directly from professionals. Patients, more than professionals, also felt that the information could help to calm their anxieties. Perhaps the most significant difference of opinion was that patients regarded computer-based education as central to their quest for information, whereas health care professionals regarded it as a supplementary source.

Williams et al. (2001) reported a study of use of a touch-screen kiosk in a single location. Substantial use of health professionals was reported during interviews with them. Nurses tended to report using the system more than doctors. Both doctors and nurses also referred patients to the terminal. Although it represented a useful resource in this sense, staff were also concerned that patients might think they were directing them to look at kiosks rather than asking direct questions of health professionals.

Nicholas, Williams, and Huntington (2001) conducted a series of one-to-one and group interviews with health professionals and surgery practice managers in medical locations where touch screen information kiosks were available for use by patients. User log data from earlier research had revealed relatively high levels of use of kiosks by children. Medical practitioners spoke of helping children both to use the system for school projects and to access pages on behalf of parents and grandparents. Hence, young people were encouraged to use this new technology for constructive purposes. This did not mean that inappropriate use never occurred; indeed, this was reported also by a number of the doctors interviewed in this study.

Practice nurses were often more proactive than doctors in encouraging patients to use kiosks, and perceived many health-related benefits to accrue from referring patients to a kiosk. The kiosk could provide access to far more information than it was physically or economically viable to provide in leaflet form. It catered to the need to empower patients by providing them with readily accessible and digestible information from a credible and trusted source. In practical terms, referral to the kiosk was used by some doctors to signal the end of a consultation. Health professionals themselves also acknowledge use of kiosks to obtain up-to-date information on a variety of health matters, with nurses being more frequent users than doctors.

GOVERNMENT INITIATIVES IN BRITAIN

To improve access to health information and health advice, the British government established NHS Direct in 1998. Although the main point of contact for this system was a telephone helpline, the further establishment of NHS Direct Online extended the service to Web-based and kiosk-based platforms. Jones (2003) reported that kiosks were used an average of 12 times a day, with around one in four kiosk users also having used the Internet for health information, but with a larger proportion (36%) having not used the Internet.

Nicholas and his colleagues (Nicholas, Huntington, & Williams, 2001b, 2001c; Nicholas, Huntington, Williams, & Chahal, 2001; Nicholas, Williams, & Huntington, 2000; Williams, Huntington, & Nicholas, 2000a; Williams, Nicholas, & Huntington, 2001) have conducted a series of important investigations with funding from the U.K.'s Department of Health to examine in greater detail than ever before the use and impact of touch-screen kiosks located throughout the U.K. Some of these studies have already been noted in this chapter. Here they are examined chronologically and more closely. The technology in this case had been developed by leading consumer health information company InTouch with Health.

To start a kiosk session users had to enter their age and gender and were then lead to a main index page. This page offered six options: Medical Conditions, Surgical Operations, Health News, Support Groups, Healthy Living and Health Directory. A tab indicating *More Subjects* was situated at the bottom of the screen. This led to two more entries: A–Z of the NHS and Travel Clinic. Although the construction and layout of each section was not quite the same, activating any of the main menu items led to a further list of contents. Some information sections contained far more content than others and required users to search through more layers to reach the most detailed information available on specific topics.

Nicholas, Williams, and Huntington (2000) reported initial findings from a study of over 70 kiosks in locations throughout the U.K. The research was based on evaluation of user logs and focused on an analysis of amount and patterns of use, the characteristics of users and variations in use that were associated with the physical (e.g., hospitals, surgeries, etc.) and geographical locations of kiosks.

In an initial pilot study, Williams, Huntington, & Nicholas (2000a) evaluated use of kiosks installed by *InTouch With Health* in four locations, Truro, Penzance, Oxford and Stockport, over a 6-month period from September 1999. During the period, 8,685 people used the kiosks and viewed 82,442 pages. There was an inverse relation of use with age. The heaviest users were aged 36 to 55 and 16 to 35, and the lightest users were aged over 75. Most interest was shown in Medical Conditions (41.5% of all enquiries), followed by Surgical Operations (17.2%), and Healthy Living (16.3%). The Healthy Living pages that were most viewed dealt with alcohol, good eating, exercise, weight, cancer prevention, back pain, abnormal heart rhythm, smoking, stress, and asthma.

Nicholas, Huntington, and Williams (2001a, 2001b, 2001c) reported a further analysis of InTouch with health touch-screen kiosks situated across the U.K. Nicholas et al. (2001a) presented data for more than 50 such kiosks. Again, they examined how much kiosks were used, how many people were users, and whether there were differences in levels of use geographically.

At the time of the study, there were 79 kiosks operating. Questionnaire data were obtained for 50 kiosks and log data of continuous real-time behavior usage were available for 56 kiosks. The log data covered varying lengths and periods of time for different kiosks, ranging from 1 to 9 months in each case. The log data provided measures of amount of use, number of users, number of pages printed, page view time, session time, and number of pages consulted per session. Questionnaire data provided additional information about the reasons for kiosk installation, its physical location, its promotion to the public, and its use by health professionals (Nicholas et al., 2001c).

In total, over one hundred thousand (116,647) user sessions and nearly a million page views (961,162) were recorded. Kiosk use varied significantly across geographical locations. Females used the system a little more than did men and most users were aged under 35 years.

On average 1.75 pages were printed off per kiosk hour. Fewer pages were printed off in doctor's surgeries, however, than in other locations. On average, a little more than eight pages were viewed per session across all kiosks.

In another paper, Nicholas et al. (2001b) presented log data from kiosks over a 2-month period from the end of April to end of June 2000, although did not unequivocally state the actual number of kiosks involved. The abstract to the paper states that the research formed part of a study evaluating 70 health kiosks, whereas the introduction states that the authors were studying logs from *nearly* 70 health kiosks. The methodology does not pin this figure down. It is reported that during the analysis reported in this paper, 17,076 page views were recorded and that further analysis would be used "to demonstrate the kind of metrics that can be derived from the logs and the associated problems in their analysis" (p. 64).

The 17,076 pages involved 1,821 users, with usage levels gradually falling from a high of 2,200 pages a week at the beginning of the analysis period to 1,229 in the last week, a drop of 44%. However, there is another discrepancy in the results at this point. The paper states the last week of analysis as *Week 24,* whereas the originally stated period of analysis (April–June 2000) ran only for 8 to 9 weeks. The number of users per kiosk also fell over the period of analysis from a high of 298 users per week to a low of 135 users—a drop of 55%.

The same authors explore other metrics within this paper. Earlier it was mentioned that with kiosks, the number of pages printed serves as an indicator of the nature of kiosk use that goes beyond basic online interrogation. Nicholas et al. (2001c) reported that 656 pages out of the more than 17,000 viewed (about 4%) were printed off. This figure needs further qualification, however, because the base total includes views made of menu pages. If the latter pages are excluded from the base figure, the proportion of information pages viewed that were also printed rose to 12%. Supplementary ad hoc research with kiosks owners and operator and direct field observations of kiosk use further revealed that many printers malfunctioned and this meant that the printed-off figure could well have been higher still but for technical glitches (Williams, Huntington, & Nicholas, 2000b). Just more than one in four (27%) of users were found to use the print function on kiosks and of those who did, 8 in 10 (80%) printed off just a single page of text.

Nicholas and his colleagues (2001b) also examined the number of pages viewed per search session. This indicated how thoroughly users searched for health information. More than three fourths of search sessions (77%) had a session length of 10 or fewer pages viewed. Some users viewed just one page (6%), whereas one viewed as many as 97 pages. A more significant finding was that one in four search sessions (26%) entailed searches of between one and three pages. Given the hierarchical structure of the content, however, this level of searching meant that only menu pages could have been viewed. This meant that a significant proportion of kiosk users failed to access health information content.

In parallel with the above observation, a further finding revealed that average session time length was short—just a second or two under 3 minutes. More refined data analysis reduced this result down to an average session length estimate of a little more than 2 minutes. Indeed, most users recorded sessions of no more than one minute and 40 seconds. Although other kiosk studies had recorded longer average sessions, in one case amounting to 12 minutes per session (Jones et al., 1999), the latter related to one particular group of users with a special health-related information interest (cancer sufferers). When a page was accessed, average statistically adjusted page view time was about 12.5 seconds. A narrow majority of users (54%) were interested in only one topic and accessed information pages from only one topic section on the kiosk (Nicholas et al., 2001b).

INDIVIDUAL DIFFERENCES IN USE OF KIOSKS

Demographic differences in the use of health information kiosks have been observed in a number of studies (Navin et al., 1996; Nicholas et al., 2000, 2001c). One consistent result is that older people are less likely to use kiosks than are younger people. Difficulties faced by older users are not simply explained by less widespread computer literacy among this age group. Diminishing sensory faculties may be another causal factor. Medical respondents in one study indicated that elderly people with poor vision would use a finger to guide their eye when reading on screen. This could affect navigation because they might when doing this accidentally activate the touch-screen and call up pages they did not want (Williams et al., 2001).

Despite these usage problems, older people have been found to appreciate touch-screen health information systems. Research with cancer patients found that older patients (especially males) expressed greater satisfaction with kiosk content than did younger users (Pearson et al., 1999). It remains the case, however, that young people tend to be more frequent and more widespread users of these ICTs than are older people. Teenagers, for instance, have been found to respond well to computer-based health information systems, although they did raise issues about privacy (Douglas et al., 1995).

One section of society to which government in the U.K. has drawn attention is ethnic minorities. In a multicultural society, any roll-out of online services must take into account the significance of the different orientations toward new technologies that might exist across cultural and ethnic groups. To assess the impact of touch-screen health information in a multiethnic community, Nicholas, Huntington, Williams, and Chahal (2001) administered an online questionnaire to 329 patients in a multicultural surgery in Nottinghamshire. England. The survey sought background demographic information about respondents as well as data based on their reported use and perceptions of the kiosk in their local doctor's surgery. Nearly one in three respondents here were Pakistani in origin.

Respondents who were born in the U.K. and held professional or skilled jobs found kiosk use easier than did those who were born outside the U.K. and had unskilled jobs. The oldest respondents, aged over 75 years, were by far the most likely to report difficulties in using the kiosk. The easier the system was to use, the longer users used it and the greater number of pages they searched and viewed.

The amount and length of kiosk use were associated with both the age and gender of respondents. Women aged under 55 and men aged 56 to 75 made greater use of the kiosk than other groups. These two groups made more visits and loner visits than others. Users were more likely to find the kiosk easy to use than not, and on balance had positive rather than negative opinions about it.

Hence research indicates that some success was enjoyed by the early roll out of this ICT in the way it was received and assessed by users and in terms of its ability to reach demographic or social groups that are recognized by government as important targets for health information. Two key groups are the elderly and ethnic minorities. Evidence has emerged that kiosks certainly attract the interest of older men. But older users were also critical of the information system and experienced some difficulties navigating around it. Meanwhile, ethnic minority respondents born overseas were relatively light users. There may be issues of information structure and ease of navigation compounded with language difficulties at play with this group.

Huntington, Williams, and Nicholas (2002a) examined age and gender user differences of a touch-screen health kiosk, using electronically recorded user transaction files collected over a 6-month period. In all, 1,378 user sessions covering 17,039 page views were analyzed for this study.

Women made slightly less use of the kiosk than did men. Usage levels dropped away with age, with the biggest users being under 35 and the lightest users being aged over 55 years. On average, users spent just more than 11 seconds viewing a page and just less than 2 minutes (114 seconds) on a single viewing session. Around nine pages were viewed per session. Differences between men and women in terms of time spent with the kiosk were slight.

One important metric in analyzing the use of online information systems in which content is organized hierarchically is the degree of penetration into the system. Calculations were made of the proportions of kiosk sessions users ventured up to four pages in, up to 10 pages in, or still further into the system. This calculation was repeated for each age group.

The results showed that older users tended to be much less likely than younger age groups to go beyond four pages into the system. Given that it was often necessary go beyond four pages before reaching information health content, this finding indicated that many older users failed to get beyond initial menu pages.

In a small-scale analysis of a single kiosk location, Nicholas, Huntington, and Williams (2001b) attempted to produce a user typology on the basis of reasons given by local users for searching content on the kiosk. They produced a four-fold typology: curious (55%), specific inquiry (17%), instructed to use it (12%), and other (17%). Curious users were more likely to look at healthy living issues, whereas those with a specific inquiry or who were told to use the kiosk were more likely to visit specific medical condition pages. Compared to respondents classified as curious, respondents with interests in special conditions or who were instructed to use the kiosk were more likely to visit pages covering surgical operations and support groups. Kiosks users with a specific enquiry in mind tended to search longer and more extensively than other respondents for the information they sought.

In a survey of kiosk use in a doctor's surgery, Nicholas, Huntington, and Williams (2004) reported that only a minority of patients (13%) had reportedly used the kiosk, with people under 55 being more likely to say they had used it than those over 55. Use of the kiosk was also linked to whether respondents used other information technologies. Those who claimed to avoid using computers were also less likely to report use of the kiosk. Those who did use the kiosk were generally positive about its ease of use.

KIOSK LOCATION

Touch-screen kiosks can be found in many different locations, such as prisons, libraries, railway stations, walk-in centers, doctor's surgeries, pharmacies, and supermarkets. The use of kiosks has been discussed in the context of their physical location. Some writers have hypothesized that the location may have an impact on volume of use (Pearson et al., 1999). Some locations may be physically more convenient to visit than others and be open at more convenient times. In the health context, some commentators have observed that the doctor's surgery or hospital waiting area may not be the most convenient locations for many potential users, despite the fact that these are places patients will need to go (Jones, Pearson, Cawsey, & Barrett, 1996).

Early research on the use of touch-screen kiosks for health information examined user of machines in a number of different locations, including a pharmacy, health center, library, and public house. The research did not make comparisons of kiosk use by location, however, though indicated that 5 months after installation, 17% of a random telephone sample of people in the catchment area reported having used at least of the terminals (Jones et al., 1993).

Later research did make comparisons of kiosk use on the basis of their location. One researcher claimed that kiosk location was a crucial factor as was the extent to which their availability in a given location was promoted (Jones, 2003). Other research directly compared levels of kiosk use four sites: an information center, pharmacy, hospital, and doctor's surgery (Nicholas, Huntington, & Williams, 2002b). This study compared sites in terms of numbers of users, age and gender profile of users, number of viewing sessions conducted, page view time, session duration, pages viewed, site penetration, number of pages printed, and health topics viewed. There were six doctors' surgeries, four hospitals, six pharmacies, and six information centers (a library, a health shop, a health authority information center, and two NHS walk-in centers) included in this research. One of the pharmacies was contained within a supermarket.

Kiosks located in information centers were used the most in terms of volume of use, number of sessions conducted per hour, page view time, session length, and number of pages viewed. Information centers attracted more female (54%) than male (46%) users, as did hospitals (52% vs. 48%). Surgery kiosks attracted slightly more male (52%) than female (48%) users. For the other locations, there were roughly equal numbers of male and female users (Nicholas et al., 2002b).

Hospital kiosks (80.5 s per session) were viewed for the longest duration, followed by kiosks situated in information centers (78.9 s), then surgeries (63.5 s) and finally pharmacies (49.7 s). There was little difference between information centers and hospitals and between pharmacies and surgeries in average page view times (8–10 s). Notably fewer pages were viewed on pharmacy kiosks than in kiosks (5.5) in the other three locations (7.2 s).

Content penetration figures indicated that relatively few users ventured beyond looking at 20 pages, and a clear majority, regardless of location, viewed more than 10 pages. In fact, location made little difference to content penetration. There was little difference discernible by location either in terms of topics viewed. Content on medical conditions was examined most often in pharmacies and surgical conditions consulted most often in hospitals (and least often in pharmacies). There were only slight differences between locations in the times of day when peak usage occurred. In information centers, peak usage occurred between 3:00 p.m. and 4:00 p.m. In pharmacies there was a low peak midmorning and then a main peak between 3:00 p.m. and 5:00 p.m. In hospitals, there was an initial low peak at 11:00 a.m. then a high peak between 3:00 p.m. and 4:00 p.m. In surgeries, there was a peak between 10:00 a.m. and 11:00 a.m. and a higher peak between 4:00 p.m. and 5:00 p.m.

Nicholas, Huntington, Williams, and Vickery (2001) conducted an exit survey of 150 users of a touch-screen health information kiosk located in a hospital. There were two key questions: (1) whether the information found answered the users' needs and (2) whether users intended, after using the kiosk, to try to find out more information elsewhere. Two thirds of respondents (64%) said that the information found had answered their questions. More than one in four (26%) said they had more questions to which they needed answers. Sixteen percent said that after using the kiosk, however, they still had further questions and intended to talk to a health professional to obtain this information. The authors also reported that women were three times as likely as men to say that the information they had found had answered their questions.

Summing up, location did make a difference to kiosk use. Kiosks located in information centers were used the most in terms of volume of use, number of sessions conducted per hour, and duration of page views and sessions, and numbers of pages viewed. Kiosks in hospitals also performed well and recorded relatively long session times and high numbers of pages viewed. This result may be attributed to the length of time patients have to spend in these locations waiting for treatment.

Surgeries performed least well, especially in terms of the numbers of sessions conducted per hour and numbers of pages printed per hour. However, doctors' waiting rooms are not the most relaxed environments and people are faced with tighter time constraints than in hospitals and information centers. Pharmacies also performed poorly on a number of metrics, scoring just above surgeries on number of sessions or pages printed per hour. Once again, the physical environment may not be conducive to extensive searching.

Nicholas and his colleagues also conducted a separate analysis on data from a kiosk located in a supermarket. There was only one device situated in this environment, so their data must be treated as exploratory. In this instance, a higher proportion of male (55%) than female shoppers (48%) used this device. Compared to other locations, the supermarket kiosk recorded the highest percentage use by those under 15 (36% vs. 9%) and those over 75 (26% vs. 6%). Again compared with the averages for other locations, the supermarket kiosk scored a lower page view time (6.9 vs. 9.4 s) and session view time (39.2 vs. 68.5 s), but more sessions per hour (1.33 vs. 0.54). In other words, the supermarket kiosk received many more enquiries, but these did not last as long. Perhaps the most significant result was that a higher proportion of supermarket kiosk users than of users of kiosks in other locations viewed three pages or fewer (41% vs. 33%). This means that supermarket users were not penetrating into the information depths of the kiosk as far as were users of kiosks in other locations.

USE OVER TIME

An analysis of use of kiosks over time was reported by Nicholas, Huntington, and Williams (2003). This analysis was based on a sample of 20 touch-screen kiosks over a period spanning 3.5 years. The authors identified four patterns of use of time: a declining pattern, a stable pattern, an increasing pattern, and a no trend pattern. In many cases examined (75%), there was an initial strong take-up in kiosk use, with a significant rate of increase of use in the first four to five months after a kiosk is installed. This then tended to be followed by an equally rapid decline in use. Early published data on kiosk use from the same authors had provided initial signs that information kiosk use seemed to fall rapidly after an initial surge in use (Williams, Huntington, & Nicholas, 2000b). However, longer term analyses revealed that more varied patterns of kiosk use could be found.

Whether kiosk use could be maintained or any decline in use alleviated depended upon patients' perceived or real information needs, the natural propensity of patients to actively seek health information, and the extent to which kiosk use was promoted by medical staff at a kiosk location. The last factor emerged as being especially important. Any health center that took a proactive stance with regard to kiosk use tended to exhibit higher than average volume of kiosk use. Over time, such locations found that the number of patients who had any experience of kiosk use grew. Hence promotion of kiosk use enhanced its reach. Maintenance of early rates of use, however, was always difficult to maintain. Nicholas and his colleagues suggested a number of possible reasons for this. These included the possibility that once patients' information needs had been satisfied there was no further reason for them to return to a kiosk in the short term. Another possibility was that some patients were disillusioned with the information content of the kiosk that had failed to meet their specific needs. There was also an issue of difficulty in retrieving the information required from the system. In this case, patients may have concluded that the kiosk was not all that useful. Finally, the idea of *sys-*

tem fatigue was invoked, whereby the novelty value of the kiosk system may wear off after a short period, with fewer people being prepared to try it at all.

CONCLUSIONS

Kiosks have represented an important technology in the context of electronic public service developments. They have been widely used, in particular, in the provision of public health information. Although the Internet may provide larger quantities of health content from more diverse sources, kiosks operated by public bodies can provide information that people can trust and give access to electronic data sources to people who do not have access to the Internet at home.

Kiosks are located in public places and therefore are available to anyone. In the health context, kiosks tend to be situated in doctor's surgeries, hospitals, and health centers. In other words, they are present at locations where people go to receive health advice and treatment. Hence, patients can utilize these information sources while waiting for a consultation. Furthermore, health professionals may refer patients to kiosks for additional information.

Early concerns lay with the nature of the technology and its ease of use (Graham et al., 2000; Pearson et al., 1999). Initial trials found that public and patients would use this technology, although those less experienced with computers had stronger reservations (Pearson et al., 1999). Older people, in particular, exhibited slower take-up of kiosk use (Nicholas, Williams, & Huntington, 2000). Children were found to use kiosks to find out about health issues when equipment was installed in their schools (Douglas et al., 1995). Young people were also found to utilize health center kiosks (Nicholas et al., 2000b). Kiosks are also used by health professionals to check up on medical information (Patyk et al., 1998; Williams et al., 2001). Medical practitioners, especially nurses, encouraged patients to use kiosks (Nicholas, Williams, & Huntington, 2001).

Kiosks were found to be used to access information about general subjects such as healthy living and about specific medical conditions or surgical operations (Nicholas et al., 2000). Many kiosk users in health and medical locations tended not to search for long or to penetrate the system too deeply. It may be that users feel under some pressure to consult the kiosk quickly and then to make way for another user (Nicholas et al., 2001a, 2001b, 2001c). The average amount of time spent using a kiosk could vary significantly with its location. British research showed that session view times and numbers of pages viewed were lower in busy locations such as doctors' surgeries and pharmacies than in hospital waiting rooms or information centers where users may have more time to browse (Nicholas, Huntington, & Williams, 2002b). Further evidence also indicated that kiosk use sometimes drops off over time, although this can vary with the location too (Nicholas, Huntington, & Williams, 2003).

Kiosks represent one among a number of technological developments that are being used to roll out public services electronically. How widely they will be used as more and more people turn to the Internet or digital interactive television for online information and transactions remains to be seen. As kiosks evolve technologically and offer more attractive interfaces that are easier to use, their use may grow. Kiosks can offer online access to people who do not possess online technology at home. With the wider adoption of interactive, multimedia technology in the domestic environment, however, kiosk success may depend much on their location. Kiosks in busy settings may be off-putting and lack the relaxed atmosphere conducive to leisure search behavior. It will be all the more important then that users can get to the information they seek as quickly and easily as possible and that that information is presented to them in a digestible form.

Digital Health on Television: Early Adoption and Use

New media technologies are increasingly crucial in the expansion of access to information services. Numerous studies of innovation adoption have indicated that members of higher socioeconomic groups have tended to embrace new technologies such as personal computers and the Internet faster than other social groups. In the context of the roll-out of health information and advice services online, however, it is intended that such developments will effectively reach disadvantaged, poorer, and minority groups of society. If such an objective is to be achieved, then traditional patterns of new technology penetration must be changed. In relation to information services operating via personal computers, technology developments in relation to more user friendly software, more powerful and speedier hardware, and lower product prices could collectively work to make this goal achievable (Kreuter, Farrell, Olevitch, & Brennan, 2000; Morrell, 2002). In relation to health information and advice services provided via digital television, the basic technology is not new. However, interactive applications of television do represent a technological development that poses fresh challenges to viewers and promises to change the traditional mode of TV use. In essence, interactive television applications represent an innovation and the success of digital health on television will depend on the extent to which viewers adopt this new form of television utilization.

Interactive television has been considered before in the health sphere, but in the context of information provision to health professionals rather than patients or the public. In particular, interactive television has been deployed as a platform on which to provide distance education programs to health care professionals (Byers, Hilgenberg, & Rhodes, 1996). In this respect, it has been regarded as a solution to the continuing education needs of health professionals who work in remote locations and lack easy access to on-site tuition. Two-way live interactive links via tele-

90

vision can offer an alternative that has been favorably received when piloted in other fields (Biner, Dean, & Mellinger, 1994; Lyons, MacBrayne, & Johnson, 1994).

ADOPTION EXPECTATIONS

The study of innovation adoption has produced a number of population typologies that reflect the degree to which different sectors of society accept and use new technological developments. Rogers (1995) distinguished five adopter categories: (1) innovators, (2) early adopters, (3) early majority, (4) late majority, and (5) laggards. These groups were differentiated on the basis of their *innovativeness* (i.e., readiness to adopt new technologies) and rate of adoption. Laggards represented those people who tend to resist new ideas and developments and are the last to adopt them, if they ever do. The innovators are open to new developments and are the first to try them out. Both groups comprise population minorities. The remaining three types fall between the two extremes and represent the majority of the general population.

Other researchers have linked innovativeness to human personality characteristics such as sensation seeking and venturesomeness (Foxall & Bahte, 1991). Much earlier, innovativeness was conceived to have its origins in individuals' novelty seeking motives (Hirschman, 1980). Novelty seeking has in turn been linked to an individual's needs to solve problems, gain competence in coping with new environmental challenges, that are in turn associated with basic survival needs (Flavell, 1977). At the same time, a further theoretical distinction was made between the *willingness to adopt* an innovation and the *actual adoption* of a new development, labeled respectively as *inherent innovativeness* and *actualized innovativeness* (Midgley & Dowling, 1978).

In research in Britain on uptake of digital television, distinctions were made between adopters, "could be's" and "won't be's." Adopters had already obtained digital television because of the greater content choices it gave them, although some early adopters were experimenting with this new technology and had not necessarily developed a firm and lasting commitment to it. The *could be* category comprised individuals who had not yet obtained digital television but could be persuaded to do so. The *won't be* category were not interested in digital television, were happy with traditional television services, and could not envisage being persuaded to get digital television in the future (Klein, Karger, & Sinclair, 2004).

This theoretical distinction was regarded as important. Many individuals may display inherent innovativeness in the form of a broad interest in new things and a stated intention to adopt them, but the speed with which they actually do so can vary from one individual to the next. An intention to adopt does not invariably lead to instant adoption. Identifying the factors that cause the translation of intention into action in relation to different innovations is key to understanding innovation adoption.

Actual adoption is influenced by the strength of an individual's inherent innovativeness (i.e., predisposition to display an interest in innovation adoption) and other factors that may serve as barriers to adoption. Rogers (1995) listed five attributes of innovation that could affect rate of adoption: (1) relative advantage, (2) compatibility, (3) complexity, (4) trialability, and (5) observability. It is important to note that Rogers' paradigm was based on the study of adoption of new ideas and products in developing nations. Nonetheless, these innovation adoption-related concepts are believed to have relevance to the study of new technology adoption in developed countries. Before adoption takes place, potential users must be able to observe the utility and benefits of an innovation. It may also be advantageous if they can also test it for themselves on a trial basis. An innovation must have demonstrable ease of use (complexity) and usefulness (relative advantage). Its ability to provide an application and the way in which this happens must also fit comfortably within the user's environment and circumstances (compatibility). To the extent that a new technology is perceived to be likely to provide what the user needs and that the effort required on the part of the user does not exceed their boundaries of patience, the likelihood of adoption is enhanced (Bagozzi, Davis, & Warshaw, 1992).

Numerous surveys have been carried out to test the diffusion paradigm. As already noted, early studies of technology adoption have indicated that early adopters of personal computers tended to be of a higher socioeconomic status than the rest of the population (Atkin & LaRose, 1994; Dutton et al., 1987; Steinfield et al., 1989). A similar finding emerged in relation to adoption of videotext services (Ettema, 1984). Technology innovation early adopters have also tended to be younger and better educated (Atkin & LaRose, 1994; LaRose & Mettler, 1989). Links between innovation adoption and household size have also been found, with larger households being more prominent among early adopters (LaRose & Atkin, 1988). The latter finding indicates that family households have been quick to adopt new technologies such as personal computers (Crispell, 1994). Gender, however, has not emerged as a consistent predictor of innovation adoption (LaRose & Atkin, 1992; Reagan, 1995). Lin (1997) reported no gender gap in adoption of personal computers.

Another important factor in relation to adoption of new technologies is the degree to which new users had adopted earlier technologies, and especially earlier similar technologies. Hence, the compatibility between adoption of a new technology and previous technology experiences is important to new technology adoption (Blumler, 1980; Dickerson & Gentry, 1983). Experience with earlier technology was associated with adoption, for example, of cable television and personal computers (Dutton et al., 1987; LaRose & Atkin, 1988). Innovation adopters have been found to adopt functionally similar media (LaRose & Atkin, 1992). Personal computer adopters were found to be more likely to adopt videotext services (Lin, 1994). Adopters of mobile phones were much more likely to use a range of other technologies than were nonadopters (Wei, 2001).

Despite the apparent clustering phenomenon in the adoption of functionally similar technologies, the actual motives for using different technologies can be quite distinctive. As such, the utility and benefits of traditional mass media (e.g., television), interpersonal communications channels (e.g., telephones) and new online media (e.g., e-mail) may be defined quite differently (Perse & Courtright, 1993). The distinctiveness of different communications technologies has been further reinforced in studies of behavioral usage patterns. For instance, use of one communications technology can displace use of another. Computer adopters have been observed to watch less television (Vitliari, Venkatesh, & Gronhaug, 1985). The use of electronic bulletin boards was found to reduce time spent with television, reading books and telephone use (James, Wotring, & Forrest, 1995). Other researchers, in contrast, have reported no consistent relation between interest in use of traditional media and use of the Internet (Jeffres & Atkin, 1996).

TV: POTENTIAL AS A HEALTH PLATFORM

In recognition of the fact that adoption of innovations may occur more widely and more quickly where a new technology is a development of a pre-existing technology with which most people are already familiar, the third major platform that has been investigated in relation to the provision of online health information is interactive digital television (iDTV).

The 1997 White Paper, *The New NHS* (Department of Health, 1997), identified the Internet and digital television as key media through which public access to the NHS could be improved. It was envisaged that new interactive communications media could empower patients to take more care of their own health as well as improving the efficiency of health provision in Britain. The promise of iDTV stemmed, in the first instance, from the observation that most households in the U.K. (98%) possessed at least one television set. Hence, there was widespread familiarity with the medium. Although iDTV was a technological advance on standard analogue television, this represented a smaller technological jump for consumers than did the shift from traditional television to using a personal computer to access the Internet.

Although the traditional television is ubiquitous, the same is not true of digital television. In the U.K., however, digital television sets have spread rapidly within just a few years and their penetration had caught that of the Internet by 2003. Varying estimates for digital television penetration in the U.K. placed it at between 38% and 46% in 2003 (Towler, 2003; Klein et al., 2004).

The aim of online health services operating via iDTV is to provide members of the public with easy access to a range of health information and advice services from the comfort of their armchairs at home. In June 2000, Gisela Stuart, the (then) Parliamentary Under-Secretary of State for Health in the U.K. announced that the Department of Health would fund a series of pilot projects exploring the possible health applications of iDTV in Britain. The aim of these projects was to provide patients with easy and fast access at home to health advice and information

In Britain, the Department of Health spent around £6 million funding four initial pilot experiments during 2001 and 2002. The vast numbers of people with TV sets and the familiarity of the technology to most people made the TV an especially appealing medium in this context. These TV-based interactive services were designed to enable registered users to be able to access large banks of health information via their sets. Users could navigate this online health encyclopedia using a standard remote control of the kind issued with new digital television services.

In addition, experiments were run with *transactional services*. These were services with two-way communications potential. They could allow users to make appointments with their doctor or with other health professionals and services, to volunteer their own services to community health support groups, or to connect, via a live video and telephone link, with an online NHS nurse who appeared on their TV screen while talking to them over a standard telephone line.

In this brave new world of modern interactive communication technology, digital television has been regarded as having greater potential than the Internet because television is already a well-established medium. Nearly every household in Britain has at least one TV set and, despite the relative success of supermarket online shopping, more people feel comfortable using TV than the Internet. Fewer people are likely to be excluded from a service that is available via television than one that can only be accessed via a computer terminal. It is also believed that more people may therefore be persuaded to engage with interactive information services via the more familiar TV remote control than using a mouse. Whether this assumption is accurate, however, is a matter that is open to some debate. As seen in chapter 7 (this volume), the availability of interactive capability, even via the familiar TV set, is no guarantee that viewers will use this facility (Towler, 2002).

Under this new iDTV initiative, it was hoped that increased exposure through iDTV would strengthen the NHS (National Health Service) brand and position the NHS as the most trusted and responsive source of health information and advice in Britain. Interactive digital television was also seen as a platform on which to enhance the image of the NHS as an employer. As part of the iDTV pilot, an experiment was run with one consortium in which NHS careers information was carried as part of the service to stimulate recruitment into the health service.

This chapter examines evidence for the early adoption of digital interactive television services. The iDTV experiment in Britain began with four pilot schemes directed at the public and patients. This pilot ran for 1 year spanning 2001 and 2002 and included services that operated on a national and regional basis. Evaluations of these pilot projects included analyses of their early use by those within their transmission areas. Later chapters examine barriers to adoption, opinions about these services and the potential and perceived impact they had on users and health services.

THE iDTV EXPERIMENT IN BRITAIN

The purpose of this pilot exercise was to explore the potential of this medium to deliver a range of health information and advice services to a diverse range of viewers. The individual pilot projects were conducted on a national and regional scale and utilized a number of different television platforms that comprised direct to home satellite transmission, cable transmission and broadband telephone networks.

The four appointed consortia were: Channel Health Interactive Lifestyle, Communicopia Productions, A Different Kind of Television (DKTV); and Flextech Living Health. Channel health was already an established broadcast channel on the Sky Digital satellite television platform. This service had a national reach. It proposed to insert special programming with interactive links within its normal schedule for a limited period spanning several months. Communicopia offered an interactive health information service that was largely text based, but also had video material on specific health topics that could be downloaded by users on a broadband platform in Hull in the north of England. DKTV originally outlined a service that would supply two distinct health information and contact services to registered users, delivered along with a program service via a cable television platform and a broadband platform in two parts of London. Finally, Flextech Living Health offered another largely text-based health information service with content taken largely from the NHS Web site, supplemented with content from local suppliers on a cable television platform in Birmingham. It also offered an online, doctors' appointments booking facility and the video nurse service. Further details about the four pilot iDTV consortia are provided in Table 6.1.

EVALUATING THE PERFORMANCE OF iDTV PILOTS

With the launch of the iDTV pilot services, the Department of Health commissioned an evaluation study to monitor the performance of the consortia and the services they provided. The aim of the evaluation exercise was to inform national policy and local service development by providing soundly based evidence on the operation, outcomes and effects of using DiTV to provide information and services to people in their homes and workplaces.

A multimethod approach was adopted for this evaluation exercise in which a range of quantitative and qualitative data were obtained via real-time and post hoc measurement techniques (Nicholas, Huntington, Williams, & Gunter, 2003b). From the start, recognition was given to the complexity of the medium being analyzed and the fact that such interactive services represented a new phenomenon and new experience for most users. It was of paramount importance to obtain high quality data on real-time use of iDTV services because a fundamental question was whether patients and the public would avail themselves of interactive health information services via their TV sets at home. In addition, it was important to gain a thorough understanding of users' experiences with these services. Did they find them easy to use? Was the content relevant to their needs? Were they comfortable with transactional services in which they had to engage in real-time activity with iDTV providers or back-up NHS services operating through the TV platform?

The evaluation study also explored the reactions of the health professionals involved in the provision of some of these online services. How effective was booking an appointment with the doctor via the television? Did NHS nurses fielding enquiries from viewers who could seem them on their TV screens feel that a video format enhanced the standard telephone-only service they would normally supply?

TABLE 6.1
Interactive Digital Television Pilots

Communicopia
Launched in November 2001 on broadband telephone platforms operated by Kingston Interactive Television (KIT) in Hull and eastern parts of Yorkshire, England and by Video Networks HomeChoice service in London. It represented an extension of the NHS Direct Internet information service. The service enabled viewers to access content from the NHS Direct online Web site including details of more than 400 illnesses and medical conditions, support organizations, and advice about living a more healthy life. Text material was mixed with specially produced video clips. There were 20,000 pages of text and 40 hours of video clips. The video clips provided perspectives of medical professionals and patients on a range of illnesses and conditions. There were interactive options including health quizzes and a text messaging reminder service for children's vaccination dates. The service was branded and promoted as NHS Direct Digital.

Flextech Living Health
This service was launched in June 2001 and featured a range of digital TV health applications to a potential average audience of 45,000 homes. The service was rolled out onto the Telewest cable network in Birmingham, England. The main part of the service provided 22,000 pages of text information on a wide range of health issues, information about local health services, and a database of medicines. In addition, two transactional services allowed users to books appointments online with their local doctor and to contact a NHS nurse live via a telephone and video link. The pilot ran for 6 months with government funding and was then extended for a further 6 months by the parent company.

Channel Health
This service piloted a series of broadcast TV programs (titled *Bush Babies*) to a national audience of more than 5 million digital satellite TV subscribers on the Sky Digital platform. This broadcast service was linked to a text-based enhanced service, also provided nationally, and a limited interactive experiment operated in one location in west London. Programs dealt with health issues relevant to pregnant women and new mothers. There were links from the programs to the enhanced text service both of which were transmitted on Sky Digital. The local interactive experiment was conducted with nine pregnant women and comprised e-mail support links between users and health professionals.

DKTV
This company developed a service originally intended to run on cable television and broadband telephone platforms. During the pilot, the service ran on a broadband telephone platform only to a small number of residents (c500) in the London Borough of Newham. The broadband platform was operated by Video Networks HomeChoice service. DKTV aimed to work together with public sector organizations to provide national and local public service access via interactive digital television. The DKTV services enabled users to find out more about local services by clicking on menu items in a walled garden TV channel. Some of these services were health related. Each menu item was accompanied by a video front end with a spokesperson explaining more about the service and how to gain access to it. An in-built messaging system enabled users to contact local health services for further information or actual help.

Hence, the methodologies used had to be able to get to grips with these questions and provide answers that would help future policy planning and service development. Further to these issues, the evaluation exercise needed to consider the effectiveness of different technology platforms in delivering health information and advice to patients and the public. Do interactive platforms have a wider potential to affect the status of health knowledge and health-related behaviors across the public? How does iDTV compare with other NHS Direct platforms such as the Internet and touch-screen kiosks in terms of the way they are used and the nature of users' experiences?

The way in which health information services are packaged within each of a number of distinct iDTV transmission systems can vary in significant ways. Not only do these platforms provide access to potential subscriber bases that vary greatly in size, they also provide distinct reception and viewing environments that may have an impact in terms of how easy health information services are to access in the first place.

EVALUATIVE RESEARCH METHODS

Broadly, the iDTV evaluation comprised an analysis of user bases and of user reactions. Measurement of use of iDTV services was fundamentally grounded in digital logs that registered real-time user behavior. In addition, self-report evidence on use of these services was obtained in ad hoc surveys of users. Further data on use were utilized in the case of one pilot consortium drawing upon television industry audience ratings statistics. The reactions or opinion of users were measured via a mixture of postal surveys, telephone interviews, online questionnaires, and focus groups.

These methodologies were applied to investigate a number of distinct themes:

1. Patterns of Use of iDTV Services,
2. Nature of iDTV Early Adopters,
3. iDTV Service Access and Usability, and
4. Public Confidence and Perceived Benefits.

In this chapter, a number of specific findings is examined around the general usage of iDTV services. Hence, findings pertaining to Items 1 and 2 will be covered here. Data on iDTV service usability, on perceived benefits, and public confidence linked to digital health provision are examined in chapters 7, 8, and 9.

Real Time User Measurement

Using key log user metrics such as number of site visits, length of time spent visiting a site, depth of penetration into site, and reach, the volume of use of iDTV services will be explored. The big question is whether people will use these services. Fundamental to the analysis of iDTV service use were the digital logs the service generated routinely. Comprehensive digital log data were obtained in the case of two of the four consortia, and summary log data were made available for a third. Log data for Living Health and Communicopia were relatively refined and accurate and compared favorably in these respects with Web logs. Log data for DKTV were limited and their accuracy questionable (Nicholas, Huntington, Williams, & Gunter, 2003b).

A major problem in analyzing log data is that of *caching*. Interactive digital television viewed pages were cached, as are Internet pages uploaded to the client's (end user's) machine (Nicholas et al., 2003b). *Caching* is an Internet browser feature switched on at the client's machine and means that pages, once viewed, were available from the terminal being used. Thus, any pages re-viewed did not have to be downloaded again from the server, obviously saving considerable time. From the point of view of recording logs, however, this practice created a problem. Views of previously seen pages were made from the cache and were therefore not recorded by the server access log file. Requested cable iDTV pages were routed through hubs that were then sent on to the user's set. Once a page had been requested the hub would cache the page and make that page available to other users on the hub without rerequesting the page from the original server. Again, this could result in an underreporting of pages viewed. Living Health employed a method to obviate the effects of caching. The process was defeated by the inclusion of a noncacheable "gif." The idea here was that each page included an image that could not be cached by the hub and so requests were made to the server every time and a page count recorded.

Despite initial pessimism over provision of user identification data, individual subscribers could be identified via the log data supplied, but *subscriber* referred to a household rather than to an individual person. Hence, *user* in the sense employed here, may refer to a family of users. Log data enabled the measurement of overall numbers of users, and changes in these numbers over the pilot period. Usage data could be displayed in terms of the raw number of users using the service per day; the reach, and return visitor (and the numbers of users making return visits). Further measures included the length of time spent tuned in to the service and the number of pages or screens viewed during a visit. These data could be further broken down by topics viewed. Hence, it was possible to ascertain if some parts of the service were more heavily used than others (Nicholas et al., 2003a).

Self-Report User Measurement

Self-report data on iDTV service use will be utilized to identify key predictors of use. This type of analysis was not possible with log data because detailed information about the nature of users was not available. Through self-report data, comparisons will be made between users and nonusers of iDTV health information services to understand more about early adopters of these services and to find out why some people decide not to tune in to them even though they are available.

With the Living Health service, data were obtained from two postal questionnaire surveys conducted shortly after the service was launched and midway through the pilot period. The questionnaires were distributed along with promotional literature to cable television subscribers and yielded return samples of 450 and 723 respondents respectively.

With Channel Health, data were obtained from two user surveys conducted respectively during the early part and the later part of the pilot period. The first survey was conducted in part by post ($n = 114$ respondents) and in part via an online questionnaire ($n = 322$ respondents). The second survey was conducted by telephone interview and produced 251 respondents.

With Communicopia, a postal questionnaire survey was sent to all potential subscribers to the Kingston Interactive Television platform in Hull and 1,184 usable responses were returned.

With DKTV, a single telephone interview survey was carried out shortly after the launch of its service in east London. At the time of the pilot, there were 513 broadband subscribers in this locality and all were approached for interview. Interviews were successfully conducted with 281, of whom 35 reportedly used or watched the DKTV service.

In-Depth Interviews

Ad hoc surveys were supplemented in the case of most consortia with in-depth qualitative interviews carried out individually or in focus group formats.

With Living Health, depth interviews were conducted individually with six of the staff fronting the In-Vision service in which users could call up a nurse on the telephone and see her on their TV screen simultaneously. In-depth interview data were also obtained from health professionals concerning the local doctors' appointments booking service. Twenty in-depth interviews were conducted with Living Health users identified through one of the ad hoc surveys, four of whom had used In-Vision. A further 31 InVision users were identified through call center logs, 27 of whom responded to telephone interviews and four participated in face-to-face interviews.

With Channel Health, qualitative data were obtained via the consortium among a small sample of nine pregnant women or young mothers and eight health care workers. These individuals were shown a demonstration of the Channel health service and allowed to experiment with it themselves, before giving their impressions. Further in-depth telephone interviews were carried out with two pregnant women about the interactive services supplied by Channel Health.

Communicopia held consumer panels once a month from before the launch of its service, to explore issues of usability, information content and presentation. Each panel meeting involved between 10 and 15 participants, some of whom attended more than once. The sessions lasted between 90 minutes and 2 hours. Participants were presented with demonstrations of the service and opportunities to use it themselves.

Television Audience Measurement

Viewing statistics produced by Broadcasters' Audience Research Board (BARB) were utilized for Channel Health which transmitted programs nation-wide to a potential audience base of 5 to 6 million viewers. These viewing data derived from the U.K. television industry's national *people meter* panel of over 5,000 households. All TV sets and other related equipment, such as video-recorders and set-top box decoders, are linked to a data collection device in the home that automatically records which TV channel is tuned into for each set when it is switched on. Video recorded viewing is also registered. The presence of individual household members in front of a set is recorded manually by householders using a remote control-like handset.

USE OF iDTV HEALTH SERVICES

Over the 12 months of piloting, the four iDTV pilots were made available to a potential combined audience of 5 to 6 million households, equating to 11.5 to 12 million individuals throughout Britain. The only national service, Channel Health, attracted aggregated audiences of approximately 2.8 million viewers to episodes of its maternity series, *Bush Babies* (Nicholas et al., 2003b).

Based on self-report data, it was estimated that 200,000 to 300,000 people availed themselves of one another of the remaining three iDTV services, a reach figure of 2%. This reach figure is small when measurement included the contribution of the Channel Health service on the national Sky Digital platform, which provided 99% of the total potential audience base for the four pilots. Taking the Sky Digital subscriber base out of the equation, significantly higher local reach figures were recorded for the other services, each of which was offered to much smaller test markets.

The Living Health and Communicopia services respectively achieved reach figures among their local audiences of 30% and 20% across their pilot durations (6 months and 5 months). DKTV, which operated on a smaller scale, still achieved a reach figure of 35% across its 3-month pilot duration. Further, on Channel Health, 9% of respondents who had identified themselves as viewers of the *Bush Babies* television series reported using the maternity guide—the enhanced text service that supported the programs (Nicholas et al., 2003b). The specialized nature of these services and the short time spans over which they were available also need to be taken into account when interpreting the significance of these results.

Reach—Individual Services

Living Health was made available to an average of 45,000 subscribers across the duration of the pilot. The actual market size changed across the duration of the pilot from 38,000 households at the start to 51,000 at the end. Log data revealed 13,718 different visitors (households) over the 6-month pilot period. Based on this figure, it was estimated that around 34% to 39% of platform households accessed the service. This was judged to be a healthy initial figure.

Self-report data from a postal survey of households within the receiving range of the Living Health service revealed that more than 8 in 10 (84%) said they would be likely to very likely to access Living Health if the service continued to be transmitted.

Communicopia (NHS Direct Digital) was available to approximately 10,000 potential homes. Over the 5-month period monitored, 1,965 different households used the system. This gave an estimated reach of 20%.

With Channel Health, television industry audience data produced by BARB indicated that *Bush Babies* episodes aggregated (across their repeat showings) audiences of more than 300,000 in the first (6-week) phase and 2.3 million in the final (3-month) phase. According to self-report questionnaire data, 27% of Channel Health viewers had reportedly watched *Bush Babies*.

Channel Health was estimated to have a monthly reach figure among Sky viewers of approximately 15%. Given a Sky Digital audience base of around 5.7 million households at that time, with the audience for *Bush Babies* estimated to about 200,000 homes during the main phase of the project, this meant that 3.5% to 4% of all Sky subscribing homes tuned in at some point.

DKTV—during the 2-month survey period, 142 users availed themselves of the service, out of 403 to 513 households receiving it during this period—a reach figure of up to 35%.

Return Visits

Repeat use of a iDTV service can be indicative of its usefulness and appeal to users. It can be taken as a behavioral measure of satisfaction with the site and its content. A service with a high percentage of returnees can be regarded as having a "brand" following. Data showed that once someone has used a iDTV health service, there is a good chance they will use it again. About 60% of Living Health users said that they would use the service as needed. Logs showed that 41% of Living Health users visited the service again during the pilot. Living Health users who first visited the channel within the first three months after launch, on average visited the channel three times or about once a month during the remainder of the pilot period. In looking just at those users who had visited twice, the average lapsed time between the first and second visit was calculated at 26 days—indicating return visits at a rate of approximately once a month.

A slightly smaller proportion (37%) revisited the NHS Direct Digital service provided by Communicopia over the January to May 2002 period. It is also worth noting that the rate of return visiting may have been partly affected by changes to the positioning of the walled garden service in the broadband TV-on-demand environment operated by KIT in the Hull market where this pilot took place. This positioning issue is examined more closely in chapter 7 (this volume).

No log data were available for Channel Health, so assessment of patterns of use was dependent on self-report data that are probably less reliable. Subscribers were asked how often they watched the service and 56% said they watched at least once a week, 20% reportedly watched at least monthly, and 24% watched less frequently. Return visits could not be calculated at all for DKTV.

Time Online

Short online consultations proved to be the norm. Living Health viewers spent on average 6 minutes on a visit (session), whereas figures for Communicopia/NHS Direct Digital indicated 7 minutes as the average visitor session time. Longer session times were associated with viewing more pages of content. Time spent viewing also depended on the types of material being viewed. On the NHS Direct Digital service, for instance, video material was available featuring interviews and scenarios with patients and health professionals. Watching this sort of material could often double average session times. No time online data were available for Channel Health or DKTV.

Screens Viewed

For the services for which log data were available, there was evidence that once people accessed a service, they showed a significant degree of interest in it.

In the case of Living Health, 39% of users viewed more than 20 pages during a visit and these figures proved to be stable over time. In the case of NHS Direct Digital, 44% of users viewed more than 20 pages. Although the latter finding may indicate a high degree of user interest in the content being provided, it is also important to note that this was a menu-heavy service that required users to search through a number of menu screens to reach the eventually desired text or video content.

There were indications of high failure rates too. In the case of Living Health, 19% of users viewed one to three pages and these users were unlikely to have penetrated past the menu screens and would not have seen an information page, except perhaps for daily news headlines. For Communicopia/NHS Digital Direct, the equivalent figure was also 19%. It was noted, however, that these figures compared very favorably with the use of health Web sites and kiosks, where higher failure rates were recorded (Nicholas et al., 2003a).

Finally logs also revealed that only 12% of those users accessing the InVision (online nurse) service on Living Health actually completed a session (i.e., engaged in an online consultation with a nurse over the TV). These figures may indicate that early users were checking out the system for future reference, not having an immediate need (Nicholas et al., 2003a).

HEALTH CONTENT USED

It is of great importance to online health service providers to know what types of health topics are used most and found most useful. Use of health content however can be determined by a variety of factors, such as what content is provided, how visible or accessible that content is, and what medical conditions users may be concerned about. In the context of this U.K. pilot exercise, comparisons between services were difficult because of differences in content provision and platforms.

Two of the pilot consortia stood out as principal content providers—Living Health and Communicopia/NHS Direct Digital.

With Living Health, the sections that users appeared most interested in were the "Illness and Treatment" section, followed by "Women's Health" and "Men's Health." The Illness and Treatment section accounted for 36% of all pages viewed. The most popular topics in this section were about back pain, depression, impotence, Aids, and irritable bowel syndrome. Popular topics under Women's Health were orgasm problems, dyspareunia, thrush, and cystitis. For men's health, the most popular topics were impotence, premature ejaculation, sexual infections, gay sex, and sexual health help. It would seem that the privacy of one's own home provided the ideal environment in which to explore issues that may be too intimate or embarrassing to research via a publicly placed information terminal (see Table 6.2).

For Communicopia/NHS Direct Digital, the A–Z of Conditions section was the most popular section by some margin and accounted for 57% of text pages viewed. The second most popular section was "Not Feeling Well" and accounted for 13% of pages viewed. The most frequently visited topics in the A–Z of Conditions section were diabetes, lower back pain, asthma, and mellitus.

TABLE 6.2
Most Viewed Pages on Living Health

Orgasm problems

Impotence

Premature ejaculation

Keep your sex life in good shape

No Content

NHSDirectinVision

Dyspareunia

Sexual Infections

Gay Sex

Sexual Health Help

Thrush and cystitis

Preventing prostate cancer

Flatulence

Practising safer sex

Injury treatment principles

Note.   Above topics accounted for 7.9% of all information pages. Number of unique pages viewed = 2,798.
Source.   Adapted from Nicholas et al. (2002c).

For Communicopia, the most popular on-demand video topics were the "Foray for Health," "Diabetes," and "Coronary Heart Disease" productions. These three video topics accounted for 42% of topic videos viewed. Each topic was represented by a series of videos that the user could view independently. For topics where only one video was available, the hypertension (downloaded 54 times) and MMR videos (downloaded 44 times) were the most watched. There were no views of videos on testicular cancer or ulcerative colitis.

NATURE OF iDTV EARLY ADOPTERS

Interactive digital television is in its infancy, although some observers have already earmarked this as the medium of the future (Carrigan, 2001; Gronmark, 2001). In Britain, some 6 million households had subscribed to digital television services (containing around 12 million individual viewers) by the middle of 2002. This represented around 40% of TV homes (Towler, 2002). But who are the early adopters of this enhanced TV medium? Are they people who already possess a personal computer? Or are they individuals who have an aversion to PCs but would be willing to use enhanced TV technology?

In the United States, the Yankee Group (2001) identified two key customer groups likely to take up interactive television services. The first of these were termed *aggressive early adopters* and comprised individuals who already have personal computers and who wished to acquire a second interactive device for their home, but not another PC. The second group comprised *third wave adopters* who comprised a mass-market group of potential Internet users who had not yet acquired their own PC, but might be more willing to engage with the Internet via interactive television.

Further marketing evidence from GartnerG2 suggested that the users of interactive television will represent a distinct group from PC-Internet users. It was anticipated that iDTV would attract less well-off and more poorly educated consumers than PCs.

Research in Britain by the National Opinion Poll organization supported the view that interactive television consumers have a youthful profile. A NOP survey found that among the nearly 5 million 7- to 16-year-olds using the Internet, almost 1 in 10 (9%) did so via digital television, and that more than one fifth (22%) of 14- to 16-year-old boys accessing the Internet did so using digital TV (NOP, 2001).

Government-sponsored research in the U.K. reported that nearly 4 in 10 people (38%) had got digital television and that around one in eight (12%) indicated they were likely to get it soon. Three in ten (29%) felt unlikely to get digital television, but had not closed the door on it completely. Around one in seven people in Britain (13%), however, not only did not have digital television, but thought it was unlikely they would ever get it. These hard line laggards were mostly aged over 55 and were from poorer socioeconomic classes (Klein et al., 2004).

Early Use of Digital Health on TV

Varying early adopter profiles emerged across the four iDTV pilots in Britain. This was not surprising given that the services appeared on different platforms and differed in their contents, formats and target markets. The early adopter profiles for health information services provided on digital interactive television platforms indicated that the Living Health service, that comprised mostly textual information, successfully attracted older men more than younger men and younger women better than older women. With Living Health's video nurse service, men and women used it equally. The women tended to consult this online information service on behalf of their children, whereas the (older) men did so on behalf of themselves (Nicholas et al., 2003b).

Profiles for the Communicopia/NHS Direct Digital service revealed greater usage by younger people than older people, especially by young men of the text service than the video service. Among the dominant groups found for the Living Health service, older male NHS Direct Digital users were proportionately more likely to use the text service and the video service than were younger female users.

With the Channel Health service that was transmitted on a national digital satellite service, women were, not surprisingly given the nature of its content (information or pregnancy and maternity issues), twice as likely to use it as were men. Even so, the figures for men were almost as encouraging as were those for women. Among the women users, those older than 45 were four times less likely to use than were those younger than-45 (Nicholas et al., 2003b).

Early evidence in Britain indicated that iDTV can attract low-income users. Users from neighborhoods characterized by lower than average household incomes were found to be more likely to use the text information services of Living Health and Communicopia/NHS Direct Digital and more likely to use the maternity information programs and enhanced services supplied by Channel Health. This was a positive finding because government sponsors of iDTV public service experiments believed that television would embrace users groups missed by the Internet (Nicholas et al., 2003b).

Predictors of iDTV Health Service Use: A Case Study

A study was conducted a study of users and nonusers of a iDTV service provided on a cable television platform in Birmingham, U.K. (Nicholas, Huntington, Williams, Gunter, & Monopoli, 2002). This study was conducted among households that had access to Flextech's Living Health channel on the Telewest cable service. The living Health interactive channel was essentially a content database, comprising mostly text, and covered a wide range of health topics largely adapted from NHS Direct Online (the Web site operated by the NHS). Other content was provided by additional suppliers. The site also featured careers information provided by the Department of Health's Communications Directorate.

As noted earlier in this chapter, the channel also hosted two transactional services: NHS Direct In-Vision and an online doctor's appointment booking service. In-Vision provided a one-way video link between a nurse in a NHS Direct call center and the user at home along with a telephone link between the two parties. The online Appointments Booking Service allowed users to book an appointment with their GP. Three GP surgeries in Birmingham were partners in this venture. All interactive and transactional Living Health services were provided within a "walled garden" package situated apart from the broadcast channels carried on the Telewest cable television system.

Data on use were derived from digital logs for the Living Health service covering a period spanning July 18 to November 28, 2001. These were reported in the previous section of this chapter. In addition, a user questionnaire survey was conducted by post to ascertain opinions of users and nonusers of the service and their respective reasons for choosing to engage with or avoid this new interactive television service. Such self-report data are not as robust as measure of iDTV use as log data, but were used here because it was not possible to acquire personalized details of iDTV users via log data. The latter data were controlled by the operator of the cable platform on which the Living Health service was carried and were regarded as commercially sensitive. Hence, the researchers could not gain direct access to subscribers on whom log data had been obtained to acquire more personalized information from them that could then be linked to their real-time iDTV viewing patterns. It was possible, however, to obtain data from subscribers via a less direct route.

In the Nicholas et al. (2002) study, self-completion questionnaires were distributed to a majority of Telewest Birmingham subscribers—approximately 38,000 homes—along with promotional literature sent out by Living Health that was designed to raise subscriber awareness of its channel on the Telewest cable platform.

Seven hundred twenty-three questionnaires were returned and analyzed. Of these, 496 (69%) gave postcode details that were then used to classify the sample. The questionnaire was designed to obtain information about the use and nonuse of this iDTV health information service. It also asked respondents to supply personal details, including their age, gender, household income, presence in the home of young children (aged 4 or younger), interest of health condition, whether contacted NHS telephone helpline in past 12 months, and importance of the Internet as a source of health information. They were also asked if they had ever heard of or used the Living Health service.

The number of Living health users varied quite considerably over the survey period. Just after launch, service access stood at just less than 400 users a day. The number of users recorded fell significantly after September 24th and reached a low of 200 on October 9th. From the beginning of October until the end of the survey period in November the number of daily users remained in the band 220 to 270.

Turning to the user survey, more than 7 in 10 respondents (72%) claimed to have heard of Living Health, but fewer than one in four (23%) said they had used it. Just more than one in four (27%) said they had not used the Living Health service, whereas nearly one in two (49%) had heard of it but not used it. Women were more likely to report using the service than men. Fifty-one percent of women said that they were not users, but women made up 57% of those who had reportedly used the service.

In terms of age, the biggest single proportion was contributed by those aged 36 to 45 (27%), followed by 26 to 35 (19%), 56 to 65 (18%), and then 46 to 55 (16%).

Among the 66 to 75 and 56 to 65 age bands, however, the great majority of users were male (92% and 61% respectively). Among the 26 to 35 and 16 to 25 age groups, the great majority of users (81% and 69% respectively) were female.

Health Information Seeking Groups

In a further analysis of the data from this survey, questionnaire responses were supplemented by and crossreferenced to U.K. geo-demographic data. Multivariate analyses were computed to explore further the nature of users of this interactive health information television service. In an initial analysis, a comparison was made between those who did not know about the Living Health service and those who had used it (see Nicholas et al., 2002). Multiple logistic regression analysis differentiated users from the nonaware in terms of four main factors: if the respondent had phoned NHS Direct in the last 12 months, if the respondent lived in an area with a high incidence of £20,000 or more earners, if the area had a high incidence of 0- to 4-year-olds, and if the respondent had an interest in a particular condition.

People who said they had phoned NHS Direct (the U.K. health service's telephone helpline) in the past 12 months were much more likely to report having used the Living Health channel, as compared to people who had not phoned. In all, 63% of those people who said they had phoned NHS Direct in the past 12 months had also reportedly used Living Health—this was only true of 37% of people who had not used the NHS Direct phone line. This suggested that the Living Health channel and NHS Direct were used as complementary services.

Whether the user lived in an area with a high incidence of households with people earning £20,000 or more was also significant, but not quite in the way that might have been anticipated. People who came from wealthier areas were less likely to say they used the Living Health channel compared to those people who came from less well-off areas. Approximately 45% of less well-off respondents claimed to be nonusers; however, this percentage increased to 61% of reported users from the wealthier areas. This finding was encouraging in that it supported the argument that iDTV may throw an online lifeline to those who have missed out on the digital revolution—the poor and socially excluded.

The incidence of households having young children (0 to 4 years old) was also significant. People from areas with a high incidence of 0- to 4-year-olds were more likely to say they used the Living Health channel compared to users who came from areas with a low or medium incidence of children within this age range. This may reflect parents' needs for health information relating to their children. A similar result was reported for touch-screen kiosk users (see Nicholas et al., 2001c; see also chap. 5, this volume). Here the proportion of 0- to 4-year-olds in an area was related to the average number of people using kiosks per hour. Kiosk use was higher in areas with a higher proportion of households with young children.

Respondents who had an interest in a particular medical condition were also more likely to say they used the Living Health service. These respondents were much more likely to report using the service compared to those with little or no interest in a particular condition. Seventy-nine percent of those people with no or little interest in a particular condition had not used the service, compared with 56% of respondents who had an interest in a particular condition who said they had used the service.

In a further multivariate analysis, comparisons were made between those respondents who reportedly did use the Living Health service and those who had heard of the service but did not use it (Nicholas et al., 2002). A multiple logistic regression model revealed three explanatory variables: whether the person had reportedly used NHS Direct in the past 12 months, how important to them the Web was as a tool for medical information, and whether the user had an interested in prescription drugs.

Respondents who said they had phoned NHS Direct in the past 12 months were much less likely to be people who had heard of Living Health, but not used it, compared to reported Living Health users who said they had not phoned the NHS. This confirms the result reported above in the comparison between Living Health users and individuals who were not aware of the service.

Respondents who considered the Web important as a source for health information were more likely to have heard of Living Health but not used it compared to those who did not consider the Web as an important source. This relation suggests that those using the Web for their health information needs are not switching to digital television although they know about the existence and availability of this alternative service. For these people, the early iDTV appears not to represent a substitute for Web-based information. Further research needs to clarify whether these are distinct new media markets and if they are likely to remain so.

Respondents who reportedly had an interest in prescription drugs were less likely to have tuned into this service than were respondents with no special interest in prescription drugs. Of those who did reportedly use the Living Health service, approximately 55% said they had used the service either before or after a consultation with their doctor. Hence the significance of prescription drugs in the model may well be an indicator variable of those users who are unwell. Another interpretation of this finding therefore might be that respondents who were unwell were more likely to be users of the Living Health service.

Reasons for Using the Service

Survey respondents who reported using Living Health were asked how they found the service in the first place. The largest single proportion (45%) had just started using it and indicated that they found the service by exploring the menu on Telewest's cable network—browsing in other words. Nearly one in five users (19%) said they found out about the Living Health service from the company's promotional literature, whereas 12% said they read about it in a newsletter and 8% reportedly found out about it from other publicity material. Word of mouth did not emerge as a significant source (4%), although its low rating may simply be a function of how little time the channel has had to establish itself.

A further analysis examined the main reasons for using the service—users could tick more than one option. Just browsing for health information proved the most popular reason—more than two thirds (68%) of users reported browsing as a reason for use. More than one in three users (34%) said that they searched for information before consulting their doctor. In all 55% of users queried the system for information regarding their consultation with the doctor before, after, or before and after a consultation.

When asked, what information they were looking for the last time they used the service, most users (44%) said that they were looking for information on their own medical condition. A further one in four (25%) said that they were searching on behalf of either a friend or a member of the family. Others (17%) claimed to be making a general enquiry about health matters.

Users were asked about the general usefulness of the site and how easy the site was to navigate, how they found the menus, if the site was easy to read and understand, and if the site was full of medical jargon. More than one in two respondents (55%) said the site was easy to read all of the time. Further, 45% and 39% of respondents respectively reported that the site had easy menus and easy navigation all of the time and 59% said that the site was not at all full of medical jargon. Significant majorities of users said that the site had easy menus, was easy to read and was easy to navigate either most of the time or all of the time. On a less positive note, however, only 23% of respondents reported that the site was useful all the time, although more than one half (58%) found it useful most of the time (Nicholas et al., 2002b).

A relation was found between how useful respondents found the service and gender. More men than women reported that the service was useful all of the time: 32% compared to 17% respectively. Furthermore, women were more likely to say that the service was useful only some of the time or not at all compared to men: 25% compared to 12% respectively.

Users' interest in health topics was also found to impact on whether the user found the service useful. Those users saying that they were very interested in health information were more likely to report that the service was useful all of the time compared to other users: 34% compared to 15%. Users who were quite interested or not interested in health information were more likely to report that the service was only helpful some of the time or not at all compared to users who were very interested in health information: 24% compared to 12%.

Respondents were asked how useful they found each part of the service. The Illness and Treatment section (82% saying it was very/quite useful) was considered the most useful section followed by Healthy Living (76%), Men's Health (74%), Women's Health (70%), Today's Health News (67%), Local Health Services (51%) and Children's Health (51%; Nicholas et al., 2002b)

Nonuse of Service

Nonusers of the service were asked to fill in a separate part of the questionnaire. The first part asked respondents if they agreed or disagreed with the following statements: "My doctor/nurse tells me all I need to know, so I do not bother with the information on 'Living Health'"; "I prefer to receive written/printed information from the doctor about a condition"; "I do not use the Living Health service because I am not very good with technology"; and "I tried to use the Living Health service but could not find what I wanted" (Nicholas et al., 2002b).

Twenty-four percent of nonuser respondents said that they preferred to get information from their doctor and 40% said that they preferred printed information handed to them by their doctor. Seventeen percent said that they were no good with technology, whereas 7% said that they could not find what they wanted from the service.

A relation was found between a preference for printed information and for the doctor to explain condition with both gender and age. Twenty-nine percent of men compared to 20% of women responded by saying that they agreed that the doctor told them all they needed to know. Furthermore, older users were more likely to agree with this than younger users. About 45% of those 55 or older said that they agreed with this statement. Only 20% of those younger than 55 agreed with it.

Forty-eight percent of males compared to 33% of women agreed with the statement "I prefer to receive written/printed information from the doctor about a condition." Again, older users were more likely to agree with this statement. Approximately 70% of those aged 65 or older said that they agreed with this statement. Only 25% of those younger than 45 agreed with it.

Age was also found to impact on nonuse as a result of a perceived problem with using the technology. Older users were more likely to report that they did not use the service because they thought themselves as not being good with technology. Approximately 30% of users older than 55 reported technology as a barrier to using the service, whereas 12% or less of users younger than 45 reported this as an issue. And not surprisingly then, older people were also more likely to say they could not find what they wanted.

CONCLUSIONS

Experiments in Britain with digital interactive television as a platform for the provision of online health information and advice produced encouraging results. Interactive digital television health services can attract significant numbers of users. This conclusion was reinforced by findings that even new services in multichannel television environments were visited by significant proportions of households who subscribed to the supplying platforms. Although these services achieved significant audience reach, most users visited these sites only occasionally. This indicates that online health information services on television are likely to be used by people only every once in a while, and when they are driven to seek out health information by a specific need.

What is also clear from early findings is that such is the importance of health as a topic that it can be used to encourage viewers to engage with television in a more interactive fashion. This spin-off effect, if it is sustained, could have significant implications for future interactive television market strategies. People seem prepared to enter interactive mode with the television in order to seek out health information either for themselves or for a member of their family.

Equally, although, it is clear that interactive television users may not always be prepared to search for as long or as extensively as do Internet users for the content they seek. This reflects the idea of the Internet being conceived as a medium that automatically demands effort on the part of its users, whereas the same is not true of traditional television viewing. As chapter 7 (this volume) shows, there are other factors linked to service usability and the effectiveness of interactive applications operating via the television to deliver the services users need, that also determine overall use of iDTV-based information services.

The complexity of the interactivity is another factor related to use. The more sophisticated transactional services piloted by some of the iDTV health consortia in Britain—such as the video nurse, doctor appointments booking service, and maintenance of online medical records—were utilized by very few individuals. Thus, although many early iDTV users were prepared to attempt to access text and video information services, far fewer found the transactional services as easy to use or as useful.

Despite the slower pace of take-up of transactional services via the television, iDTV may attract a different demographic profile of user than the Internet. This is encouraging evidence because it indicates that the Internet and iDTV may operate as complementary services. Of particular significance was the finding that iDTV users are better represented by socially disadvantaged groups who tend to feature at the lower end of the digital divide. Hence in time, this divide may be closed by iDTV.

Finally, further initiatives in Britain serve to illustrate the commitment of government to utilizing television as a health platform. The potential of using television sets at hospital bedsides to provide patients with access to health information is being explored in British hospitals. Bedside television and telephone systems are being installed under a program titled *Patient Power*. The service is restricted to hospitals with at least 150 beds. It will carry a general health information television channel, other subject-specific health information channels, videos on-demand dealing with various health topics, a health radio service, and access to the Internet. It could also be used as a system for storing patient records and to access clinical decision support software for medical professionals (McWhirter, 2003).

The perception of the promise of interactive digital television as a platform for the dissemination of health advice and information in government circles was underlined in Britain with the proposed launch of a nationwide television service, NHS Direct Digital TV that would provide information on a wide range of health topics, directories of medical and health professionals, self-care health advice, and news updates on health issues (Department of Health, 2003). Making a service and technology to carry it available is one thing, getting the public to use it is another. The next chapter turns to the subject of usability and interactive digital television.

Chapter 7

Digital Health on Television: Service Usability and User Psychology

The establishment of new technologies involves three sets of processes: technology diffusion, adoption, and use. In the first instance, a new technology must become established in a society. This takes place through the process of adoption by individuals. Diffusion may be driven by user demand, but such demand is more often projected than known for sure in advance. A certain amount of pump-priming of new technologies is needed by parties with the financial resources to make such significant up-front capital investment. Following diffusion, through which an innovation is made widely available, adoption takes place in recognition of uses to which the innovation can be put and needs it will effectively service. The use of a new technology stems from recognizing the functionality of the technology and its relevance to individuals' needs.

In the last chapter, the character of early adopters and their behavior in relation to online technologies and new health information services were examined. Earlier comparisons between initial adopters and nonadopters of a new iDTV health service indicated that early users of this service had differed from nonusers in their perceptions of its functionality for them. The current chapter turns to issues of usability in the context of iDTV as a health information platform. Although technology and service access are critical factors in the first instance, eventual take-up of an online service innovation will depend upon their usability.

Previous research into innovation diffusion indicated that new technologies must be founded upon a recognition of a need and be designed to satisfy that need for users. A new technology must be marketed to potential users in full cognizance of their needs and must aim to present a solution that will, on a number of levels, prove attractive to them. The appeal of an innovation in a marketing context will be defined by the advantages it offers to users, its convenience and ease of use. It must also be made sufficiently visible to potential users that they become aware its availability and potential and are tempted to try it (Rogers, 1995).

Once adopted, however, it is essential that users continue to use a new technology. The attributes that support successful marketing and distribution may not be enough to guarantee continued product or service loyalty. It is important that the innovation is effectively assimilated or integrated into the user's daily life (Latour & Woolgar, 1979; Silverstone & Haddon, 1996; Thomas & Mante, 2001).

One model of technology adoption has identified five stages through which an innovation becomes *domesticated* or integrated into the everyday life of the user, ranging from initial awareness to consumption, integration into daily life and daily routine, through to modified definition of the innovation as a result of the way it is used (Silverstone & Haddon, 1996). Thus, there is a phase when the individual buys the technology or subscribes to its use and a further phase of use in which the person integrates the technology into their everyday life. The extent and speed with which this integration of a new technology occurs can vary across categories of individual defined by their demographic characteristics and living environment (at home an at work), and may also be influenced by their attitudes, beliefs and values. To understand this process, it is important to examine adopters and non-adopters of technologies, In Europe, for instance, nonadoption of the Internet was found to be linked to a lack of need, emotional distance from new technology and resistance to innovations (Thomas & Mante, 2001).

Although many people are embracing computers and the Web, many others do not realize this technology is relevant to their lives (Morrell, Mayhorn, & Bennett, 2002). In America, a survey of older adults found that many did not log onto the Web because they saw no purpose for it in their lives (Morrell et al., 2000). Many nonusers were ignorant of what the Web could do for them, or even about how it works. There was clearly a need to motivate some potential users and to educate them. Although training programs can be provided to encourage and cultivate use of online services, another solution may be to adapt a familiar technology to inter-active ends. This is the idea that underpins the movement toward television as a conveyor of online public services. With a familiar technology, service providers do not need to encourage people to adopt the medium. Nonetheless, they are faced with the challenge of cultivating a different form of use of that medium. The ease with which people can learn to use a familiar medium for new purposes is a critical variable that will drive its adoption.

Television can be technologically adapted to serve as an interactive medium. But this does not guarantee that it will be readily used by people as an interactive medium. It has already been noted that despite the rapid growth of the digital television market in the U.K., for instance, relatively few subscribers to this new television technology use the interactive services it provides (Towler, 2003). Further British research has identified a series of stages for consumer decision making in relation to the adoption of digital television. First, consumers must feel comfortable, symbolically, with digital television. It must have meaning for them and they must decide that it is a good thing and not a bad thing. Next, consumers must be attracted by the content offered. The fact that more content is offered may not be enough. The services being provided must be regarded as relevant and useful to consumers. Finally, consumers must decide whether they can cross practical hurdles of purchasing, installing, and using the new equipment (Klein et al., 2004).

A key factor in both initial take-up and lasting success of a new technology therefore is usability. A positive orientation toward a new technology and a perceived need for the services it providers are a fundamental starting point. Both, however, may be undermined by a technology that is difficult to use. This chapter therefore turns to an analysis of usability issues in relation to the adoption and utilization of online health care services—and in particular those presented via digital interactive television (iDTV).

USABILITY OF ONLINE HEALTH SERVICES

The previous chapters have provided an evaluation and review of the online provision is a range of health-related services. Although much of the online health care provision has taken place on the Internet or via touch-screen kiosks, in Britain, digital interactive television has been identified as another platform that has the potential to reach large numbers of people who may not have access to the Internet and prefer to consult health information at home rather than in a public location.

The policy document *Information for Health* was underpinned by the notion that widespread public access to the right kind of health information is a core ingredient of modern health care (NHS Information Authority, 1998). The realization of this online objective for health has been manifest in terms of the major NHS Direct initiative that deploys a battery of information services available over the telephone, on the Web, via touch-screen kiosks and iDTV. The use of ICTs has been identified as providing a potentially economical solution to the enhancement of wider public health awareness and promotion of self-care (Wanless, 2002). Thus, iDTV, alongside the Internet, has been highlighted as a key technology in this context.

Behind all these initiatives lies the assumption that the very act of providing people with information and access to online transactional services (e.g., booking appointments with health professionals, online consultations, etc.) will lead to a better health outcome for society. In theory, patients will be able to consult with their doctor or a nurse or other type of health professional over remote text, audio, or video links from within their own homes. It has been hypothesised that such a system will offer greater convenience for patients and service economies for the National Health Service (NHS). To what extent, however, will the anticipation be matched by the actual success of such services? Given the cost of up-front investment in ICTs that is required to put these online services in place, the effectiveness with which they eventually operate cannot be left to guesswork and should not depend solely on long-term trial-and-error experiences. There is a need for systematic and carefully contrived formative research to explore how such services will be used and how people will respond to different types of online application on different communications platforms.

It is already known that patients do welcome health information that they can take away and peruse at their leisure. Furthermore, they attach credibility to the information they receive from authority figures such as their GP. Written information can increase patient compliance with their doctor's instructions (Arthur, 1995; Ley, 1982). Information leaflets have also been found to contribute to better health outcomes (Greenfield et al., 1985; Mazzuca, 1982). The provision of information online is another matter however. Important questions have already been raised about the quality of online health information, especially where the source of that information or its authority and credentials are not disclosed (Ferguson, 2002; Impicciatore et al., 1997). Yet, there is evidence that patients are turning to online sources such as the Internet and are using health and medical information they find there to second-guess their GPs (Rumbelow, 1999).

ACCESS AND THE USER

The integration of technology with the provision of public services is regarded by government as an important democratic development. It is all about putting the citizen first. The prevailing perception is that the public wants better access to services and that putting them online is one way of satisfying the public's needs. The emphasis so far, however, has centered very much on technology access. In the U.K., the Government's priority is to ensure that as many people as possible are linked to online technologies. In parallel with this development, there has been a drive to get as many public services online as quickly as possible. To facilitate ambitious technology roll-out targets, the broad aim is to provide online services over as many communications technology platforms as possible. This means using the PC-based Internet, touch-screen kiosks, mobile phones and other mobile technologies, and iDTV (cable, satellite broadband). Although access to technology is a prerequisite of online service use, it does not by itself guarantee that use will take place.

From an access perspective, evidence has emerged that iDTV does reach parts of the population the PC-based Internet does not. Research in Britain, for instance, has found that markedly more people aged 65 and older subscribed to digital television (on satellite, cable, terrestrials, and ADSL platforms) than had a home computer with Internet access (30% vs. 13%). Digital television and PC-based Internet users also exhibited different socioeconomic class profiles. PC-based Internet access was more prevalent among professional middle-class (and more affluent) respondents (56%) than among semiskilled and unskilled, working-class (and less affluent) respondents (31%). The reverse was true for digital television (51% vs. 60% respectively; Towler, 2003).

The multiplatform scenario is likely to deliver greater service reach because different communications technologies are not taken up to the same extent by different segments of the population. New ICTs can take time to become established in a usability context, even though access has been widely achieved. Upgrades to longer established technologies may prove more fruitful because those technologies are already widely used. The latter distinction is illustrated by the respective potential of the PC-based Internet and iDTV. Television as a technology is already widely established, whereas the Internet is the new kid on the block. The full potential of the Internet as a service delivery technology will not be realised until a broadband platform has been more widely rolled out at a price people are prepared to tolerate. At this point, broadband technology will increase the capacity of the Internet to facilitate transmission of complex, dynamic multimedia content and bring it into more direct competition with broadcast television as a provider of home entertainment and information.

USER PSYCHOLOGY

Even established technologies such as television may not guarantee the success of online public services—in terms of their use—when utility of such services requires a different psychological orientation toward the medium. This issue goes beyond the acquisition of basic skills in ICT use. Certainly, although we may be able to access the Internet via a desktop PC at home, our ability to use it will restrict the effectiveness with which it is used. In addition to this fairly obvious observation, however, is a less frequently considered issue of whether we feel comfortable engaging in any kind of transaction over the Internet. This last consideration is a psychological one.

Television may be a familiar technology to most people and certainly more familiar than the PC-Internet. Television, however, is traditionally a passive medium. Accessing online public services on an iDTV platform invokes a shift in psychological orientation whereby television is treated as an interactive medium. Another way of putting it is this. The PC is a "lean forward" technology, whereas the television is a "lean back" technology. With a computer, users are accustomed to engaging with the technology interactively because that is part of the inherent nature of the machine. With a television set, users are accustomed to switching it on and letting its content wash over them in a more passive mental mode.

It is certainly the case that early experience with digital television has been found to produce more positive than negative responses. One pilot study of the effects of conversation to digital television among a small sample of homes in central England found that after 3 months of iDTV experience nearly 4 in 10 participants (38%) wanted to get digital television for themselves as soon as possible and more than one in three others (35%) said they wanted to get it within the next few years. Few (7%) said they definitely did *not* want digital television (GoDigital, 2003). Wanting digital television and feeling comfortable with the idea of using its interactive features are, however, two different things.

Research commissioned by Office for Telecommunications (OFTEL) in Britain, confirmed that digital media consumers perceive the TV set and PC differently. They have a distinct psychological orientation toward each technology. The

PC is regarded as a technology that needs to be worked at. The TV set, in contrast, is considered as a technology you relax with. Effort is expected with a PC, and is anathema to TV set usage. Furthermore, the use of interactive services on iDTV is regarded by some digital consumers as an unwelcome disruption of normal viewing behavior or simply as an inappropriate use of the medium (OFTEL, 2001).

Hence access does not success in the context of online public service roll-out. Less familiar technologies have to become not only more widely distributed but also more familiar to more people. With more familiar technologies that have established usage patterns and psychological orientations, users must be reconditioned to approach them in a different way. Television viewers must be able to shift readily from *watching* mode to *transacting* mode. The achievement of this objective means that more attention should be focused on usability issues.

USABILITY ISSUES

Online public services must be easy and effective to use if they are to be accepted and utilized as widely as government would like. During the development of such services, therefore, more attention should centre on establishing the usability and application effectiveness of these services for users. *Usability* here is taken to mean that the interface through which users engage with online services is easy to understand and utilize. *Application effectiveness* means that the most appropriate communications formats are utilized for given services. These factors underline the need to understand user psychology as well as demography.

As user research reported in chapter 6 (this volume) showed, although early adopters of new digital health services on television exhibit a particular demographic profile, other factors, related to people's psychological dispositions towards computer technology and preferred sources of health information, were significantly predictive of nonuse.

PLATFORM AVAILABILITY AND PLATFORM USE

The argument under this heading is that merely because people have a technology platform available to them does not mean that they will use it. This point is underscored by evidence for the U.K. on penetration and use of PC-Internet and iDTV technologies.

In 2002, a survey commissioned by the Independent Television Commission (ITC) found that 43% of television set owners in the U.K. (98% of the population) owned PCs with Internet access (Towler, 2003). The same survey reported that 44% of U.K. television viewers had access to iDTV.

Among iDTV viewers, one in seven (15%) said they used interactive services on this platform at least once a week in 2002, down from 19% in 2001. A clear majority of these viewers (66%), however, said that they *never* used interactive services, an increase on the year before (62%). Although interactivity was fairly limited, amounting to choice of camera angles in sports broadcasts and access to more detailed story content in news broadcasts, what these findings indicate is that availability to interactive services on television does not guarantee their use. Furthermore, the interactive services available at the time of this survey were not complicated to use.

Other evidence has indicated that viewers are prepared to interact with their television set if an application really grabs their interest. Sky Digital, the direct-to-home commercial satellite broadcaster in Britain, released an interactive game called Gamestar in March 2002 and attracted 1.4 million players a week. These games, however, attracted mostly young people and the success of iDTV as a purveyor of public services in the future will depend upon its ability to persuade a much wider demographic cross-section of the public to treat television in a "lean-forward" manner.

In the digital health context, some cable television subscribers who had access to a new digital interactive television health information service did not use it because they had a self-professed mental block about technology (Nicholas, Huntington, Williams, & Gunter, 2002a). This belief was linked to demography, being more widely held among older people, reinforcing classic technology adoption findings (Reese, Shoemaker, & Danielson, 1987; Rogers, 1995). The significant point, however, is that this psychological orientation cut across age-bands and predicted increased likelihood of nonadoption of this iDTV health service, even among young people.

SERVICE ACCESS

If iDTV is to prove an effective platform for interactive public services, users must be able to find the service they want from among the multitude of other services provided in a multichannel television environment. Online public services could literally be swamped in a digital television package containing perhaps 200 or more services. Online public services in an iDTV environment will therefore have to address their digital visibility in this crowded digital environment.

Accessing services in this type of television environment takes place through the electronic program guide (EPG). This is not simply an on-screen television guide that provides advance information about programs. It is the gateway to the services themselves. The EPG is both a menu of the services on offer and an access point through to the underlying content—whether interactive or noninteractive. EPGs tend to be hierarchical, offering at first a short list of superordinate service or channel category headings giving access to a second level that offers lists of the services under their specific category heading. At the second level, the service lists can get quite long, typically running to more than three screens. Each screen may contain 10 services. Some channels—usually the historically longest established, mainstream television channels and premium subscription channels (e.g., movie channels and major sports channels)—occupy prime positions at the heads of these menus.

The service lists are likely to grow longer in the future. Because many interactive public services will be offered as *walled gardens,* that is, services that are separately listed alongside mainstream television channels (rather than as enhanced services lying beneath and linked to sequential program services), they will have to be searched for and identified from the service lists. If such services are placed far down the list and not clearly labeled for what they are, users may have difficulty finding them and could easily miss them even when they have reached the right screen.

Digital media consumers have been found to regard the EPG as one of the most significant developments associated with digital television. It is seen as an essential innovation given the extensive number of channels in the iDTV environment. Nonetheless, consumers also recognised that a position near the top of a channel list places a service as a distinct advantage. Channels further down the list are more likely to be overlooked by users when scrolling down, especially if they lack a prominent brand image (OFTEL, 2001).

As evidence to be presented in the next part of this paper indicates, television viewers have a low tolerance for working hard to find interactive services in multichannel environments.

FINDING INFORMATION ON iDTV SERVICES

The public's confidence in online public services piped through their television sets will be enhanced if these interactive services can be readily used. Once a public service has been located on a television platform, it must be easy to find information on it. This does not mean simply being able to locate the service among a large suite of other channels. It also means that once the service has been found that the information and transactional capabilities it contains are themselves easy to access. This point is especially important give that many users or potential users of interactive public services on a television platform may lack the technology literacy of early adopters of the Internet.

Self-report survey evidence from among nonusers of a iDTV health information service on a cable network indicated that one of the key predictors of nonadoption was reported inability to find the information they anted. This response was rare among people aged 45 and younger (5% or fewer), more prevalent among people aged 46 to 75 years (10%–13%), and most common of all among those older than 75 years (26%; Nicholas, Huntington, Williams, & Gunter, 2002a, 2003b).

The fact that a service has been accessed does not mean then that service information can also be readily accessed. This point was illustrated in evaluating the iDTV pilot projects in Britain. One analysis reinforced the significance of ease of movement from the initial platform environment interface to specific service content.

In this case, a service called NHS Digital Direct was produced by Communicopia and transmitted on the broadband platform operated by Kingston Interactive Television (KIT) in Hull. At the time of the research, in 2002, the KIT platform was made available to 10,000 broadband subscribers. The service comprised text and video-on-demand information covering a wide range of health topics. The service was provided alongside a range of other entertainment and information services in the KIT environment. Over a pilot period extending several months, a number of changes occurred to the position of NHS Digital Direct on the KIT platform (see Nicholas, Huntington, Williams, & Gunter, 2002c).

Most of the text health content was supplied to Communicopia from the NHS Direct Web site. The content of this site was divided under the following headings: Not Feeling Well, A–Z of Conditions, First Aid, Medicine Cabinet, Healthy Living, Local Information, Search & Index, and About This Service. The service also included 95 videos on a wide range of health subjects that had been originally produced for this operation.

In an initial period spanning around 12 weeks, two menu levels were in operation. One of these was the platform homepage for the overall range of services provided by KIT. Within this was a further Local Link menu. At this time, NHS Digital Direct could be accessed both directly from the homepage and also via the Local Link menu. Users therefore had more than one route through to the service and did not have to explore very far to access health information content.

In a second period, that spanned around 4 weeks, there were again two relevant menu levels: the homepage and the Local Link menu. At this time, however, the direct link to NHS Digital Direct from the homepage was removed. Users now had to click through to the Local Link page and then click again to reach the health information service. In a third period, the menu structure shifted again from a two-level system to a three-level menu. This comprised a homepage menu at level one, a further platform operator menu (KIT page) at level two, and then a further page (Community Centre) within the level two menu that revealed a level three menu through which digital health content could be accessed. At this stage then, users had to navigate three screens to find the digital health service as compared with two screens in the two earlier phases.

Digital logs were used to monitor real time use of this service. These logs registered levels of use for different parts of the service and yielded a number of user-related metrics. Measures were taken of the numbers of text screens and videos viewed across the three periods previously outlined. Volumes of use fell across these periods as access to the digital health service required progressively more effort on the part of users.

From period one to period two, when access to the digital health service shifted from being one click away to two clicks away, there was a 33% decline in number of text screens viewed and a 29% decline in numbers of video viewed. From period two to period three, when access shifted from being two clicks away to three clicks away, there was a 45% decline in text screens viewed and a 35% decline in videos viewed. NHS Digital Direct attracted an average of 50 users per day who viewed about 1,700 text pages and 140 videos during the latter part of period two. This level of use fell to 15 daily users viewing about 500 text pages and 40 videos during period three.

Not only did the number of text pages and videos accessed decline as the amount of effort required on the part of users increased, there was further evidence of deteriorating use of the service on other metrics. The average number of daily users declined across the three periods. There was a 29% decline in average daily users from period one (35) to period two (25), and a 36% decline from period two to period three (16). The amount of time spent viewing pages on content declined across the three periods. There was an 11% decline in page view time from period one (36 s average page view time) to period two (32 s) and a 34% decline from period two to period three (21 s).

Of course, in this case, another explanation might be offered. A reduction in page view time could be influenced by the numbers of repeat users who, having learned the menu structure, are able to move more swiftly through the page hierarchy to reach the content pages. Because the numbers of repeat users was also found to have declined over time, with removal of direct access to the health information from the platform homepage, this factor is likely to have had a steadily weakening influence on the nature of service use.

Another—and perhaps a more powerful way—of looking at use of the service is to see how it attracts new users and returnees over time. Coming back to a service constitutes conscious and directed use. People might arrive at an Internet site or TV channel by accident —and, of course, that constitutes *use* according to the logs, but they are unlikely to arrive at the same service on repeated occasions by accident.

A further analysis was computed on log data to examine repeat use of the Communicopia NHS Direct Digital service across the three menu periods during which access to health information content was moved progressively further away from the initial iDTV platform home page. The data relate to new and returnee users between periods—return visits within period were not included. The data were adjusted for differences in length of period. In period one, of course, all users were new. In period two, when NHS Direct Digital was removed from the homepage, one half of use was accounted for by returnees from the first period and one half were new to that period. The number of new users declined by about 60% from period one to period two.

The decline in new users in period three was not so sharp (44%) compared to period two. Returnees from period one still made up 50% of use in period three, however, in absolute numbers, there was a decline of 40%. However, there was a marked decline in returnees in period three from among users who were new users in period two. Again, the changed position of Communicopia's health information service within the KIT broadband environment could have contributed to this decline. New users in period two accessed the service via the second level Local Link menu. In period three, this changed and the service was then available from a third level menu called *Community Center*. At this point, it appeared that fewer and fewer new people were finding the service.

Another way of comparing the menu periods is to look at the number of screens viewed during a visit. This metric is about measuring how deep users penetrate into the site or service. This was determined by counting the number of pages viewed by a particular user during a visit to a site or service. It indicated something about the depth (and length) of engagement, and the extent of navigation. Compared to period one, when the NHS Direct Digital service was available straight from the main menu, periods two and three had a greater number of users viewing more than 21 pages, 51% to 52% of users did so compared to 43% in period one. This suggested that users making the additional effort to find the service by navigating the new menu levels were likely to be more regular users of the service. They were committed core users of the service who persevered through two changes in the menu structure.

These findings indicated that access and use of the NHS Direct Digital health information service declined over the several months of the pilot on a number of metrics. As the service became more difficult for users to access, by being ever more removed from the opening menu page of this interactive television environment, the numbers of visitors and amount of use made of the service dropped away. This research provides a clear illustration that in a "lean-back" television environment, interactive public services must be readily accessible once the service as a whole has been located on the platform menu. Any extra effort that is imposed upon users by the service supplier or platform operator—even as little as one additional click on the remote control—could have significant implications for overall levels of service use.

APPLICATION EFFECTIVENESS

Application effectiveness depends upon finding the most suitable format for conducting certain types of information enquiry or communication transaction. Traditionally, the choices of communication channel have been limited, comprising spoken face-to-face, telephone, and written (hard copy) forms. In the digital communications environment, the options have expanded to include video links, e-mail and voice mail. Electronic communications can be conducted one-on-one or in a group format. Such communications can be asynchronous (a message is sent and a reply despatched some time later) or synchronous (two-way simultaneous communications). Once a user has located an interactive service on a multi-channel platform and navigated their way through to the required service content or transactional link, does the format offered provide the most appropriate or satisfactory modality through which to complete an enquiry or transaction?

Application effectiveness is likely to be a key factor that underpins the longer term success of interactive public services. the first barrier to cross is to convince digital consumers that the use of online services per se is an appropriate activity for the TV set. Many people with iDTV still do not recognize interactivity as a legitimate function for television. Many certainly do not use interactive services even when they are available (Towler, 2002, 2003). Then, even if interactivity is accepted as an aspect of using the television, this perception may not apply equally to all kinds of interactivity. For example, even iDTV subscribers express discomfort over the idea of conducting online banking over the TV set because it does not fit with safe and legitimate usage of the (typically main) digital TV set (OFTEL, 2001).

In the health context, for example, most users may be perfectly happy to search text-based information in undertaking a general information enquiry. A person suffering from a specific medical condition, however, may draw additional comfort from viewing video that features real people who also suffer from that same complaint. One reason for this may be that the sufferer may seek emotional support and reassurance as well as factual information with regard to their condition, and this can be supplied more effectively in a video format than in a text format. In both these cases, the communication links are asynchronous. There may be occasions when synchronous links are needed.

Someone suffering from a medical condition that is currently giving them cause for concern may need to speak to a health professional immediately. Watching a prerecorded video will not suffice. They need immediate advice or diagnosis. In this case, the opportunity to speak to a qualified professional on the telephone or actually being able to see that person via a live video link may be more appropriate.

Social Presence

One important concept associated with application effectiveness in the interactive communications context is *social presence*. The social presence model claims that communication media vary in the degree to which they can convey the physical presence of communicators (Short, Williams, & Christie, 1976). The model arranges media along a continuum from low (written numeric or textual content) to high social presence (e.g., face-to-face communication). It is further contended that individuals will select the medium that they perceive to have the highest social presence.

Another related model is media richness theory (Daft & Lengel, 1984). This theory posits that people select communication technologies based largely on the attributes of the medium. Again, media can be arranged on a continuum from *lean* to *rich* based on their speed of feedback, variety of channels, friendliness of source, and richness of language used. Media richness theory also considers the context of use and proposes that individuals will seek to match the richness of a communication medium with the complexity of the task for which it is used.

Some of the earliest research reported that newer media, particularly when involving text-based communication, were rated by users as more appropriate for information exchange tasks requiring lower social presence (Rice, 1993; Trevino, Lengel, & Daft, 1987). Compared with direct face-to-face communication, for example, computer-mediated communication (CMC) was reportedly ranked low in social presence (Perse & Courtright, 1993). Later research challenged this notion of CMC, however. Indeed, engagement with computers was reported frequently to take on the same tenor as interpersonal communication (Reeves & Nass, 1996). CMC can be used for socioemotional tasks just as readily and effectively as can face-to-face communication (Joinson, 2001; Parks & Floyd, 1996; Walther, 1996). The rules determining the nature of communication via computers often resemble those that govern the way individuals interact face to face (Lee & Nass, 2002). Although certain communication cues in face-to-face situations are missing in the CMC context, skilled exponents of CMC find ways of enhancing the form of communication in that environment and may nevertheless engage in emotionally fruitful encounters with others in that context (Tidwell & Walther, 2002). This background is important to the establishment of public services online, especially where such services may involve a range of different types of CMC interaction between members of the public and public service providers.

Alternative theoretical perspectives have emerged in the field of CMC such as the social identification and deindividuation model (SIDE; Lea & Spears, 1992, 1995), social information processing theory (SIPT; Walther, 1992; Walther & Burgoon, 1992), and the hyperpersonal perspective (Walther, 1996). Each of these models have indicated that individuals can compensate, in different ways, for the nonverbal cue limitations of CMC.

The SIDE model offers an explanation of how individuals adjust cognitively for the limitations of CMC by drawing upon social stereotypes in forming impressions of others, once information about their group identity has become apparent through textual exchanges. This process enables one communicator to form a more complete (although not necessarily more accurate) impression of another that would normally be informed by appearance cues in face to face contact (Lea & Spears, 1995).

SIPT proposes that individuals can adapt available cue systems—including linguistic features available in e-mail systems—to compensate for missing nonverbal information about those with whom they are communicating. In addition, the *mood* of a CMC user's verbal messages to another online user can be affected by their anticipation of future contact with that person. More effort may be made, in terms of good *netiquette,* when further contact is expected (Walther & Tidwell, 1995).

The hyperpersonal model extends some of the features of SIDE and SIPT and focuses more explicitly on the processing of information sought and given online. Similar to SIDE, the hyperpersonal perspective proposes that receivers engage in compensatory attribution processes to fill in the gaps in direct information about others with whom they are communicating and, in doing so, may form distorted or exaggerated impressions of those others by building inaccurately on limited feedback information. Research conducted to test this model has also indicated that, under some circumstances, CMC can lead to firmer bonds between correspondents than would occur through face-to-face encounters (Walther, 1996).

Seeking Health Information Via the TV

In iDTV health research in Britain, although not systematically investigated, the significance of social presence and media richness emerged through a number of the findings (see Nicholas et al., 2002c). One iDTV pilot—Living Health—provided information in text and video form and offered access to transactional services such as online appointments booking with GPs and other health professionals and live telephone and video links to NHS nurses. Text information about medical conditions that was provided online via the television was valued by many of its users.

In relation to this pilot, which operated on a cable television system in Birmingham, the second largest U.K. city after London, a postal survey indicated that more than 4 in 10 (44%) sought information relating to their own medical condition, whereas 1 in 4 (25%) sought it for friends and family. More than 8 in 10 users of this information (81%) said they found the text information useful. Over four in ten users (43%) said that the health text information helped a lot in dealing with their doctor.

There were other individuals, however, who did not use this digital health service although it was available to them at no extra charge as existing cable subscribers. Among these nonusers, lack of use among some was attributed to not being very good with interactive technology (17%) or not being able to find the content they wanted within the digital health service (7%). Far more of these people, however, said that their doctor tells them all they need to know about their medical condition (24%) or that they preferred to receive printed information from their doctor about a condition (40%; Nicholas et al., 2002c). These findings suggest that avoidance of an interactive television health information service may occur among some potential users because they prefer to go direct to their doctor for such information. Interactive digital television may lack sufficient media richness for these individuals as compared with direct physical contact with the GP.

Video Versus Text

In further analyses of iDTV pilots in Britain, an attempt was made to examine the differential use and response to information provided online via different platforms and formats (Nicholas et al., 2003b). Two of the pilots introduced in chapter 6 (this volume) presented a significant amount of content in video format as well as in text format. One company called Channel Health broadcast a series of programs on maternity issues (called *Bush Babies*) on a national digital satellite platform, coupled with text information attached to each program as an enhanced service. Another pilot consortium, Communicopia (branded also as NHS Direct Digital), provided a video-on-demand service comprising material on a variety of health topics, alongside an extensive online library of health information in text, on a broadband telephone network.

Of Channel Health's *Bush Babies'* respondents who were surveyed, 7 in 10 (70%) reportedly watched just the television broadcasts, whereas more than 1 in 5 (23%) said they viewed the text and video, whereas less than 1 in 10 (7%) reportedly just viewed the text behind the programs. Both video and text formats proved popular with Communicopia/NHS Direct Digital users. More than 4 in 10 (41%) of those surveyed who had used the NHS Direct Digital service claimed that they only used the text part of the service and that they had not requested a video; 6% said they had only used the video part of the service, and more than 1 in 2 (54%) said they had used both text and video.

Text proved to be the most popular in terms of the personal opinions of NHS Direct Digital users, with 6 in 10 (60%) saying they preferred the text service, whereas just less than 4 in 10 (38%) preferred the video service. This pattern was reversed for men younger than 36 years. Young men preferred videos: 63% of men younger than 36 said that they preferred to watch videos rather than read text, compared to 26% of females in this age group. In follow-up focus groups, participants felt that some information presented in video form would have been better as text. It was suggested that information on medication, for instance, could have been better presented in tabular form (Nicholas et al., 2003b).

Users of NHS Direct Digital were also asked to rate the importance of each service—text versus video. The average scores were similar, although there is suggestive evidence that videos were found easier to understand compared to text and that they were also found more interesting than text. These survey findings were reinforced by the views expressed by focus group participants. However, videos were not invariably perceived to have a significant advantage over textual information. One in three NHS Direct Digital users (34%) who were surveyed agreed with the statement that watching a health video was a big improvement on reading the text, with similar proportions disagreeing and having no opinion (Nicholas et al., 2003b). Such evidence indicates a need to explore in more detail what the relative advantages of video and text might be in relation to the different information needs of users.

Transactional Services: Video Diagnosis

The digital health television services piloted in Britain in 2002 explored the potential of iDTV as a two-way medium where the user becomes an information sender as well as a receiver of content. Such applications represent more advanced forms of interactivity and require a different mindset on the part of users who engage in a customized activity geared to addressing their specific problems rather than one of a more general nature. These are genuinely new applications of television.

The applications tested in the pilots included visual interpersonal communication with a National Health Service nurse (InVision), an online doctor appointments booking service (both supplied by Living Health), and the maintenance of personal medical records online (Communicopia/NHS Digital Direct). In addition, one consortium (Channel Health), tested a small-scale e-mail support service for a specific group—pregnant women (Nicholas et al., 2003b).

With the Living Health InVision service, users could telephone the call-center and simultaneously see on their television screen the nurse to whom they were talking. The user at home could ask the nurse any questions about their medical condition and the nurse would either offer advice and information. The visual element could be further utilized by the nurse who could show pictures, charts, and video clips to the user where they provided relevant as part of the response to the enquiry.

Apart from the visual element of the service, for which special training was given to call-center nurses, the procedure followed was the same as that established for telephone-only callers. This involved a Clinical Assessment System (CAS) protocol. With this procedure, a flow diagram is produced where the questions are generated by the system depending on answers and information supplied by callers. The nurse works through this to arrive at the recommendations to be offered to the caller. This could be advice to visit a doctor within the next 24 hours, to seek or receive home help, or some other course of action. In extreme cases, calls can be routed through to the emergency services to enable instant assistance to be provided.

To set up the service, the caller accessed the InVision page on the television and followed simple on-screen instructions. These generated an InVision reference number. The caller then telephoned an NHS Direct call-center and quoted the number. The InVision connection was then made, and the nurse appeared on screen at the same time as the audio connection over the telephone was made.

As part of the larger project to evaluate the performance of iDTV health information pilots, a special study was made of the video nurse service (Nicholas, Huntington, Williams, & Gunter, 2002b). This study examined how and why members of the public used this telemedicine service. More detailed findings on its impact are discussed in chapter 8 (this volume). In the present context, however, the study provided data that illustrated the emotional value of live video formats.

Data were derived from four sources: users of the service who were interviewed by telephone ($n = 27$) or face to face ($n = 4$), personal interviews with call-center nurses ($n = 6$), call logs, and call scripts ($n = 64$) generated by CAS interactions between users and nurses.

The service was warmly received by users and nurses, but used by few people. A total of 163 users emerged from a potential audience of over 38,000 subscribing households at the beginning of the pilot, rising to 51,000 at the end. Over the period of study from the end of July to end of November 2001, there were 1,380 requests for the InVision service. This was a relatively small number of visits compared to the use of other services offered by Living Health. This could indicate that a consultation with a nurse comprises a higher level of interactivity than checking out text content on health. In all, 1,062 of these requests (75%) were cancelled, 806 by the user (for reasons not yet known), and 411 were terminated because of a time-out code, a busy signal, or because the service was closed. Just 163 InVision sessions (12%) were completed. It was speculated, although not proven, that low use of the service could be explained by the small potential user base for the iDTV health service as a whole, by discouragement in marketing literature of causal use of the InVision part of the service (a confidential service to be used only in the case of a genuine need for immediate medical advice), lack of publicity, and the possibility that many people were not yet ready to engage with this kind of service on television (Nicholas, Huntington, Williams, & Gunter, 2002b).

More women (55% of total users) than men (45%) used InVision. A majority of users (57%) were younger than 45. Two out of three users (68%) had reportedly contacted the call-center on behalf of someone else—most often an enquiry related to a child. Of those who had made contact on behalf of themselves, a clear majority were men (62%). Most female callers (56%) had called on behalf of a child.

The nurses' call scripts broke down enquiries into four broad categories:[1] (1) treatment advice (i.e., for a specific condition that has just arisen, such as a personal injury, or that is not being treated)—45 (70%); (2) reassurance (i.e., queries about the seriousness of a particular condition)—23 (36%); (3) diagnosis—15 (23%); and (4) general information (i.e., queries such as whether one can mix two drugs; medicines that do not contain animal products, etc.)—9 (14%).

Users of this online video link found the service helpful. What was particularly interesting, however, was that many callers (36%) sought reassurance as much as specific medical help. For these callers, using a service in which the nature of the communication was richer than text or voice-only was advantageous in that the more "human" element conveyed greater reassurance and this was enhanced with the visual element.

The nurses gave a number of examples of callers who were more concerned with being reassured or with simply communicating with a nurse than with bald medical or treatment facts. One female caller, for example, was distressed about her husband's drinking and violence. In this case, the nurse decided that the facility of the system to show images or video clips was not relevant here. Instead, the nurse decided that this caller needed reassurance that help was available and gave her details of relevant support groups.

Users' remarks provided qualitative evidence that video links offer a richer format than text or even audio links. For certain types of health-related enquiry, users need to see as well as hear whom they are dealing with. Where there is an emotional need in addition to an information need, pictures may speak louder than words.

Other user remarks indicated that the video link made the online consultation seem not only more personal, but also more confidential. The video link simulated face-to-face contact and hence made the nurse seem closer. Although the visual element was clearly valued, it is notable that only one user said it would be useful for the video link to be two-way. It might be that this would be considered too intrusive by many.

Such was the enthusiasm of callers about the visual element of the InVision service that further research needs to be carried out to measure more precisely the benefits of this kind of telemedicine. The need for further enquiry is reinforced by the mixed evidence available to date. Thompson and Ogden (1995) found that the ability to see the respondent in a telephone conversation gave only a small improvement to understanding. Whittaker (1995) felt that the additional cost of a video-based service did not warrant use in terms of the minimal increase in benefits. Studies in an educational, rather than medical setting, however, show more positive results. In his review of multimedia research, Mayer (1997) concluded that animated images do enhance learning, particularly when accompanied by verbal explanation.

Despite question marks over the cost effectiveness of video diagnosis, the degree to which early users referred to the reassurance it gave them points to the po-

---

[1]Percentages add to more than 100 as some queries contained elements of more than one category.

tential of this type of online health service. Interestingly, psychological studies (e.g., Sellen, 1995) looking at video-conferencing purely in terms of communicating or conversing, have indicated that teleconferencing and audio-only telephone conversations do not differ markedly in terms of conversational behavior (degree of formality, turn-taking, etc). Nevertheless, the element of the exchange that might be expected to promote reassurance or trust—social presence—is enhanced by a video communications channel (Greef & de Ijsselstejn, 2001).

Transactional Services: Booking Doctor's Appointments

Use of Living Health's doctor appointments booking service was very low with just 30 people making an online appointment with their doctor over the 6 months pilot period. There were just three doctor's surgeries involved in the pilot and they did not promote the service very enthusiastically. The procedural complexity associated with signing up to this pilot project, its limited duration (6 months) and lack of effective promotion meant that take-up was minimal (Nicholas et al., 2003b).

Transactional Services: Medical Records Keeping

Communicopia/NHS Direct Digital offered users an opportunity to maintain personal vaccination records online that they could access via their TV sets. This online vaccination updating service accounted for 0.14% of use for the entire NHS Direct Digital service. In all, just 28 people used it. The service comprised a reminder of when a jab was needed and users had to enter all relevant personal details. The take-up was disappointing, but the value of this service must be questioned, especially when it was only in place for a short time (Nicholas et al., 2003b).

Age and Usability

Older people are a primary target group for health information and advice services on digital interactive television. Interactive digital television may offer a more convenient way of giving them access to health information and advice at home. But they often tend to lack the digital familiarity of younger people. In the iDTV pilot work in Britain, age was found to be linked to ease of understanding of interactive television health information services. Users older than 65 were more likely to report that they had experienced difficulties (Nicholas et al., 2003a, 2003b). Qualitative research with older users of such services revealed that elderly people reported some anxiety about the march of information technology. Older participants often did not regard themselves as likely participants in this digital revolution (Nicholas et al., 2003b).

ERGONOMIC ISSUES AND USABILITY

Online technologies do not always present easy to use information systems. Research with the Internet, for example, has shown that many Web sites lack usability

(Nielsen, 1998). The lessons that have been learned in studies of the Internet may be applicable also to the use of iDTV. This may be especially true in relation to the use of online information services by older people. Many Web sites have been found to disregard the visual requirements of users (Clark, Knupfer, Mahoney, Kramer, Ghazali, & Al-Ari, 1997; Luck & Hunter, 1997). This may be especially true with older users (Jakobi, 1999). It is important for online information site designers, regardless of the technology platform, to understand how human cognitive information processing works and how cognitive capacity and the ability to process different types and quantities of information can change over a person's life span (Echt, 2002).

It is important to realize that human beings process information differently in different formats and via different modalities. It is not enough simply to acknowledge that people process pictures differently from words. They may also process text differently from the page as compared to the screen. Both the Web and early iDTV health information sites have emphasized text presentation. It has been recognized for some years, however, that many people do not like to read long text from the screen (Echt, 2002). Although text information is read linearly, screen information may be browsed, scanned, and skipped over in a nonlinear fashion (Nielsen & Morkes, 1997).

The Web offers many options for information searching. Users, however, often employ selective attention strategies when processing information from a screen (Marks & Dulaney, 1998; McDowd & Shaw, 2000). Information attributes guide the gaze of the eyes and attention is readily directed to areas that are more relevant to the search goal (Scott, 1993). The greater sensitivity to physically salient attributes when reading from a screen means that processing of electronic information is potentially more prone (than when reading printed text) to distraction. On-screen features that stand out because of shape, color, or movement and that are not supportive of core information may impair processing (Aspillaga, 1996; Vora, 1998).

Older adults tend to make less exhaustive searches than do younger people (Johnson, 1990). This may be because older adults have trouble finding and extracting information from visual displays and do so more slowly (Kline, 1994; Madden & Allen, 1991). There is consistent evidence that people read slower from screens than from the printed page (see Echt, 2002). The clarity and size of text on the screen can also pose problems for readers. Older people are using computers more. Even so, many older computer users (more than 40%) have been found to report difficulties reading text on screen (Hutchison, Eastman, & Tirrito, 1997). Older adults have also been found to express more dislike for reading from a computer screen than do younger adults (Meyer & Poon, 1997).

Taking into account research on visual ageing and information processing from the screen, some researchers have provided guidelines for the presentation of printed medical information and instructions concerning the special needs of older users (Hartley, 1999; Morrell & Echt, 1997). There have been few empirical tests of the efficacy of such guidelines, but where they have occurred, the results have confirmed the significance of certain presentation attributes (Echt & Pollack, 1998). Echt (2002) listed features such as typography, layout, organization, navigation, and graphics as being among those worthy of close consideration by Web site designers. For example, 14-point font was found to be an optimal point size for legibility, bold text worked better than italics, and upper case was to be avoided. With layout, black text on a white background generally worked best. Text was easier to assimilate when headings and subheadings were used to break it up.

Many of these guidelines could also be applied to the design of health information sites transmitted via digital interactive television. Hence, it is not enough simply to opt for television as a platform in the belief that the less computer literate segments of the population (e.g., the elderly) will then automatically be drafted into the online world. Usability features connected directly with the interface between users and services will play a crucial part in bringing on board late adopters of new communications technologies.

In research with the iDTV health service experiments in Britain, readability tests were carried out among older people (aged 61–75 years) on the text service of the Living Health consortium. Menu items were regarded as clear and easiest to read and understand. However, some older people experienced difficulties with the service. Questions were raised about the usefulness and value of the service, with participants reporting that they did not always find it easy to locate the information they were looking for. One suggestion was made for the use of more picture material, such as diagrams and images, to enhance the text (Thompson, Williams, Nicholas, & Huntington, 2002).

CONCLUSIONS

The roll-out of digital technology is obviously essential if society as a whole is to reap the benefits on online public services. Without access to the delivery technology, the public can not receive electronic services. Putting the infrastructure in place has therefore been at the forefront of planning for the future digital world. As the analysis presented in this paper has indicated, however, infrastructure is not everything. Even when virtually all public services have been e-enabled and most people have reception technology either at home or within easy reach at a public location in their community, the effective utilization of these services requires a number of other important considerations.

Two key elements that will underpin the success of the online public service provision are the usability and application effectiveness of these electronically communicated services. These two concepts invoke a change of orientation toward understanding digital consumer psychology. In particular, there is a need to recognize that even when adapting an established medium such as television to provide interactive capability, viewers will not universally shift their mindset toward the medium. Although there may be certain advantages in utilizing television in the context of closing the digital divide, where the latter is envisaged primarily as a matter of demographics, such a development omits to take fully into account the significance of audience psychology.

Even when most viewers have been cultivated to regard television as a "lean-forward" as well as a "lean-back" medium and can engage with the medium in both ways, there remains the issue of finding the best formats for particular kinds of information enquiry and for conveying specific types of transaction. Recognition of the differential social presence and media richness afforded by different communication formats is a matter of paramount importance.

In addition to the application effectiveness of new communications technologies, it is important to ensure that usability in terms of interface design will also enhance the attraction of online information services.

Interactive digital television is a new platform. It represents a development in the nature of television as a technology and as a viewing medium. The use of iDTV as a communications channel through which to transmit health information and advice is a pioneering innovation. Even on a familiar platform, it may take some time for a new service to become established in terms of its market share.

In the case of the iDTV pilot experiment in Britain, both the services and platforms were relatively new, not just in terms of content, but also in terms of the way users were invited to engage with the services being offered. Although people may be used to the idea of being *interactive* when using a personal computer for access to the Internet, this is not true of television viewing. The long-conditioned psychological orientation toward television is one of passive reception. Interactivity on television is limited to channel surfing via the remote control, video recording of off-air broadcasts for later viewing, and latterly, choice of camera angles at sports broadcasts. Full-on interactivity with the television that involves content mining or two-way communications, with the viewer being a sender as well as a receiver of messages, is a new phenomenon for most viewers that will entail some reconditioning of their usual orientation toward the medium.

Future research with online technologies in the public service context must establish the most appropriate and effective formats for different types of online task, and ensure that they are designed to appeal to users. Only then can the digital divide truly be closed and online public services enjoy longer term acceptance and success.

Digital Health: Perceived Benefits and Health Impact

The roll out of online health advice and information services represents part of a wider initiative to capitalize on information and communication technology (ICT) applications in consumer markets and in the context of digital government (Cawson, Haddon, & Miles, 1995; Dutton, 1999; Miles, 1988). From the early 1990s, many new products emerged that enabled two-way messaging via fixed and mobile technologies in text, audio, and video formats. Interactive ICTs were envisaged as transforming the way in which public services could be delivered to citizens (Dutton, 1999). This is a worldwide phenomenon, although it is more advanced in some countries than others. Furthermore, even in countries with relatively advanced ICT developments, these have frequently failed to reach all sectors of society equally (Norris, 2001). This observation is particularly true of the Internet, which has represented the cornerstone of much e-government thinking.

In Britain, the government aims to have all or virtually all central and local government services available online by 2005. Regardless of how achievable, in practice, this target may be, it has recognized the need to consider a number of different ICT platforms on which such services could be carried in order to avoid the pitfalls of what some authors have called the *digital divide* (Norris, 2001).

What this means is recognizing that the Internet is not the only platform of significance in this context. Although steadily increasing numbers of households have become linked to the Internet, there are many more late adopters or laggards who have yet to do so. Yet, virtually every home in the country has television, and new technological advances in interactive digital television (iDTV) may render this medium an alternative channel through which public service access for all could be achieved.

133

New electronic communications systems have provided opportunities for public dialogue in a variety of contexts. Information sharing can be facilitated horizontally among citizens as well as vertically between citizens and government. The evolution of computer-mediated communications (CMCs) has opened up communications channels that can, in some cases, provided effective substitutes for face-to-face conversations—or so it is hoped.

In a health context, for instance, there are hopes that these ICTs can be used to cultivate a climate of self-help among the public and patients, whereby some information transactions at the level of general enquiries about health conditions, symptoms, treatments, and preventive measures, and may be even simple levels of advice and diagnosis, can be conducted online rather than in person. Thus, in addition to the carriage of health campaigns targeted at the general population, interactive media can be deployed to roll out large quantities of health-related information that members of the public and patient groups can consult in their own time whenever the need arises.

In considering the impact of digital health provision, therefore, distinctions can be made between deliberate attempts to raise public awareness or to change attitudes and behaviors in relation to specific health issues, nondirectional information services that are available 24/7 for online consultation, interactive online facilities for facilitating networking between geographically dispersed individuals who share common health problems, and transactions between public and health professionals concerned with personalized enquiries about health problems.

HEALTH CAMPAIGNING:
SELECTING THE BEST CHANNELS

Media health campaigns have typically relied heavily on media such as television, radio, newspapers, and other mass-market printed media (e.g., magazines). These media have provided opportunities to reach large numbers of people, but they have not always been universally successful in terms of eventual health impacts. There are other channels available for carrying health messages such as billboards, posters, theater slides, music, and new electronic media such as the Internet, computer games, and CD-ROM disks (Salmon & Atkin, 2003).

Deciding which channel or medium or combination of channels and media to use requires an analysis of the relative advantages and disadvantages of each modality for the presentation of health messages. Channels vary in the audiences they reach, how much attention they command, and the way they present information. The impact of health messages can be measured in terms of how many people are reached, whether the right people are reached, whether audiences pay attention to and understand health messages, the degree to which the messages have perceived relevance for recipients, the credibility of the message and its source, and its ability to raise the public profile of the issue.

There are also differences between channels and media in terms of the kinds of messages they can most effectively present, the ability of different kinds of messages to produce the desired effects, the cost of producing messages for that channel or medium, and the cost of the channel or medium itself in relation to the access it can provide to the intended or targeted audience.

Using posters and billboards, for example, may be cheaper than using television. Television advertisements and programs can be expensive to produce and airtime can be costly too. But although posters and billboards may offer less expensive options, they may reach far fewer people. Further, given the typical exposure settings of these different media, there may be differences in the levels of attention to health messages on billboards or posters as compared with television.

Advertisements on television may reach large numbers of people, but attention to them may be poor. Viewers often use commercial breaks as convenient points in their viewing to do other things that entail looking away from the screen, or they may change to a new channel or leave the room temporarily (Gunter, Furnham, & Lineton, 1995). Even if the viewer stays with the break, a campaign message may be competing with five or more other commercial messages within that commercial break for the viewers' attention and memory. Embedding health messages within entertainment programming (e.g., soap operas), however, may provide a more subtle method of getting the messages across. If a health message is effectively integrated into the storyline, viewers may learn from it without being consciously aware of having done so. Through association with attention-grabbing dramatic events in the program, the message may hit home more powerfully than it would have done if presented as a public service announcement or within a factual program. This method can be very successful in getting health messages across (Singhal & Rogers, 1999).

The use of newer media, such as the World Wide Web on the Internet, also holds promise for conveying health information and persuasive messages to people. Such communication technology can carry large quantities of information in a variety of modalities (text, audio, and video). Large numbers of people can be reached through this channel these days, though significant proportions of the population would still be excluded in virtually all countries. Messages can readily be produced in a number of versions, each targeted at different subgroups of the general audience. There may also be opportunities for more dynamic involvement of audience members by utilizing the interactive capabilities of the Internet. According to Salmon and Atkin (2003), Internet Web pages can be very good in terms of offering wide access, targeting special subgroups, and having the capacity to carry large amounts of content. They can be moderately effective in terms of reach across the public as a whole and the credibility attached to the information being conveyed. The Internet was rated as poor, however, in terms of its current agenda-setting capabilities.

In understanding the health impact potential of mediated health information therefore it is important to examine the specific variables that make a difference to the way members of the audience respond. Audience, channel, and message factors can be distinguished in this context. Audiences can not be treated as a homogeneous mass. Members of an audience may exhibit different personal characteristics, interests, and needs. All these factors can play a parting shaping their current health status and personal health information requirements. Such factors may also influence how they respond to specific health messages (Rimal & Adkins, 2003).

The impact of health campaigns can be affected, as already noted, by the choice of communication channel through which to deliver health messages. The selection of communication channel must also be informed by the type of audience at which messages are targeted. In addition, the purpose and objectives of a campaign can also affect channel choice. Raising awareness of a health issue with the wider population can be quickly and economically achieved through a major mass medium such as television or newspapers. Changing people's health-related behaviors, however, may be more effectively achieved through interpersonal communication (Rogers & Storey, 1987). Television advertising campaigns can inform large numbers of people of the health risks associated with smoking, but may lack the potency, for example, to persuade smokers to give up smoking. For that, more direct intervention in their behavior may be necessary, such as attending self-help groups, receiving counseling, hypnosis, wearing nicotine patches, and so on. The choice of communication channel for health campaigning must therefore be informed by the kinds of outcomes its producers and sponsors hope to achieve.

A further crucial factor that can underpin successful health campaigning is the tailoring of messages to audiences. People respond best to persuasive messages they perceive to be relevant to them. Message producers must therefore learn as much as they can about the personal characteristics, interests and needs of their target audiences so that they can customize message content to appeal to specific recipients. Audiences can be segmented, not only demographically but also psychologically into different types and subtypes. In consequence, with some health campaigns it may be necessary to produce more than one version of a health message. Each version would be designed to have a strong appeal to specific audience subgroups (Kreuter, Farrell, Olevitch, & Brennan, 2000).

Hence, effective health campaigning must take into account audience, channel, and message characteristics. In the older media environment, complex conceptual modeling of campaign design in this way could create a financially unrealistic solution requiring the production of many different messages, designed for different media, and targeted at different sectors of the audience. With media such as television or radio or newspapers or magazines, this solution could be financially prohibitive because of costs of campaign message production and space access in these media. Furthermore, these media, being largely aimed as mass audiences, represented a somewhat cumbersome method of targeting specific audience segments (Rimal & Adkins, 2003).

The tailoring of health messages can not be so readily achieved through older mass-media technologies. Tailored messages are important in the health context because they are designed to have special significance for targeted recipients. As such, they can also be expected to have a greater impact upon recipients (Brug, Campbell, & van Assema, 1999; Bull, Kreuter, & Scharff, 1999; Kreuter, Oswald, Bull, & Clark, 2000; Rosen, 2000). Messages based on target recipients' motives and readiness to change their behavior and that used participants' own names were more effective in the context of promoting physical activity change than were messages that omitted these elements (Bull et al., 1999).

Message tailoring must take into account factors such as a relevance, perceived risk, self-efficacy, and the type of feedback provided to message recipients (Rimal & Adkins, 2003). The relevance of messages is influenced by the degree to which they are in tune with the motives of recipients to change their behavior and present arguments that are deemed credible. When a message is perceived to have personal relevance, it will be cognitively processed more effectively. Further, recipients will be able to process a greater number of more complex arguments once their engagement with the message is more focused. Perception of the personal relevance of a message will enhance this process (Petty & Cacioppo, 1979).

As well as relevance, an individual's perceived risk from a health problem also plays a significant part in determining responses to health messages. The greater the perceived personal risk from a health problem, the more the individual is motivated to seek self-protective measures. Under these circumstances, the individual may be more receptive to health content that will inform those measures (Rimal & Adkins, 2003).

Self-efficacy is another factor underlying behavior change. To what extent do individuals perceive they possess the ability and drive to change? Individuals who feel they have greater self-efficacy are more likely to face up to serious challenges and to persevere (Bandura, 1986). Self-efficacy is also important in relation to the maintenance of health behaviors (Fuchs, 1996). Information seeking about heart disease was found to be more determined among individuals who perceived themselves both at risk and able to do something about it through their own actions (Rimal, 2001).

Feedback on behavior change is important because the attainment of positive results can itself be motivating. Good feedback can lead to behavior change (Brug et al., 1996; Gask, 1998). Feedback can be even more effective, however, when the reinforcements have personal relevance to the individual (De Vries & Brug, 1999). One advantage of computer-mediated communication, the Internet, and other interactive technologies such as interactive digital television lies in being able to customize health messages for lots of different types of user. The interactive nature of such technologies also allows them to mimic interpersonal communication to some degree, as well as to provide communications to large numbers of users (Rimal & Adkins, 2003). Indeed, communicating via interactive technologies has been found to give rise to a phenomenon in which the human users responds to the technology in the same way as they would to another person (Reeves & Nass, 1996).

IMPACT OF RETRIEVED ONLINE INFORMATION

Ultimately, the success of digital health provision must be measured in terms of health benefits to users, with knock-on economies and efficiency benefits for the health services. In Britain, online health information and advice is intended to promote self-help and self-health care through enhanced public awareness and knowledge about health. This impact may occur as a direct result of exposure to health information or as a function of more fruitful interactions with health professionals that benefit from this enhanced awareness. In the latter instance, patients may ask their doctors more informed questions about their condition following advance consultation with online health information sources. Alternatively, patients may seek further clarification or confirmation of what their doctor told them via subsequent reference to online health information.

Research has indicated the effectiveness of information in hard copy form in relation to health benefit gain for patients. For example, written information can increase patient compliance with their doctor's instructions and so help the healing process (Arthur, 1995; Ley, 1982). Information leaflets have also been found to contribute to better health outcomes (Greenfield et al., 1985; Mazzuca, 1982).

In regard to electronic information, one study found that as a result of using the Internet, approximately one half of all health information seekers advised a family member or friend to see a doctor, changed their exercise or eating habits, or made a positive decision related to their health treatment (Cyber Dialogue, 2000). Research in the U.S. by the Pew Institute (2000) revealed that as well as consulting the Internet for general information about health and health care, one in four Internet users (27%) visited health Web sites to arm themselves with specific information prior to visiting a doctor or clinic, whereas one in three (34%) consulted online sources after seeing a health professional. Nearly 1 in 10 (9%) sought information about specific doctors, hospitals, or medicines. The same survey uncovered self-report evidence of Internet impact upon health. More than one half of Pew survey respondents (51%) said that Internet health information affected the way they eat or exercise, and nearly one half (47%) said it affected decisions about health treatments. Among the latter group, over one in four (28%) said that Internet information affected their decision about whether to see a doctor.

In a British study of digital health information on the Internet, it was reported that such content had a significant impact upon the perceived health of the user. Two thirds of users said that such information had "helped a lot" in being better informed and just less than one half felt that the information had helped in their dealings with the doctor. More importantly, over one in three respondents said that their condition had improved after having visited an Internet site (www.surgerydoor.co.uk; Nicholas, Huntington, Williams, & Blackburn, 2001).

The Internet can be used by specific groups of users, defined by personal health problems, to retrieve information about their particular medical condition or information that may be relevant to them, given their lifestyle. Such information may be of value to people who place themselves at risk through their lifestyle. The Internet is regarded as a potential valuable information source in learning about avoidance of sexual transmitted diseases. However, in a U.S. survey on this issue distinction were made between using different Internet information applications in this context. Although most respondents (61%) expressed a willingness to visit a Web site to retrieve information about sexually transmitted diseases, fewer would engage in e-mail contact (45%) or chat room discussions (30%) about this topic (Bull, McFarlane, & King, 2001). Among respondents to this survey, men who have sex with other men and those with a reported history of testing for sexually transmitted diseases were more likely to endorse sexually transmitted disease prevention through chat rooms and via e-mail links (Bull et al., 2001).

The Internet has been investigated in relation to its ability to deliver nutrition education. The aim of this online application was to raise awareness of nutrition issues and ultimately to influence consumption of fat, fruit, and vegetables. In this investigation, the impact of a Web-based, computer-tailored nutrition education program for adults in the Netherlands was measured. Participants who had been exposed to the program exhibited significantly enhanced awareness of recommended intake levels for fat, fruit, and vegetables and a greater intention to change to a healthier diet, as compared to other adults who had not been exposed to this program (Oenema, Brug, & Lechner, 2001).

IMPACT OF ONLINE SUPPORT NETWORKS

The retrieval of health information from online databases represent "on-tap" resources for the public and patient groups to utilize whenever they have the need, with spin-off benefits in terms of enhanced personal knowledge, more informed patients, and perhaps also users who feel more empowered to take control over their own health. In addition, online technologies can provide other kinds of digital health service. Some applications may used for emotional support as much as for clinical knowledge acquisition (Finn, 1999; Sharf, 1997).

In this vein, important work has been carried out on the impact of the Internet on various specialist user groups, principally with regard to online support groups. Support groups vary between those that cover many health issues and those that specialize in a single health topic. They can offer opportunities for information exchanges between participants in chat rooms, on bulletin boards and in mail groups. Usually they communicate about specific topics such as body image and eating disorders (Gleason, 1995), hemophilia (Scheerhorn, Warisse, & McNeilis, 1995), cancer, heart disease, and AIDS (Rolnick et al., 1999; Shaw, McTavish, Hawkins, Gustafson, & Pingree, 2000).

Online support groups can be beneficial for individuals who can not or do not wish to attend face-to-face meetings. Communication via text links only (e.g., e-mail, chat rooms, etc.) may lack the social presence of face-to-face contact but can nonetheless provide feedback that contains information and reassurance for users. Further, because the feedback derives not just from medical professionals but also from fellow sufferers, it may have more personal relevance for users (White & Dorman, 2001).

Many online support networks have become established on the Internet covering a variety of health topics and medical conditions. Support groups can have positive health benefits for participants in terms of more informed decision making and even increased health (Cline, 1999). Most online support groups communicate on specific health topics, rather than on general health matters. These networks represent virtual communities in that their members share common interests and concerns although they may never meet one another in person (Burrows et al., 2000; Turkle, 1996).

Many benefits have been associated with online support groups (Finn, 1999; Madara, 1997). Feedback to participants on their enquiries or problems may be available 24 hours a day, seven days a week. The use of asynchronous feedback allows time for both parties to formulate their responses to each other and therefore to obtain the maximum benefits from participation. Such services are available to any participants who have access to these online networks and one-on-one or group interaction is possible regardless of the geographical location of participants. Online support networks also afford participants anonymity which means they may be more likely to be forthcoming when discussing sensitive topics. Indeed, online interaction reduces embarrassment, such as might be experienced in face-to-face interactions, and thus encourages self-disclosure (Ferguson, 1997; Klemm & Nolan, 1998; Madara, 1997).

The absence of visual or aural cues means that gender, age, racial identity, and social status remain hidden. So too do physical appearance and social skills abilities. Thus, the biasing effects of these factors on the way participants might interact are removed from online interactions (Davison et al., 2000).

Disadvantages associated with online support groups include that they are restricted to people who possess a computer and have online (i.e., Internet) access. This criterion may eliminate certain sectors, such as the elderly, who could benefit from online support networks. Participants must also be sufficiently computer literate to be able to utilize online technologies (Davison et al., 2000). In some online support groups, large numbers of participants may generate large quantities of messages. Reading all this content can be very time consuming. Further, not all this material will necessarily be relevant to the individual participant (Shaw et al., 2000). Online messages can be misinterpreted. In the absence of nonverbal cues, such as appearance, eye contact, and mannerisms or vocal qualities such as tone of voice, accent, and articulacy of expression, many of the subtleties that guide impression formation in face-to-face communication are missing (White & Dorman, 2001).

Online networks can also be characterized by the phenomenon of *lurking*. This comprises visitors to online sites who read others' messages but do not contribute any disclosures of their own. It is easier to remain passive in the online environment than in a face-to-face setting, where a moderator or counselor may call upon silent participants to speak up and take part (Dickerson, Flaig, & Kennedy, 2000). Online support networks may also be susceptible to deception whereby some visitors may be liberal with the truth about their own condition or situation to invoke sympathy from others (Dickerson et al., 2000).

Gann (1998) reported, for example that participation in such networks is particularly heavy in the field of Acquired Immune Deficiency Syndrome (AIDS). Other online networks—not always facilitated through the Internet—have also been established for individuals who are HIV positive or display AIDS (Bosworth &

Gustafson, 1991; Brennan, 1996; Owens & Robbins, 1996). Reeves (2001) reported that HIV and AIDS sufferers used the Internet to find information, make social connections, fight for the rights of fellow sufferers, and to escape from their everyday problems. Communicating online could help them to forge a sense of community with fellow sufferers and be used to establish a lobbying platform to debate social policy issues and change the climate of opinion about HIV and AIDS.

Online activities therefore have included peer support and sharing of information on treatment advances and clinical trials. Brennan (1996) reported an electronic network called *Computer Link* that offered online social support and assistance to homebound individuals with disorders such as AIDS and Alzheimer's Disease. It had a bulletin board, e-mail, question-and-answer sections, and an online encyclopedia of information about diseases and care giving. Research indicated that all these sections were used, and that e-mail was used especially often (Brennan & Ripich, 1994). Caregivers found it as useful as did sufferers to exchange information and experiences with others in a similar position to themselves (Brennan, 1996).

Quick (1999) studied the role of online support groups for those suffering from kidney disease. Results did not yield clear evidence to support the hypothesis that users benefited from the contact with other sufferers, although users did participate in discussions and remained members of the group throughout the duration of the fieldwork.

In a similar study, Finn (1999) found that a disability groups' communication exhibited many of the same features as face-to-face self-help and mutual aid groups, with an emphasis on problem solving, information sharing, expression of feelings and mutual support and empathy. Online support groups can offer encouragement to participants, provide updates on the latest treatments, and offer the reassurance that comes with knowing that they are not alone (White & Dorman, 2001). Such remote support can be as powerful as face-to-face meetings (Finn, 1999). This impact can be felt especially among those users who might find self-disclosure more difficult in a face-to-face environment. This observation has been supported by research into the use of online support networks by men (Klemm & Nolan, 1998; Salem et al., 1997).

As well as these mushrooming networks of online mutual support groups, there is a growing movement within the medical profession for promoting partnerships between patients and doctors. Jadad (1999) considered that the Internet will have a profound effect on the way patients and health professionals interact. Anecdotal evidence has emerged that families using the Internet are already starting to demand different treatment from doctors because they believed that Web sources were better informed (Rumbelow, 1999).

PERSONAL SATISFACTION WITH ONLINE HEALTH ON TV

Television has been regarded as an alternative platform to the Internet in the provision of online health information. Different formats have been tested in regard to the use of television in the health care context. Digital interactive television has been used to provide generalized health and lifestyle information as well as more specific content on specific medical conditions in text and video formats that can be viewed on the household TV set (Gunter, Nicholas, Williams, & Huntington, 2001). Another format is teleconferencing in the form of live, interactive, two-way television that offers many opportunities to bridge the geographical distance between patients and health care professionals (Jones, 1997). Innovative uses of telemedicine have made it possible for physicians to consult with patients at locations many miles away (Fishman, 1997b) and to deliver continuing education programs to professionals practicing in rural areas (Byers et al., 1996).

The benefits of this type of service have been measured by asking users of such services about their satisfaction with the information and advice provided. Another approach is to find out whether use of digital health services is believed by users to have had any impact on their use of offline health services. First, what is the evidence for perceived personal satisfaction with these services?

Byers, Hilgenberg, and Rhodes (1999) reported a project using a two-way audio and video teleconferencing system to provide instruction to pregnant women and their partners to prepare for childbirth. A registered nurse taught a class at a regional hospital site. The class was transmitted live to an audience at a small rural hospital at a remote site. A site facilitator assisted at the remote site. The nurse received special training in the use of the technology. The site facilitator was employed to personalize the experience for the patients. She was also a nurse. Three separate series of classes were spread out over 6 months. Support literature was also made available to patients. In addition to a prepared presentation, there were opportunities for the patients to ask the instructor questions. The patients had to practice some of the techniques being taught. The instructor could monitor this practice via the two-way video system.

A survey indicated that patients were largely pleased with the remote course delivery, found that this interactive TV approach met their expectations and that they learned from it. The main problems were technological ones, for example associated with quality of sound. Remote classes were found to be more convenient. Some patients indicated a greater likelihood of missing classes if they had had to drive to a remote hospital to receive instruction face to face.

British research reported by Nicholas, Huntington, Williams, and Gunter (2003b) indicated that users of pilot digital television health information services indicated widespread satisfaction with them. As outlined in chapter 7 (this volume), there were four iDTV pilot projects run during 2001 and 2002. The companies concerned with Living Health, Communicopia/NHS Direct Digital, Channel Health, and DKTV. Living Health provided a text information service and two transactional services (doctor appointments booking and video nurse). Communicopia provided a text and video-on-demand information service and an online medical records service. Channel Health broadcast programs on pregnancy and maternity issues supplemented by back-up, online text information linked to each program, and available on-air. DKTV provided an online communications channel to local health and other public services operating via digital television.

A total of 45% of Living Health viewers said that the service had been very useful, 48% said that the service had been quite useful, whereas 7% said that the service
had not been useful. The main reasons people gave for finding the service helpful
was that they felt reassured by the information given—50% said so; 15% of users
said that the advice helped them deal with the condition themselves, whereas 20%
said that the advice helped them to contact the right service. Interviewee respondents also indicated that the service was very useful, enabling them to avoid visiting
the doctor, research a condition for friend, and check information about medication.

The Living Health InVision service went down extremely well, and comparisons between the telephone equivalent are instructive. Respondents rated the service either very satisfactory (76%) or satisfactory (24%)—100% satisfied in other
words, versus 97.8% for the NHS Direct telephone-only service. Additionally,
100% of InVision customers polled said they would use the service again and recommend it to friends or family.

Finally, 88% of those who had used both InVision and the telephone service preferred InVision (the rest had no preference). These results suggest that the nurses were
able to offer an equivalent service while having to engage the camera and operate the
InVision system in addition to the normal clinical assessment system (CAS) software.

People who used Communicopia/NHS Direct Digital generally found what
they were looking for. A total of 15% of NHS Direct Digital viewers agreed and
69% disagreed with the statement that in general users could not find what they
were looking for on the service. Of the users, 81% said that if they needed health
advice they would consult health information on KIT.

Most people who used the program and accompanying text information service
(Bush Babies) on Channel Health thought the service quite useful—60% said so.
Those in lower socioeconomic strata were less likely to say that the information
would be useful for them: 17% said the information would be useful for them,
compared to 40% for higher socioeconomic groups. Those living with a partner
said the videos were useful to them: 56% said this compared to 37% of married and
8% of single users. For those users who were pregnant, 83% said the information
was useful to them compared to 29% who were not pregnant.

The 35 respondents who claimed to have viewed or used DKTV were asked to
rate their overall satisfaction with the service along a four-point scale from very
satisfied to not at all satisfied. Two respondents were very satisfied, 21 were quite
satisfied, seven were not very satisfied and one was not at all satisfied. The remainder did not know. The average satisfaction score indicated that these respondents
were only "quite satisfied" with the service. When asked how often they thought
that they or their family would use DKTV in the future. Most of these respondents
(20) thought they would use it about the same as now, with nine saying they would
use DKTV more often and six saying less often (Nicholas et al., 2003b).

IMPACT ON THE USE OF HEALTH SERVICES

Research on digital health in Britain, focusing on provision of interactive health
information and advice services via television, has shed light on the different ways

in which the remote, electronic provision of health-related services might impact upon the way public and patients use health services. Nicholas, Huntington, Williams, and Gunter (2002a, 2003b) studied users of a pilot interactive digital television service, carried on a cable television platform to a large cosmopolitan area in central England. This channel (Living Health) was essentially a content database, mostly in text, covering a wide range of health topics largely adapted from the U.K. National Health Service's Web information service (NHS Direct Online). In addition to this standard content, material was used from other suppliers that provided update daily news bulletins, medicines and services directories, and public health alerts. NHS careers information was provided by the Department of Health's Communications Directorate.

The channel also hosted two transactional services, the first being NHS Direct InVision and the second an On-Line Surgery Appointments Booking Service. InVision provided a one-way video link between a nurse in a NHS Direct Call Center and the user at home; the video link was supplemented by a telephone link to provide oral communication between the two parties. The On-Line Appointments Booking Service allowed users to book an appointment with their doctor. Three doctors' surgeries were partners in this venture.

This pilot operation ran from the end of June until the end of November 2001. Nicholas, Huntington, Williams, and Gunter (2002b) surveyed a sample of users at around the half-way point of this period. Users' reactions were obtained from a postal questionnaire sent out with literature promoting the television service. Data were obtained from 723 respondents, of whom just less than one in four (23% or 167) had viewed the interactive health service, of whom just more than half (53%) were female. Of particular relevance to the current discussion, respondents were asked to indicate the health benefits of using the channel. They were asked (1) how the information they discovered had helped them in dealing with their doctor, (2) whether they felt that their condition had improved as a result of the information found, and (3) if the information had helped in understanding their condition.

The findings showed that iDTV can create health consumers who feel better informed. Two thirds of Living Health's users (67%) said that the information they obtained had either helped or helped them a lot in becoming better informed about their condition. This survey finding was corroborated by data from in-depth interviews, with respondents remarking on the usefulness of having so much information readily to hand (Nicholas et al., 2003b).

Perceived Benefits for Doctor–Patient Relationships

Evidence has emerged from several studies of online health information use that such content can assist people when they see their doctor. Users have reported that they often feel better informed after consulting an online health information service (Cyber Dialogue, 2000; Nicholas, Huntington, Williams, & Blackburn, 2001). In Britain, both kiosk users and interactive digital television users commented on the benefits obtained from using these online health information sources in the context of consultations with health professionals.

A study of kiosk users reported that a clear majority reported how helpful its health information had been in connection with dealing with their own doctor (Nicholas et al., 2004). In a separate study of users of an iDTV health information service (Living Health), 4 in 10 (40%) said that the information they found had helped in their dealings with the doctor and one in five (20%) said it had helped a lot (Nicholas et al., 2003b). In addition, two out of three (67%) users of this iDTV health service said that the information had either helped or helped them a lot in becoming better informed, nearly one half (47%) being "helped a lot." Nearly one third (31%) said that the information found either helped or helped a lot in improving their condition (Nicholas, Huntington, Williams, & Gunter, 2002b).

These views were echoed by users of a second iDTV health information service (Communicopia/NHS Direct Digital). Here, more than 7 in 10 users (73%) felt that the information they found had helped to some extent in their dealings with their doctor. Just more than one in four users of this service (27%) said they would use the service to look for information that they would not want to discuss with their doctor (Nicholas et al., 2003b). The same finding also emerged for a third pilot consortium, Channel Health, many of whose users felt they were far better armed when they met their doctors, midwives and obstetricians and praised the maternity issues television series on this channel for giving them a knowledge base regarding their condition (Nicholas et al., 2003b).

Explaining Perceived Benefits

Users' ease of understanding a iDTV health information service mediated the service was felt to have improved their condition or helped them in understanding their condition. Users (56%) who said that the system was either not very or not at all easy to understand were more likely to say that the system did not improve their condition compared to users (30%) who reported the system was easy to use. Further, users reporting a difficulty in understanding the system were also less likely to say that the system helped or helped a lot in understanding their condition: 59% compared to about 36% (Nicholas, Huntington, Williams, & Gunter, 2002b).

Whether the user found the iDTV service easy to view or read impacted upon whether they perceived any positive health outcome. However, the relation was not the one that might be expected. Those users who reported the system easy to read most of the time were more likely to rate the system of limited help. Sixty-five percent of users who reported that the system was easy to read either some or none of the time also said that the service either helped improve their condition or helped it a lot. This compared to nearly one in five users (19%) who described the system as being easy to read most of the time. This unexpected relation can perhaps be explained by the fact that ease of reading reflects educational background, and more educated users may have already been familiar with the medical information found on the Living Health channel (Nicholas, Huntington, Williams, & Gunter, 2002b).

Interactive digital television users who rated the menus as easy to follow also felt that the information provided by this service enhanced their understanding of their own health condition. Users who found the menus easy to use "all the time" (62%) were much more likely to perceive personal health benefits than were users who experienced some difficulties with the menus, either part of the time or all of the time (35%).

Using Health Information as Alternative to Visiting the Doctor

Further questioning of iDTV users revealed that they did not simply access online health information to make their doctor's appointments more fruitful, but sometimes also regarded online services as a substitute for visiting the doctor. Around one half of early users of the pilot Living Health service on cable television in England reported using its health content instead of going to see a doctor (Nicholas, Huntington, Williams, & Gunter, 2002a).

A logistic regression model was used to explore further which factors characterized those respondents more likely to use information in this way. Results indicated that use of alternative medical information sources to visiting a doctor was predicted by the perceived importance attached to the practice nurse (located at the doctor's surgery), respondent age, responsibility for the health of another person, interest in prescription drugs, interest in health living, and interest in alternative health. Significant in the current context was the finding that using the DITV health service also emerged as a predictor variable (Nicholas, Huntington, Williams, & Gunter, 2002a).

Greater reliance on the general practice nurse, being younger, having responsibility for someone else's health, interest in prescription drugs, and interest in healthy living or alternative health were all predictive of greater use of medical information found from various sources as an alternative to seeing the doctor. In addition, use of the iDTV heath information service also emerged as a significant predictor variable in this context. Users of this iDTV health service were more likely than nonusers to say they had used medical information sources they had found instead of seeing the doctor. Although this result does not confirm that iDTV health services can provide a substitute information source to a person's own doctor, it does indicate that users are characterized by having a stronger tendency than nonusers to utilize medical information sources in that way (Nicholas, Huntington, Williams, & Gunter, 2003b).

In a further study, Huntington, Nicholas, Williams, and Gunter (2003) explored the usefulness of a video-on-demand health information service supplied to the public via interactive digital television. The video service ran in parallel to a text-based information service that concerned topics also covered by the videos. The service was supplied by NHS Direct Digital over a broadband TV-on-demand system (HomeChoice) in London. Over a 4-month pilot period, user sessions could be divided into four types: (1) sessions where users actively downloaded a text screen, but no video (6%); (2) sessions where users actively downloaded a video, but not text (40%); (3) sessions where users actively downloaded a video and text (15%); and (4) sessions where users did not download any information content and only introduction and menu pages were viewed (38%).

Most users of this service were one-off users (72%). More than one in four (28%) were repeat users, and these users visited the site between two and five times. The most popularly used videos dealt with diabetes (23%), coronary heart disease (15%), pain management (15%), and first aid (12%). Further user analysis indicated that videos were often only watched part of the way through. There were some gender differences, with women being more likely to download videos about cervical cancer and men more likely to download videos on exercise for the elderly. Most users (67%) said they found the system easy to use and nearly all users (97%) reported that they had found downloaded videos to be useful. Three in four users (76%) said that the last video they had watched had answered questions they would otherwise have put to a doctor or nurse. Most users (91%) said that the videos would help them (a lot—41%, and a little—50%) in managing their medical concerns.

IMPACT OF DIGITAL VIDEO DIAGNOSIS

Evidence has emerged that the public and patient groups will utilize prerecorded video materials about health issues when they are made available online. In addition, video formats have been utilized to provide direct links between patients and health professionals in relation to health advice and consultation. When used in a therapeutic context, video links can be adapted provide treatment as well.

Early examples of this type of online application include video links directed at elderly communities to provide counseling in nutrition and diet, and about health and social services (Brenk, 2002; Swindell & Mayhew, 1996). Some online, video-based exercises have involved peer-to-peer support group video-conferencing facilities. These facilities have been developed to enable carers and health professionals to interact remotely with each other. Such networks have been effectively applied to provide professional support and training. There is also evidence that remote, video links can prove to be as effective for information exchanges as are face-to-face meetings (Brown, Pain, Berwald, Hirsch, Delehanty, & Miller, 1999). Both patient and professional user groups have expressed satisfaction with video links (Callahan, Hilty, & Nesbitt, 1998; Clarke, 1997), although it is not always clear what it is about a video-conferencing system that gives rise to user satisfaction or dissatisfaction. One observation has been that it may be oversimplistic to ask users whether they are satisfied with online health services of this kind (Mair & Whitton, 2000). It might be more fruitful in relation to future service production or configuration to obtain more detailed feedback about specific remote video links in relation to real-time application.

Digital health research in Britain included an investigation of the impact of a more dynamic and, some might argue, more truly interactive service. One of the four iDTV contractors (Living Health) provided an experimental, interactive medical advice service. As described in chapter 7 (this volume), the service (called InVision) enabled users of Living Health to establish a two-way audio (telephone) link with a nurse in a NHS Direct Call Centre accompanied by a one-way visual link through which the digital subscriber at home can see the nurse on his or her TV screen. Thus, the nurse is seen live on-screen as the telephone conversation takes place. The nurse answered the caller's enquiries in the usual way, but was also able to show photo images, graphics, and short films on-screen when appropriate to enrich the information given to the caller. The impact of this service was gauged by assessing the way the service was used and the degree to which advice given was followed. In addition, an attempt was made to assess the impact of the use of InVision on referrals to back-up health services (Nicholas, Williams, Huntington, & Gunter, 2003a).

The potential significance of this type of service stems from the perception that online health services can be used not simply to provide a health content reference library, but also an infrastructure through which more dynamic advice and diagnosis services can be conveyed (Wanless, 2002). In a two-way communication format, users send as well as receive information. In a health context, any advice or diagnosis offered by a health professional is dependent, to a significant degree, on the information about symptoms supplied by the patient. Research has shown that computer-mediated communication (CMC) may have certain advantages over face-to-face communication in some situations.

In the context of patient self-disclosure, people often tend to reveal more about themselves in a computer-mediated environment than when in a face-to-face interview (Joinson, 1998). When using CMC, people are less constrained or inhibited than they would be a direct face-to-face situation. For example, it has been found that intravenous drug abusers interviewed about HIV risk behaviors, disclosed more about themselves in an audio computer-assisted self-interview than in a face-to-face interview (Des Jarlais et al., 1999). Women who attended a public family planning or sexually transmitted disease clinic tended to admit to more socially undesirable behaviors (e.g., sex with multiple partners) in a video-enhanced computer-assisted interview than in face-to-face interview (Kissinger et al., 1999). Similar findings have been reported for the computer-assisted version of the Risk for AIDS Behavior scale (Navaline et al., 1994) and a computerized survey of sensitive information (e.g., male–male sexual experiences, injection drug use) for adolescents (Turner et al., 1998).

The reasons for this increase in self-disclosure and lack of inhibition are unclear, as is the overall veracity of the socially undesirable behaviors reported. Joinson (1998) proposed a number of social psychological models to explain these phenomena. The absence in CMC of the visual cues present in face-to-face can lead those who interact through CMC to be more formal and direct with each other. Visual anonymity can result in reduced intimidation and embarrassment leading to greater self-disclosure (McKenna & Bargh, 1998). Although it has been argued that CMC is a more impersonal communications medium than face-to-face interaction (Kiesler et al., 1984), it has also been acknowledged that emotionally involving relationships can be established even in a computer-mediated environment (Reingold, 1993). In fact, such relationships and the exchanges that take place between participants can be even stronger than those that occur within a face-to-face format (Walther, 1996). It appears that CMC is an ideal way to gather information from people in an efficient and comprehensive manner. Additionally, CMC appears to be useful for querying people about sensitive, difficult to talk about topics.

Another attraction of CMC health-related programs for health providers and sponsors is that they have been calculated to save the cost of health care delivery in the U.S.. This does not apply across all aspects of health care provision, of course, but in relation to those that can feasibly and effectively be delivered in this mediated fashion. For instance, clinical assessments that might be conducted in a health center via paper-and-pencil tests can be conducted online. This has been achieved already in assessments of children (Yokley, Coleman, & Yates, 1990) and addiction assessment (Budman, 2000).

Another attractive feature of CMC health programs is that they can be tailored to the needs of the individual. The individual can be initially classified by gender, age, relevant knowledge level, severity of disease, and risk factors, and then a diagnostic programs devised that caters to that specific user's needs. Turning then to the InVision service provided via iDTV on a cable platform, was there any evidence that the strengths of CMC characterized this televised helpline?

Impact of Video Nurse on iDTV

Nicholas, Williams, Huntington, and Gunter (2003a) reported a study of a video nurse service provided via iDTV. This service enabled subscribers to establish a two-way audio (telephone) link with a nurse in a call-center accompanied by a one-way visual link through which callers could see the nurse on their television screens. The nurse answered callers' enquiries in the usual way (to the protocol used with telephone-only callers), but was also able to show photo images, graphics and short films on-screen when appropriate to enrich the information given verbally.

The study was largely qualitative in nature, obtaining data through interviews from patients and nurses. The call scripts maintained by the nursing staff were also analyzed. Qualitative data were supported by quantitative data from computer logs that recorded volume of caller traffic via the iDTV site. In all, 27 callers agreed to complete a telephone interview and four others agreed to be interviewed face to face. Interviews were conducted with six participating call-center nurses.

Over the period of study (20 weeks), there were 1,380 initial requests for the video nurse service. Of these, 1,062 (75%) were canceled, 806 by the user, 411 because of a time-out code, a busy signal, or the service was closed. In all, 163 video nurse enquiry sessions were completed.

With the small interviewee sample, low number of calls taken by each individual staff member and small number of nurse scripts available, it is difficult to generalize about either the callers or the information required. It was noted in the chapter 7 (this volume) that calls were categorized into those requesting treatment advice, those seeking reassurance, those requesting diagnosis, and those asking for general health information.

Even when interviewees indicated that they wanted instructions or basic information, they agreed that seeing the nurse on the screen was reassuring. They were asked if they would use the service for more detailed information, but felt either that this would not be fair on others waiting to make calls, or that it would not be a suitable medium, as a lot of information would be difficult to take in.

Interestingly, despite these very positive evaluations of the information only one in five of questionnaire and interviewee respondents (19%) received more than they would have via a traditional telephone service (in terms of advice, all callers received the same information). However, statistics generated from the system showed that only 20% of all calls were handled using images. Of the 64 call scripts analyzed, only two were considered to warrant images. With the patient interviewees, however, the lack of visual input by the nurse was, in all but one case, a consequence of the type of information required.

One third of respondents (33%) said that the advice they received related to self-help and health information generally. A similar proportion of users (32%) were told to see their doctor and 1 in 10 (10%) of respondents were told to see their doctor within 4 hours, and 5% were told to go to hospital. Seventy percent of respondents said they followed all the advice given, 22% said they followed some of it, and only 7% claimed they did not follow any of the advice.

It was apparent from remarks made by respondents who had called the video nurse, that callers had intended to rely less on their doctor for certain kinds of health-related enquiry. Although it is clearly recognized that serious health conditions require face-to-face diagnosis, with more general enquiries, other (online) sources of information can be used where available. This no only reduces the doctor's workload, but may often be more convenient for the patient who would otherwise have to make time available during the day to visit their doctor in person (Nicholas et al., 2003a).

IMPACT ON USERS' HEALTH STATUS

There are a number of options available to researchers to investigate the impact of use of online health information services on the health status of the public. One option would be to compare users and nonusers of such services in terms of their general state of health, lifestyle, and attitudes to well-being. Another option would be to conduct an epidemiological study of parts of the country where digital interactive television reception is available and areas where there is no such reception comparing visits to the doctor, occurrence of various illnesses and ailments, while controlling for known, pre-existing geographical differences and their known or presumed causal agents.

Neither of these approaches was possible in the context of the current pilot exercise because the penetration of iDTV health information services was low and the existence of such services too short to exert effects that can only be realistically measured over a long term. Instead, insights into the possible impact of the Living Health service on users' health status was gained from volunteered information about health status among users of the service. Data from iDTV health information service users were reported by Nicholas, Huntington, Williams, and Gunter (2002c) and by Nicholas et al. (2003b). Although that survey was designed primarily to obtain data on the use and nonuse of digital television for health information, specifically in regard to the iDTV service, additional questions were included that examined users' perceived health benefits of this kind of service. Further questions explored the kinds of health information users sought from the service and whether such information was sometimes used as a substitute for going to see the doctor.

One third of Living Health users said that the information found either helped or helped a lot in improving their condition. Nearly 62% of Communicopia/NHS Direct Digital users said that the information found either helped a little or a lot in improving their condition and 15% said it had helped a lot.

In the case of Channel Health, three out of four women who used the enhanced text service, which supported the broadcast programs, said that they found its information reassuring. In-depth interviewees tended to say that they approached their pregnancy in a healthier fashion because of seeing the programs. Its advice about diet and exercise was found especially useful.

Whether an iDTV service improved the user's condition or helped in understanding it appeared to depend on the extent to which people understood the nature of the Living Health service. There were usability issues at play here which have implications both for site design and for user digital literacy.

Whether the user found the system easy to use impacted on whether that person expressed a positive health outcome as a result of receiving digital health information, but the relationship was the inverse of what might have been expected. Among Living Health users, of those who said they found the system difficult to use, 56% said it did not improve their health compared to 30% of those who said the system was easy to use (Nicholas et al., 2002b). Hence, those finding the system easy to use were not the users who experienced the strongest positive outcomes. There is a sense here that the harder you have to work at it, the more appreciative you are of the benefits.

CONCLUSION

The sponsorship of e-health services by governments represents an attempt to empower citizens as health information consumers. The objective of these initiatives is to enhance a mentality of self-help among public and patients and to take the strain off health professionals in relation to information provision functions. There is also a possibility that some superficial diagnoses could be conducted on a remote basis. The aim of digital health is not to supplant face-to-face interactions between patients and health professionals, but to cut down on the occasions when public consult with professionals. Very often, members of the public seek an audience with their doctor for little more than health-related information or reassurance about their health. Online health services may be able effectively to take over some of these functions, leaving health professionals to devote face-to-face consultations to more serious forms of diagnosis and treatment.

Users of online health services have generally reacted in a positive way. Most users have found official health service Web sites helpful. Similar reactions have occurred in relation to pilot schemes involving digital interactive television. What has also emerged from early research in this field is that it is not just the provision of information per se that is important, but also the way in which information is imparted. There are numerous potential applications of online health services. The provision of factual content is one application, but the giving of emotional support and reassurance is another feature. Hence, for some generalized enquiries a text information database will suffice. For other types of application, however, users prefer a more personalized transaction. Visual forms of presentation may then become significant.

When giving instructions in behavioral techniques, for example, video footage providing visual demonstrations may be needed (Byers et al., 1999). Online health service users who need reassurance about a specific medical condition or treatment may find video vignettes featuring health professionals and fellow sufferers more valuable that factual content in text format (Nicholas et al., 2003b). Although text information can enhance consultations with doctors by giving patients clues about the right kinds of questions to ask or by offering a second opinion, a video nurse may offer a more direct form of reassurance to callers who need immediate feedback on what to do about a condition that is troubling them (Nicholas et al., 2003a).

The use of mediated campaigns to promote health issues may be especially important to people with low health literacy. It is therefore important consider the health literacy levels of target audiences for health campaigns. This factor must be seen as a more distinctive one than general educational level (French & Larrabee, 1999). Different health communication approaches may be needed with people with high and low health literacy. Low health literacy people, for example, may be reached better with interpersonal and multimedia channels than with printed materials. Health communication also needs to take into account the culture of target audiences. People from different countries and different cultures may have different preferred sources of health information. Health communication professionals should therefore work with members of a target group or community to identify what are the best approaches to take.

Consistent evidence has emerged that people may be more willing to disclose sensitive or controversial information in a computer-mediated environment (Locke et al., 1992; Turner et al., 1998). With people of low health literacy, however, there may remain a problem of being able to articulate the details of their condition or concern given their relative ignorance of health matters.

Inexperienced computer users may lack the technology literacy to take full advantage of online health services. It is important therefore than online services are user friendly and that service providers make arrangements to ensure that users can learn to make the best use of the interfaces to these services.

Online health services, operating via the Internet or television, may not have the potential physically to heal, but they can provide valuable psychological support that may have a temporary, but at the time significant benefit for individuals. Such services can, through the information and emotional support they supply, have perceived and real effects on the health status of users. The challenge that lies ahead is to refine the understanding of how effective different online formats can be in relation to achieving positive health-enhancing results for different types of enquiry.

Digital Health: Public Confidence and Trust in Sources

◇

The research reviewed in previous chapters indicated that the early uptake of electronic health information services indicates that digital health may contribute significantly to the cultivation of a climate of patient proactivity in health care. Furthermore, television has the potential to work effectively alongside the Internet and touch-screen kiosks in public locations in the provision of health reference sources and two-way interactive advisory and diagnostic services.

One of the key areas of concern about the growth of online health services has focused on the quality of information and help provided. In this context, *quality* is defined in terms of the clinical accuracy of information and the credibility and trustworthiness of the online source. This issue was referred to earlier in relation to the Internet. The current chapter presents new findings from Britain on the perceived trustworthiness of both Web and digital interactive television as online health information platforms.

During the latter part of the twentieth century, a number of quality rating systems were published relating to health Web sites. This activity illustrated the degree to which health information professionals had become concerned about the quality and authority of health information on the Internet (Kim et al., 1999). Digital health information offered directly to the consumer is of special concern because it may be acted upon by the individual without the further mediation or control of a qualified health professional. Under such circumstances it is vitally important that the information or advice provided is clear and unequivocal. Even then, an online patient may misinterpret the advice given. Turning the trust issue around, however, members of the public may be suspicious of online health services even when they derive from official sources because of suspected implications about provision of standard health diagnostic and treatment services in doctors' surgeries, clinics, and hospitals. In other words, are online services being offered as a substitute for rather than as a supplement to traditional face-to-face diagnosis and treatment of medical conditions? An important question to ask about online health services therefore is how much are they trusted by the public? Furthermore, are different online platforms, such as the Internet and interactive digital television (iDTV) trusted equally or differently?

The digital environment is in its infancy. It is relatively new and also fast changing in terms of content, formats, and sources. As a marketplace, the provision of online health information is immature and dominant service providers have yet to emerge (Hunt, 1999). It is important that services that capture the public's apparent interest in and need for readily accessible health content are reputable and place patients' health needs at the top of their agenda.

Evidence has already emerged that indicates that it may be difficult to judge authority in relation to online health information services because there are so many parties associated with their production. This feature has become apparent in relation to touch-screen health information kiosks. For instance, a kiosk may be the property of one operator, supply content produced by a different operator and may be physically located in premises owned by a third operator (e.g., a supermarket). Under such circumstances, with which operator does authority reside in relation to the information being offered? There may be some confusion in consumers' minds over this issue (Nicholas, Huntington, & Williams, 2002b).

AUTHORITY ON THE INTERNET

Research into issues of the authority of Internet sites has almost exclusively centered on examinations of the intrinsic quality of information itself, and how this can be assured, rather than the perceptions and attitudes of the information users. Although establishing the professional authenticity and accuracy of online health information is important, the apparent lack of interest in public perception is a serious omission. This is particularly true given that online technologies have been used to target different groups with varying dispositions toward the medical profession, information sources, and technology platforms.

In British research with a panel of young people, aged 16 to 24 years, trust in different information sources was found to vary widely. An overwhelming majority (83%) said they trusted highly the news on the BBC. This source far outstripped, in terms of prevalence of this degree of trust, the news on commercial television (44%), news in quality newspapers (30%), and even information from the respondent's own doctor (30%). In respect of e-mail circulars, there was zero trust. With online news Web sites, just more than 6 in 10 respondents (61%) exhibited some degree of trust (Coleman, Griffiths, & Simmons, 2002).

Although the Web has been regarded as presenting a major opportunity to reach large numbers of people with useful health care information, it is the absence of editorial controls over content on many Web sites that has raised the issue of authenticity, with many observers questioning the quality of the information provided (e.g., Silberg, et al., 1997). Other research has indicated that even "official" information published by government sources can be of dubious quality (Coulter et al., 1999a, 1999b). Such research has indicated a multitude of problems with Web-based health information: Much of the information was inaccurate and out of date, technical terms were not explained, and few materials provided adequate information about treatment risks and side effects, to name but three.

The rapid growth of the Internet has ensured that, in addition to these so-called "official" channels, there are also thousands of unregulated, unidentifiable, and, possibly, unscrupulous sites readily accessible through the World Wide Web. As earlier chapters indicated, the authority of these sites has come under much scrutiny. The quality of Internet sites that contain both generalized information and detailed information on specific medical conditions has been assessed (e.g., Griffiths & Christensen, 2000; Impicciatore et al., 1997). Such audits uncovered numerous problems in terms of inaccuracies in the information provided or cases where the information was not as up to date as it could have been.

Griffiths and Christensen (2000), for example, surveyed 21 Web sites that provided information about depression and assessed the quality of site information along a number of criteria. Nicholas, Huntington, Williams, and Gunter (2003) noted that these authors "classified sites according to their stated purpose, ownership, involvement with major drug companies, and whether they showed evidence of a professional editorial board. They scored site information against U.S. federal best practice guidelines embodied in the code published by the Agency for Health Care Policy and Research. They also assessed the identification, affiliations, and credentials of authors associated with the sites. Findings indicated that quality of content varied and was often poor in terms of these criteria. Furthermore, accountability criteria as indicated by the reported credentials of content authors might be poor quality guarantees. Instead, evidence of ownership and the existence of an independent editorial board were more useful quality indicators" (p. 216).

Policies and procedures for guaranteeing the quality and authority of Internet health information are needed not just to enhance the public's view of the authority of the provider, but also to avoid wrongly diagnosed ailments or other manifestations of poor information provision that could have fatal consequences. To this end, a number of health bodies and information providers have already attempted to formulate policy statements, guidelines and principles regarding Web-based health information (e.g., Kim et al., 1999).

Concern has been expressed, however, about the quality of quality rating bodies and systems themselves. For example, one study that assessed the rating criteria of a number of systems, found that only three gave information about their own editorial boards—despite attribution, authority and openness generally being stated criteria for evaluating medical sites (Hernandez-Borges et al., 1999). Another audit of auditors analyzed sources that reviewed and rated health information sites, and concluded that the evaluation instruments were not comprehensive and many did not actually measure what they claimed. Their presence, therefore, was not necessarily as informative as desired (Jadad & Gagliardi, 1998).

THE PUBLIC AND ONLINE HEALTH INFORMATION

Another important question is how the actual user of the information—often the lay public—thinks about quality and authority issues. Over a brief period of time at the turn of the century, the National Health Service (NHS) in Britain was hit by a number of scandals, including one case of controversial heart surgery performed on children (Kennedy, 2000) and another case involving the removal, retention, and disposal of human organs and tissues without parental consent (Redfern, 2001). Such highly publicized problems have given rise to much public scepticism of the NHS.

A survey for the London *Evening Standard* newspaper in February 2001 on Londoners' opinions of the NHS found that significant differences existed according to political allegiance (Kings Fund, 2000). Labor government supporters were found to be more confident than others of obtaining high-quality medical treatment and were more likely to assert that the NHS had improved over the previous 4 years. Nevertheless, nearly 4 in 10 (39%) of all respondents—a substantial minority—felt they would not receive high-quality medical treatment. In the same survey, more than 4 in 10 respondents (42%) supported the opinion that "the government should encourage the take-up of private health insurance," with slightly fewer (37%) agreeing that "the NHS should rely less on its own hospitals and pay private hospitals to provide more care." This evidence indicated that the NHS did not have the total trust of the general public.

Perhaps more damaging to the authority of the NHS in Britain were opinion polls indicating that, after a so-called *honeymoon period* following the 1997 Labor Party general election victory, when dissatisfaction with the health service fell from 50% to 36%, public opinion about the NHS became more negative again (Mulligan, 2000). A Market and Opinion Research International (MORI) nationwide opinion poll in the U.K. in July 2000, for example, found that nearly two thirds of respondents (64%) thought that the NHS had not improved since Labor came to power, similar to a National Opinion Polls (NOP) poll taken for BBC1's *The Dimbleby Programme* in March of the same year, that indicated that 66% of the British public felt there had been no improvement (see Mulligan, 2000). A later poll (September 2001) conducted by British Market Research Bureau (BMRB) on behalf of the BBC found that almost 6 out of 10 people (59%) who were questioned thought that Labor had made no difference to the NHS since it came to power in 1997, and one in six (16%) thought that the Labor government has made things worse (BBC Online, 2002).

The findings of these opinion polls were important in the context of the roll-out of online health services on the Internet and interactive digital television. If the NHS brand is not trusted, this could have significant implications for the acceptance, uptake and use of online NHS services. Trust in brands has been found to affect the success of online services beyond the health domain. Trust in an online source is known to play a crucial role in the believability of online information and in the extent to which users will engage in a transaction with that source. Trust creates more favorable user attitudes toward service suppliers and engenders customer loyalty.

Trust is important to people whether dealing with other people or with technology. This last point is reinforced by evidence that people engage with interactive communications technologies in much the same manner as they would another person. Technology users assign human characteristics to interactive technologies (Nass, Moon, Fogg, Reeves, & Dryer, 1995; Nass, Reeves, & Leshner, 1996; Reeves, & Nass, 1996).

A number of sources of trust have been identified in connection with the online environment. These include user presumptions, initial appearance of service provider, service-related experience, and the reputation of online sources. Users will often make presumptions about online service suppliers on the basis of second-hand knowledge, such as media reports, other user recommendations, and social stereotypes whereby the supplier resembles another supplier that is known to the user. First impressions of a supplier based on initial inspection of the site where the service is located can affect the confidence the user will have in that supplier. Early experience of the service will then play a key part in determining longer term loyalty. In addition, accreditation of the service by reputable and authoritative sources can also create a favorable disposition toward it among new users (Bailey et al., 2003; Tseng & Fogg, 1999).

In a case study of an online service, Bailey, Gurak, and Konstan (2003) reported that many of the above features were linked to service success. In this instance, the site under investigation provided health, beauty and pharmacy products. The Web site from which it operated was easy to use as well as easy on the eye and hence generated good first impressions. The operator worked hard to keep customers loyal by providing them with regular updates about new products. Endorsements of the service by previous customers and by authoritative sources were also published on the site for new users to see.

In research in Britain, new online health services, sponsored by government, on the Internet and interactive digital television were evaluated in terms of users' reactions. One study examined the issue of service authority in a usability study of the a health information Web site operated on behalf of the NHS by a company called SurgeryDoor (Williams, Huntington, & Nicholas, 2002a, 2002b). Twenty information science students examined the site and were asked for their opinions on navigation, information content, aesthetic appeal, and other features. Advertisements on the site were perceived as considerably lowering its authoritativeness. These were displayed as banners across the top of each page, where they occupied a larger area than the title or logo of the supplying company itself. Further, they contained flashing, eye-catching, and distracting images. This gave the impression to many users that the site was more concerned with generating revenue than with promoting healthy living or providing useful health information.

The extent of advertising led some respondents to question how the organization was funded. Questions were also raised about nature of links with the Department of Health and National Health Service. One observation was that advertisements on these sites could be excused on the grounds that revenue to maintain the sites had to be found from somewhere. Other users, however, felt less comfortable with the presence of advertising and preferred health sites to be run and funded exclusively by bone fide health organizations.

This sensitivity to the commercial aspects of a health Web site may indicate that the public (in Britain at least) have reservations about any close association between a public service such as health and advertising. For many people, the idea that health information can be regarded as a means of moneymaking may still be anathema. It may be, however, that other factors related to the nature of the online environment come into play here. The issue of branding, advertising, and brand recognition has taken on a new dimension on the Web. Simon (2001) noted that the range of content choice online has produced a shift in consumer attitudes toward a more skeptical disposition. Increasingly, users are not prepared to tolerate advertising on health sites.

Issues concerning the whether the presence of advertising and sponsorship on health Web sites can lead to biases or distortions of health information and advice are clearly important. In Britain, the migration of health content from an open public medium such as the Internet, that is largely free of regulation, onto a medium such as television that is centrally regulated means that issues of information service branding may become even more sensitive. Much of the remainder of this chapter is devoted to a study conducted in Britain on user opinions about a pilot health information service transmitted on digital interactive television. In this study, comparisons were also made with perceptions of similar information provided on an Internet-based service.

AUTHORITY, TRUST, BRANDING AND MEDIA

Issues linked to the authority and trust that can be placed in different media as sources of information have been debated and investigated over many years. This debate becomes particularly focused in the context of health information because of the possibility that people may act upon such information and their actions may have significant implications for their personal well-being.

In the broader debate about trust in mediated information sources, television has often emerged as the most trusted mass communication. In the context of news of major international and national significance, for example, for several decades, people have rated television above the other major news media as the premier and most trusted news source (Gunter, 1987; Stanley & Niemi, 1990; Towler, 2002). Television is widely regarded as the source from where people get most of their news from (Gunter, 1987; Gunter, Sancho-Aldridge, & Winstone, 1994; Gunter & Winstone, 1993; Towler, 2002). The major departure from this pattern occurs in the case of local news for which people turn more to their local newspapers (Gunter et al., 1994), although even here, television has begun to pose a serious challenge (Towler, 2002).

Television has a positive image as an information provider. It is believed to report events accurately by more people than believe newspapers, radio, or magazines do so (Rubin, 1983). When faced with conflicting reports about major national or international events, people are more likely to believe television than the press (Lee, 1975). However, when each medium's credibility is rated separately rather than comparatively, the gap in trust between media narrows (Stanley & Niemi, 1990).

Differences in perceived credibility of different information media can vary with the types of information people are asked to consider. Research in Britain asked people to evaluate television news in comparison with radio and newspapers in terms of five attributes: the most fair and unbiased news coverage, the most complete news coverage, the most accurate news coverage, bringing the news most quickly, and the clearest understanding of events and issues. These ratings were applied separately to international and national news and to regional and local news (Gunter & Winstone, 1993; Gunter et al., 1994).

In respect of national and international news, television was rated highest on all attributes. It was seen as providing the most complete, most accurate, quickest, and clearest account of news. Newspapers and radio competed for second position throughout. Radio was rated higher than newspapers for bringing news more quickly. Newspapers were perceived more often than radio as offering the most complete coverage and clearest understanding. Turning to regional and local news events, television was again rated most highly on all attributes. The gap between television and newspapers on most dimensions, however, was much narrower. Again radio scored higher than newspapers only in relation to speed of delivery.

Other British research reported that television was rated higher than either newspapers or radio as the most accurate and detailed source of news about issues such as the police, unemployment, and the Common Market (Collins, 1984). The same study showed, however, that positive views about television were not unconditional or without limit. Although most respondents trusted the accuracy of television, only a minority (35%) said they had been influenced by it. A significant proportion (46%) also felt that news and current affairs programs on television could sometimes be deliberately misleading.

The emergence of the Internet as a public medium in the 1990s saw a new information source become quickly established. Although the Internet emerged as a major source of news, its users went online more often for information linked to hobbies, leisure, and entertainment, followed by that associated with health and science (Pew Research Center, 2000). Although the Internet offers an abundance of information, the multitude of information suppliers can pose a problem for consumers in terms of judging the sources they can trust. Information consumers usually rely on the reputation of mediated information suppliers to decide whether the information they provide is credible. On the Internet, the appearance of established and familiar news brands in the form of known newspapers or broadcasters who have their own Web sites can help. Where such brands are missing, however, then it can be difficult to decide whether the information provided by an online source can be taken at face value. With experience, this kind of problem can be overcome. The more a person uses any medium, the more they generally come to trust it (Carter & Greenberg, 1965; Rimmer & Weaver, 1987). Regular users of a medium may also apply a higher level of scrutiny to the information it provides. Although it has only had a relatively short life span, even with the Internet, more experienced users perceive it as a more believable medium than do less experienced users (Flanagin & Metzger, 2000). Overall, however, television still emerges as the most trusted information source in comparison not only with newspapers, magazines, and radio, but also the Internet (Flanagin & Metzger, 2000).

AUTHORITY OF ONLINE HEALTH INFORMATION: SOURCE CREDIBILITY

Television has been championed as having a key part to play in e-government initiatives. Although forays into the online world by public services have focused on the use of the Internet, the problem of the digital divide, whereby not everyone has equal access to the Internet nor equal computer literacy, has encouraged experimentation with the far more familiar medium. There is another reason why television may also prove be a platform with more potential than the Internet, once technologically it has evolved in its interactive capabilities. Television is a medium that people trust as an information source.

The research into online health information provision that has already been reported in earlier chapters included an analysis of the importance of source branding and perceived authority of health content made available online through the Internet or interactive digital television. Users' perceptions of the authority of interactive health content on the Internet and on television were investigated. Parallel services were provided through both media.

On the Internet, a Web site that offered official National Health Service (NHS) information was operated by a company called SurgeryDoor. It comprised more than 5,000 pages of content with access to an additional 40,000 pages of local health service maps and listings via Web links to approved organizations (M2 Presswire, 2000). In respect of digital interactive television, authority, and trust perceptions were examined in relation to three of the four plot consortia introduced in earlier chapters—Living Health, Communicopia/NHS Direct Digital, and Channel Health. These pilot projects provided online health information in text, video-on-demand, and regular broadcast program formats, together with transactional services that provided links to health professionals. There was a significant degree of overlap in text content between the NHS Web site operated by SurgeryDoor and material offered in Living Health and Communicopia on cable television (see Nicholas et al., 2003b).

Data were derived from an online survey of users of the SurgeryDoor Internet health site and from postal, telephone, and online surveys with iDTV service users. Details about the iDTV methodology were presented in chapter 7 (this volume). The online questionnaire was hosted on the SurgeryDoor Web site and yielded 1,068 responses (5% of the 21,118 unique IP addresses that were recorded as visiting the site during the period the questionnaire was in place).

Perceptions of Health on Internet

Users of the Internet health Web site were asked how they rated the trustworthiness of the site. An overwhelming majority of respondents were very positive about the site, rating it either excellent (34%) or good (51%) in terms of its trustworthiness. Around one in seven (15%) thought the site was just *OK* in terms of trustworthiness, and just two respondents rated it as poor.

Further analysis examined links between perceived trustworthiness and attitudes toward advertising on the site. The presence of advertisements on the site impacted on the site's perceived trustworthiness. Users were asked if the advertising content on the site was either *excellent, good, OK,* or *poor.* Users who rated the advertising as excellent (77%) were more likely to rate the trustworthiness of the site as excellent too, than were those who rated the advertisements as *OK* (23%) or poor (38%).

A person's trust in the authenticity of a site was also found to be a significant factor on health outcome, with those users demonstrating the greatest trust being more likely to claim a positive health outcome. It was found that those rating the site's trustworthiness as either good or excellent were more likely to say that they had been helped a lot and were less likely to say that the site was of no help (Nicholas et al., 2001a).

Perceptions of Health on iDTV

Perceptions of authority and trust of health information on interactive digital television focused not simply on the medium as source, but also on the NHS as source. Should the NHS be involved in this kind of venture? Did the fact that it was named as a source lend credibility to the information supplied? Feedback on these and other related questions were obtained from users of three out of the four iDTV services that were piloted in Britain in 2001 and 2002 (Nicholas et al., 2003b).

Most of the health information content for the Living Health pilot channel, for example, was provided by the NHS and all pages were branded with the NHS symbol. Of users of this service, 6 out of 10 (60%) said they would trust health information found on iDTV for most things. The involvement of the NHS in the content on this site was noted by nearly two thirds (63%) of respondents. For three out of four respondents (75%), the NHS was regarded as a symbol of trust. Even more respondents (83%) said they trusted the information on this iDTV service because the NHS was involved. Notably, however, just over one in two respondents (51%) said they would carry on using the service even if the NHS was not involved, whereas more than 4 in 10 (43%) would not use the service if it lacked the NHS brand.

For certain types of people, the NHS brand really meant something. Interactive digital television subscribers who had either used the Living Health service, which carried NHS branded health information or had heard of the service, were more likely to say that the NHS was a symbol of trust compared with iDTV subscribers who had not viewed this particular service. There were, however, some iDTV users who did not buy into the NHS brand. Interactive digital television users who visited the doctor less frequently and those less interested in health information were less likely to accept the NHS as a symbol of trust, were less likely to recognize the NHS symbol, and were less likely to say that the NHS branded information could be trusted. Younger respondents were also less likely to recognize the NHS as a symbol of trust compared to older respondents. Of those individuals who had not been to a doctor in the previous 12 months, more than one in four (27%) said they did not trust online health information, knowing that the NHS was involved with it. This indicated a significant percentage of early users of this interactive digital television pilot service who did not trust the country's National Health Service as an information authority.

Overall, these findings indicated that use of the NHS symbol on the Living Health channel did not reduce public perceptions of the NHS as a symbol of trust. In fact, the evidence is that the presentation of NHS branded information on iDTV, although it was delivered by a third party, promoted trust in the NHS symbol. People who had either used the Living Health service or had heard of the service were more likely or twice as likely to say that the NHS was a symbol of trust for them compared to cable television subscribers who had not used the service. Thirty percent of respondents who had not used the Living Health channel did not see the NHS as a symbol of trust. However, this figure fell by more than one half to 12% for those who had used the service. Interestingly, the figure fell to 18% for those users who had heard about it but had not used it. It would seem that users were generally impressed by what they saw. The positioning of the NHS logo within the information services of a third party provider and delivered by another did not dilute the NHS as a symbol of trust.

With two other iDTV consortia, further data were obtained about the trust invested in health information and advice services. Communicopia/NHS Direct Digital users were asked to rate the trustworthiness of health information sources out of five. Sources where the NHS brand was present scored well. Hence, the telephone helpline, NHS Direct and the iDTV service NHS Direct Digital, although rated as less trusted than NHS doctors and nurses seen in person, were placed above health magazines and medical books (Nicholas et al., 2003b).

With Channel Health, which broadcast programs and linked text content on maternity issues to a nation-wide audience on a digital satellite transmission platform, around one half of viewers who were surveyed for their reactions were aware of NHS involvement and their reactions to this were generally positive. NHS branding was seen as offering more authority and credibility to the content (Nicholas et al., 2003b).

CONCLUSION

This chapter has examined the issue of authority, credibility and trust in online health information. If online health information services are to be successful in the longer term they must secure public and patient trust. If users have doubts about the quality of an online service in terms of the authority of its information, they are likely to discontinue using it.

Credibility of information sources can vary with the medium through which the information flows. Television has been a highly regarded medium in terms of its role as a news source. Not only do most people identify it as their main news source, they also trust it the most. In comparisons with newspapers and radio, television more often than not is rated higher for the quality and objectivity of its information.

The emergence of the Internet has presented new competition to the longer established media as information suppliers. Users can obtain far larger amounts of information via the Internet than from other media. However, as a new medium, the Internet does not yet have the brand strength of the other major information media. In fact, in the few comparisons that have been made, television remains the most trusted source, ahead not only of print media and radio, but also ahead of the Internet (Flanagin & Metzger, 2000).

It is not just the reputation of the medium that is important in terms of information authority. Information consumers also look at the source of the content. In the context of online health information, source reputation may be a key factor that influences users' perceptions of content.

Research into online health information provision in Britain looked at two very different aspects of the perceived authority of information. A study of a health Web site examined some of the issues related to the trustworthiness of a commercial Web site that carried advertisements, whereas a study of a iDTV service looked at information that was predominantly NHS branded and used the NHS logo as a symbol of trust although this information was made available via a third party. Direct comparisons between the two studies were not made, although it is felt that the results can be generalized between platforms.

Seekers of health information on the Internet may search many Web sites. Visiting a number of sites maybe a way of checking the authority of the sites and supports the contention that authority is there for the taking (Hunt, 1999). Interviews with users of various online systems have indicated that people might simply go from site to site looking for information that best fits their own preconceived ideas, thus conferring authority on the source of the most appealing information, regardless of other criteria. Despite this phenomenon, the NHS was regarded as trustworthy even among users of other sources (Nicholas et al., 2003b).

One important finding was that the presence of advertisements on health Web sites tended to undermine their perceived trustworthiness (Nicholas et al., 2003b; Williams et al., 2002b). This result has significant implications for the reception given to health Web sites that may be run in partnership between public sector and private sector organizations. In Britain, for example, the NHS represents a trusted health information brand. Any close association with commercial advertisers in the online world, however, could change this perception.

Evidence also emerged from among iDTV users in Britain, that frequency of contact with health professionals together with degree of wider interest in health may mediate perceptions of the NHS as a recognizable symbol of trust. This finding was consistent with the observation elsewhere that those who use NHS services tend to be more positive about the NHS generally (Mulligan, 2000). The significance of amount of actual contact with health services to public opinion about them, might also offer some explanation for the finding that younger respondents trusted online health information less than did older respondents.

Hence, trust in the primary health services may affect the degree to which individuals will use iDTV information and advice services for which those health services are information providers. In Britain, if NHS branded health information is highly regarded, people are more likely to utilize iDTV health information from that source. Where the source is not trusted, iDTV subscribers will not visit the TV health channels with which that low-credibility source is associated. But if greater contact with a health service can result in improved opinions about it, as has been observed with the NHS in Britain, more regular contact with health services via television may have a similar effect.

It is one thing to establish whether trust in a health information source exists. Another important question concerns the issue of what factors go into a person's evaluation of authority and trust. Do people analyze the information presented to them and make judgements about its quality? Or do they take it at face value, making judgments instead about the source rather than the content of the information and whether the provider can be trusted or not? Why do people trust certain sources? These are all critically important issues, particularly with the commitment by the government to continue rolling out digital health information to the public.

People value and need an information source they can trust when they go online. This is especially important in relation to health information because of the potentially critical effects inaccurate advice might have for the individual. Health information is being made available across a range of technology platforms to ensure maximum population coverage. Will health information consumers regard the health information they obtain over their mobile telephones the same way as that they obtain through their television sets or over the Internet or via a touch-screen kiosk? In the case of a kiosk, will the nature of the public location (e.g., a supermarket versus a health center) make a difference to how users reach judgements about the quality of content and who, ultimately, is responsible for that content (Nicholas, Huntington, Williams, & Gunter, 2003b)? These are questions that will need to be further investigated in order to understand users' orientations toward online health sources and which sources are perceived to have authority and why.

Chapter 10

The Future Potential of Digital Health

◇

A rapidly ageing population in the developed world has led to intensified efforts to enhance health services and to produce more economical and effective ways of treating illnesses and chronic conditions. The evolution of information and communication technologies has yielded platforms on which health information and advice can be distributed to large and remote populations and created channels through which even certain forms of diagnosis may be possible. Such developments have formed part of a wider range of initiatives by governments to bring public services online. Experiments in e-health, e-education, e-taxation, and e-voting are designed to make public services more accessible, to empower citizens, and make an increasingly alienated electorate feel more involved (Keighron, 2003; Norris, 2001).

There is a hope that the increased flow of health information via online systems will enable citizens to become empowered health consumers. Placing citizens in this position may cultivate a climate of self-care and encourage preventive medicine over treatment of ill-health. The use of online support services and remote contact with medical and health professionals may yield certain economies for health care systems (Robinson et al., 1998). What is less certain is whether online health services will have purely positive and beneficial effects. Although they might represent convenient one-stop shops for information about illnesses and treatments, and about which professionals and sources or sites of health care are highest rated, there could be a downside to online health care.

The "informed patient," created by this online health environment, could be more likely to question a doctor's diagnosis. This might increase the time taken to reach an agreement about treatment, as primary-care health professionals debate with their patients over second opinions derived from online sources. There may be increased occasions on which patients decide not to follow the advice of their doctor with dire potentially consequences if that is the wrong decision to take in their case (Wilkins, 1999). Despite their apparent convenience, online diagnoses with health professionals may not lead to better diagnoses (Bader & Braude, 1998; Wilkins, 1999).

The impact of online health care might therefore have a number of important implications for the future. Certainly, online platforms offer alternative sources of health information to face-to-face contact with medical and health professionals. Remote consultations and remote support groups operating via electronic networks may open up opportunities for citizens to obtain advice about health without the need to travel or leave home (Gregory-Head, 1999; Oravec, 2000). The use of online health information sources may encourage a more proactive disposition toward self-care and prevention. It may also cultivate a more critical disposition toward information and advice from professional sources rather than taking that information at face vale (Neff, 1999). In this last case, a more critical attitude might place health professionals under greater strain, rather than, as has been hoped, relieving it. There could also be significant cost implications for health service providers with patients requiring more time to accept diagnoses or recommended treatments (Appleby, 1999; Lincoln & Builder, 1999). There may also be health implications when patients refuse to accept the treatments offered by their doctors (Eng & Gustafson, 1999; Lamp & Howard, 1999).

One consequence of the wider dissemination of health information and advice online could be a shift in the balance of power over health as health professionals no longer hold exclusivity over health information (Wilkins, 1999). An optimistic view of this scenario is that professionals and patients will act in partnership (Thomas, 1998). A pessimistic view is that it will create conflict, pressure, and complication in the physician–patient relationship (Grandinetti, 2000; Lamp & Howard, 1999).

THE EMERGENCE OF ONLINE PLATFORMS

The rapid growth of the Internet in the 1990s fueled in part by the rapid rise (and fall) of many dot-com companies first drew public attention to the varied applications and potential of online services. Millions of Web sites became established within a few years. Among these, one of the most popular categories of information sought via the Internet was health. A survey by Cyber Dialogue (cyberatlas.com, 2000c) found that 36.7 million people in the United States alone had used the Internet to search for health-related content. These health information consumers had more than 20,000 health-related Web sites to choose from.

The role played by information and communication technologies (ICTs) in health is not limited to the distribution of information on the Internet. Computer-mediated communications (CMC) systems have been applied that are non-Internet based. Such systems can convey information as the Internet does, but they also provide two-way links between health professionals and patients for the purpose of customized provision of health advice and diagnosis. CMCs permit flexible use of video, audio, graphic, and text formats to supply information of a general or more targeted nature. Increasingly attention has switched from the Internet per se, to the role that might be played by a longer established medium with a far wider penetration—television. Traditionally a passive medium for the reception of content, the emergence of interactive digital television has opened up a variety of new possibilities for television as a communications medium with which its users can become more actively engaged. Given the significance of pictures in many interactive services, it is not surprising that television should emerge as a key platform in this context. Early trials with iDTV have already indicated its potential as a conveyor of public and consumer services (Keighron, 2003; Niiranen et al., 2002).

Multimedia formats can be used on the Internet, but they have lacked the quality and resolution of health videos and CD-ROMs. The emergence of broadband Internet and iDTV technologies may change all this. Such technologies will bring down barriers between what computers can do on and off the Internet.

The majority of Internet users are connected to dial-up Internet service providers (ISPs) through their normal telephone lines. Although this is inexpensive, convenient, and nearly universal, the amount of data that can be downloaded through a standard phone line in a given period of time is limited. Complex multimedia data formats can take a long time to download through narrow-band connections. The growth of broadband will make a big difference. In the United States, a survey by Forward Concepts cited by Cyberatlas.com (2000) projected that by the year 2005, there will be more than 35 million American broadband users. These high-speed Internet connections (via DSL, cable modem, direct satellite connection) will provide Internet access to users at rates of speed that are 50 to 100 times faster than today's 56k standard, with even faster connections to come.

What this means for health communication via ICTs utilizing CMC is that the kinds of rich multimedia formats used on CD-ROM, with video, audio, text information, and high-resolution graphics will be readily communicable over the Internet. Digital television, also, is regarded as providing a cornerstone platform for the enhancement of health care services and may even open up a new health service infrastructure based on the convergence of different media. Interactivity is a key element in the implementation of health care applications through digital television. Interactive digital television can provide interactive services for those sectors of society left behind by the Internet revolution. This last point may be especially significant in the case of older people.

WHAT KINDS OF ONLINE APPLICATIONS?

It is widely recognized that ICTs will play an increasingly prominent role in the delivery of health care in future years. In Britain, the government has acknowledged that ICTs—especially the Internet and iDTV—will represent a key factor in the cultivation of a climate of self-care and its implementation that will help to improve the health status of the nation and produce economies in health care delivery

(Wanless, 2002). The skillful use of CMCs and online technology is envisaged to yield positive patient outcomes and improve the quality and range of health care delivery. Such developments are seen as particularly important in the context of an aging population. There is also a firm belief that by encouraging people to take better care of themselves before they get ill—an ethos of preventive medicine—the cost of health care to society can be further reduced.

The widespread and relatively cheap accessibility of the Internet can increase the provision of health information across wide sectors of the population (LaPerriere et al., 1998). The concept of the digital divide, however, underlines the fact that access to this platform is far from universal. Interactive digital television may not fully resolve this access problem either. Nonetheless, the Internet offers an interactive capability and it can accommodate transactional (two-way) communication flows (McMillan, 1999). This feature means that the Internet has enhanced capacity as a communication medium over longer established media that offer only one-way communication flow (from sender to receiver). The Internet can also provide access to large quantities of information relatively cheaply (Pereira & Bower, 1998).

As this book has shown, online technologies and CMCs are already established in the health context. People turn to health Web sites for health information (Eurobarometer, 2000; Fox & Rainie, 2000). Online technologies are applied to deliver remote health advice to individuals. Budman (2000), for example, identified 10 types of Internet applications from Barak (1999):

(a) information resources for patients, potential patients and therapists;

(b) self-help guides;

(c) testing, assessment, and screening programmes;

(d) guidance about going into therapy;

(e) information about specific psychological services;

(f) single-session advice through e-mail or bulletin boards;

(g) ongoing counselling through e-mail;

(h) real-time counselling through chat sessions;

(i) synchronous and asynchronous support groups; and

(j) online psychological research. (p. 1290)

Budman then added three more applications to this list:

(k) interactive, tailored expert systems intervention programmes;

(l) preventive interventions; and

(m) administrative quality assessments. (Budman, 2000, p. 1290)

This means that the Internet alone among ICTs has already become established as a provider of a varied assortment of health information and health care services.

What the foregoing list reveals is that ICTs can provide not only health content for retrieval by users at their convenience, but also a dynamic forum within which individuals can obtain direct, personalized help, advice and diagnosis in real time.

Despite the rapid spread of the Internet, the increasing widespread availability of iDTV, and the establishment of other technologies in health communication, such as touch-screen kiosks and mobile communications devices, the effectiveness of online health services depends on more than mere access. The technological determinism that significantly underpins online technology rollout in the health and wider public service contexts does not guarantee successful and effective service delivery. One message that emerges from the evidence presented in this book is that online technologies must be used appropriately and provide access to service delivery that users are comfortable with and perceive as an acceptable way of engaging with such services. It is therefore important to understand the psychological orientation of individuals toward online technologies and toward the specific service presentation formats that are devised for those technologies.

IMPORTANCE OF TECHNOLOGY ORIENTATIONS

The World Wide Web has become established as a massive information source in which anybody can publish anything. Health features among the most frequently accessed information categories on the Web. Despite these observations, the Internet in the home is mainly used for interpersonal communication (Kraut, Mukhopadhyuy, Szczypuda, Kiesler, & Scherlis, 1999). This form of CMC also contains two features—visual anonymity and limited channel (i.e., text-only) communication—that have been implicated in a variety of interpersonal behaviors. Both of these features were invoked initially to predict that CMC would lack the richness of normal face-to-face interaction and hence be high in task-orientation, but low in socioemotional content (Rice & Love, 1987). Indeed, it was further predicted that CMC would discourage awareness of others (Kiesler et al., 1984) and encourage antinormative, uninhibited and even aggressive or argumentative behavior—also known as *flaming*—because of the protection afforded by invisibility and anonymity (Kiesler et al., 1984).

If this initial assumption is correct, it conveys significant implications for the potential value of CMC and the use of remote, online channels in the context of direct health care provision. In particular, computer-mediated delivery channels may lack the sensitivity to deliver health services in which the cornerstone of support is emotional rather than purely physical in nature.

Fortunately for supporters of online health care, later research on CMC revealed that effective interpersonal interactions could be negotiated via online technologies. In fact, it is possible for users to establish rich connections online that may even surpass, in some ways, those that can be achieved through face-to-face meetings (Joinson, 2001; Rheingold, 1993; Walther, 1996). One of the important facets of this phenomenon is *disclosure*. This concept concerns the degree to which individuals are prepared to reveal personal information about themselves to others (Archer, 1980).

On the Internet, individuals may communicate one on one with others via e-mail. In this form of asynchronous communication, however, the message sender must wait for some time before getting a response. Internet users can also engage in more dynamic forms of communication by participating in online chat rooms in which the conversation may be generalized in nature or connected with a specialized subject or issue. In some instances, such forums may have the express purpose of enabling people to meet new friends or even to find romantic partners. Research has shown that significant proportions of users of these Internet services report forming personal relationships with others online. Users of these online chat rooms also report being more open in the way they converse and in the degree to which they reveal things about themselves than they would if meeting strangers for the first time face to face (Parks & Floyd, 1996).

Not everyone has access to the Internet, however, despite the best intentions of governments. The absence of home access might be compensated for in part by access through kiosks in public health locations or via desk-top computers in libraries. Online content searching often requires time, however. This may be a missing luxury when using kiosks in public locations with others waiting in line behind the user. As shown in chapter 5 (this volume), kiosk search times tend to be short and pages accessed may be few. Older people may have the greatest difficulty with this technology and in consequence retrieve the least information from it (Nicholas, Huntington, & Williams, 2002b).

Interactive digital television may be another solution for those who are not Internet savvy. It is overtaking the Internet in terms of penetration (Klein, Kargar, & Sinclair, 2004; Towler, 2002, 2003). Furthermore, iDTV offers a range of interactive services and forms of content delivery. Regular broadcast program services can operate as a front-end and provide readily digestible health-related content that is both factual and emotionally reassuring (Nicholas, Huntington, Williams, & Gunter, 2003b). Large quantities of text information can be uploaded for online interrogation at the user's leisure. Audio-visual material in the form of video-on-demand services can offer case study content as well as bald facts, with users choosing from a wide range if video vignettes the ones that deal with the health condition of personal interest (Huntington et al., 2003a). Improved content navigation systems will enhance the ability of viewer users to find content (Gunter, 2003b). Any search difficulties experienced by users of online services on iDTV can have serious consequences for service loyalty over time (Nicholas, Huntington, Williams, & Gunter, 2002c). Interactive digital television can also provide two-way communications links in e-mail and video-conferencing formats to enable users to link directly with health professionals (Nicholas et al., 2003a).

Although a potentially versatile medium, the long history of television means that particular forms of viewing behavior have become strongly conditioned. Interactive digital television invites viewers to become more psychologically and physically active with the medium, and this process may require a certain amount of unlearning of old viewing habits and reorienting toward the medium (Klein, Kargar, & Sinclair, 2004). There will also remain many questions about application effectiveness in relation to iDTV (Gunter, 2003b). This means finding out which formats work best in serving particular user information needs.

Self-Disclosure Online

One of the key aspects of online health service provision in the future could be remote therapy. Public and patients may seek emotional reassurance as much as clinical help. Any effective diagnosis or therapy is dependent on the degree to which patients disclose details of their history, condition, and feelings. People have been found to disclose more to a computer than to another person under certain circumstances. Further research has indicated that such openness to disclosure can work effectively in a health context. For example, medical patients have been found to reveal more symptoms and undesirable behaviors when interviewed by a computer than in a face-to-face interview with a health professional (Greist, Klein, & van Cura, 1973). Patients at an alcohol treatment center who were interviewed by computer tended to report 30% higher levels of alcohol consumption compared to participants interviewed in person. Patients were also more likely to reveal details about sexual problems to a computer than to a psychiatrist (Greist & Klein, 1980; Lucas, Mullins, Luria, & McInray, 1977).

The potential of online disclosure becomes especially apparent when individuals are called upon to discuss matters about themselves and their behavior that are of a very sensitive nature. Clients at a sex clinic, for instance, reported more sexual partners, more previous visits and more symptoms to a computer than to a doctor (Robinson & West, 1992). Time and again in a health context, CMC has been found to yield more open and honest replies from people than face-to-face interviews (Ferriter, 1993).

Some researchers have developed special software programs with which patients can engage to discuss personal and sexual problems (Binik, Cantor, Ochs, & Meana, 1997; Fleming, 1990). Such systems have been provided on stand-alone and networked computers. Not only are patents more willing to talk to a computer, they are also willing to reveal intimate details to strangers online. One early study of an electronic advice column found that people were prepared to engage in a significant amount of self-disclosure (Hellerstein, 1990).

The use of the Internet to provide online advice has become particularly popular with psychologists and other mental health practitioners in the United States. Counseling can be offered via e-mail, scheduled online chats, and interaction online with support groups comprising people who currently or have in the past experienced similar problems. Online support groups have emerged in relation to physical illnesses too. Groups for cancer sufferers, for instance, are designed to offer emotional support as well as facilitating the exchange of factual information.

Online support has proven to be both popular and effective for stigmatized groups who may feel uncomfortable seeking help and advice in face-to-face situations. Individuals may therefore seek online help even though face-to-face support is at hand (Binik et al., 1997; Mickelson, 1997). The anonymity of Internet support may be especially appealing to individuals with stigmatized problems that are easy to hide, but which could be embarrassing if they came to light. Online support groups might be particularly important to individuals who are clandestine drug users or have unusual sexual preferences. Such groups can help individuals to come to terms with their marginalised identity (McKenna & Bargh, 1998).

As noted earlier, central to most explanations of both prosocial and antisocial CMC behavior, including self-disclosure, is the concept of visual anonymity (Kiesler et al., 1984; Spears & Lea, 1994; Walther, 1996). Another feature of the online experience is deindividuation. A theory known as Social Identity/De-individuation Effects (SIDE) argues that the anonymity present in most forms of CMC can serve to magnify social stereotypes and associated behaviors when only small amounts of information about the social identity of the other person are revealed (Reicher, Spears, & Postmes, 1995; Spears & Lea, 1992). Thus, when an individual's own identity is not revealed to others, that person will feel more confidant expressing their mind and their true feelings without holding back and being bothered about politeness or diplomacy (Spears & Lea, 1994). When any aspect of their own identity is revealed, such openness and disclosure will reduce.

In demonstrating this point, Joinson (2001) found that individuals disclosed more about themselves when communicating via a computer e-mail link than when meeting with each other face to face. However, the presence of a video picture of one's discussion partner led to significantly lower levels of self-disclosure during computer-mediated communication. In the video condition, individuals became more concerned about the way they presented themselves and this led to a heightened sensitivity to self-disclosure. When they thought they could not be seen and they could not see others, however, they conversed online with greater openness and showed less concern about how they may have appeared to others.

One writer has warned against plugging video cameras into PCs, arguing that visual cues detract from more open communication (Walther, 1997). Long-term members of computer-mediated discussion groups were found to display reduced attraction and affinity if they had seen a still picture of their fellow participants (Walther, Slovacek, & Tidwell, 1999). One view is that online participants share a social classification as *Internet users*. In that respect they have something in common and may perceive themselves to be more similar to one another than they really are because of that fact (Walther, 1996). If they then receive additional information—especially of a visual nature—that causes them to revise their opinions of each other, resulting in reduced similarity perceptions, that could seriously affect how open and honest they are in their future communications with each other.

This evidence on the way people use online technologies could have important implications for the application effectiveness of remote health care provision. On those occasions when members of the public or patients simply need basic factual health information about a medical condition, a text-based information source may be sufficient. On other occasions, when someone suffering from a medical condition needs not just clinical information, but also reassurance, video interviews, or discussions involving fellow sufferers may prove more effective in meeting all the needs of the user. When an individual needs immediate reassurance of a highly personalized nature, a live link with a health professional is the only one likely to prove effective still. However, whether online advice or therapy is effective may depend upon an understanding of how people behave in CMC contexts.

With iDTV based health information and advice services, preliminary evidence has emerged that users welcome formats that offer greater social presence in addressing certain of their health-related needs (e.g., reassurance about a chronic health condition from viewing other sufferers talk about it on screen). However, this kind of development is not accepted unconditionally. One-way video interactions with a video nurse, for example, were believed to add an important dimension to telephone-only links. Nonetheless, some users were wary of the thought of a two-way video interaction where the user could see and be seen by the nurse, believing it to place them in a more vulnerable position (Nicholas et al., 2003a).

RATIONALITY AND EMOTIONALITY ONLINE

The provision of online health care may involve direct communication between health or medical professionals and public or patients or more open-ended discussion groups in which members share a condition or interest and exchange rational information or emotional reassurance.

Computer-mediated channels can support interpersonal interactions in a number of ways (Braithwaite, Waldron, & Finn, 1999; Rheingold, 1993; Walther, 1995). Walther (1996) distinguished between three types of communication exchange in CMC. In *impersonal CMC,* the exchanges that take place are primarily concerned with information retrieval or task completion, with little or no social interaction taking place. With *interpersonal CMC,* users engage in social interaction. Finally, there is *hyperpersonal CMC,* that involves a social exchange between participants that requires participants to fill in the gaps in the information they have about each other that often results in a more positive impression of the other person than would normally derive from a richer communication channel, such as face-to-face interaction.

The third category recognizes that interpersonal exchanges via CMC can become so rich and powerful that the participants value them above face-to-face interactions. A number of factors are involved in this process. As such, an individual may develop an idealized image of the person at the other end whom they may never have met in person. In the anonymous environment of online communication, individuals can demonstrate extremely high levels of self-disclosure. The asynchronous nature of e-mail, for instance, allows each participant to think carefully about how they respond to each message they receive from the other. In the absence of visual cues, each participant is encouraged to generate increasingly open disclosures about themselves. SIDE theory predicts that in the absence of face-to-face cues and prior personal knowledge of the other person, the few social context cues present in CMC take on exaggerated value and may lead to over-attribution of similarity between participants (Walther, 1996).

In the health sphere, online support groups provide a ripe context for the development of hyperpersonal communication because participants who join and become involved in an online group already are assuming a common identity with other group members. This perception can form the foundation of a presumed bond that may already exist among online group participants. In this context, an individual assumes the identity of having a particular problem or concern and assumes that other online members share a similar identity. Messages that are exchanged within the online group can reinforce this perception of shared identity. This context, together with the anonymity and opportunity for planned responses provides a ripe environment for senders to initiate interactions with hyperpersonal potential.

Under circumstances in which the individual is experiencing great stress, the presumption that others in an online support group are in a similar position can represent the basis for the formation of powerful social bonds. These conditions may also render interaction with similar others the most desirable form of support to the individual concerned. Furthermore, the more the source of stress is perceived to be outside the individual's immediate control, the more stressful it is experienced as being. According to optimal matching theory, individuals will seek out others to talk to with whom they perceive the greatest similarity in terms of condition and its causes (e.g., stress caused by money problems, personal relationships, or illness; Cutrona & Russell, 1990).

Failing access to a fellow sufferer to speak to, the next best alternative may be access to a video-recording of similar others talking about their problems to other people or to health professionals. Thus, video feedback—although recorded—can still offer psychological comfort and reassurance (Nicholas et al., 2003a, 2003b).

Coping with a medical illness—especially one that is life threatening—can be categorized as a negative and uncontrollable event requiring emotion-focused coping to address the fear, anger, and depression that can result. Quite apart from physical treatment, serious medical conditions can be improved or at least the patient's experience of them uplifted via emotional and social support mechanisms (Cutrona & Russell, 1990).

Some serious medical conditions can adversely affect the individual in a number of ways—loss of job and income, contact with others, physical incapacity, and relationships with family and friends. Finding support from among others with similar experience may be difficult to achieve offline. For one thing, the individual may be too incapacitated to attend support group meetings at locations distant from his or her home. The advent of online support communities, however, can bring the individual into contact with hundreds of others with whom they perceive they have something in common. Contact can be established and maintained without ever having to leave home.

Hence, e-mail and the Internet are renegotiating the boundaries of communication within medical-related discussion groups. Patients can share personal stories, medical information, and support from others with similar conditions. Research has shown that such CMC discussion groups have provided new avenues of social and emotional support for such patients (Braithwaite et al., 1999; Mickelson, 1998). Individuals join a social support online community because they are seeking information, empowerment, encouragement, emotional support, and empathy regarding their specific condition (Mickelson, 1998). Because online communication is anonymous and does not require some of the social graces of face-to-face communication, it represents a welcome alternative. Furthermore, online discussion groups are available all the time, 24 hours a day, 7 days a week.

Computer-mediated social support can complement or act as a substitute for face-to-face interaction among those with a serious medical condition. Cancer patients, for example, have been found to form hyperpersonal relationships with fellow sufferers online that they value more than the direct support they receive from others around them (Turner, Grube, & Meyers, 2001).

Even among older adults, regular users of the Internet rated the medium highly for the social support networks that could be accessed. In fact, such mediated social support was highly valued and made them feel more confident about helping themselves (Emery, Cowan, Eaglestone, Heyes, Proctor, & Willis, 2002).

What has emerged from reviews of online support groups and self-care projects, however, is that certain groups have found the Internet to provide a better source of such support than others. Individuals with different illnesses or medical conditions have different self-care needs and requirements. It has already been noted that having an illness or condition that is embarrassing, socially stigmatizing or disfiguring leads people to seek support of others with similar conditions. Even within these types of conditions, however, there are differences in the extent to which offline or online sources of help are preferred. Face-to-face support group participation in the U.S., for example, has been noted for cases of alcoholism, AIDS, breast cancer, and anorexia. The highest levels of online support were observed for sufferers of multiple sclerosis, chronic fatigue syndrome, and, again, breast cancer and anorexia (Davison et al., 2000). Although there was some evidence here for the view that online support is sought by sufferers from socially embarrassing conditions, there was an additional indication that online forums emerged for conditions overlooked by the medical community or for which there was, more generally, a poor understanding. It remains the case, nonetheless, that individuals suffering from serious, life-threatening illnesses may often still feel the acute need to experience the physical presence of others and the emotional sustenance that can only be derived from actual encounters with other people.

According to social comparison theory, in conditions of uncertainty and anxiety, individuals exhibit stronger drives to affiliate with other people, and especially with those who they believe best understand the causes of their uncertainty (Schachter, 1959; Teichmann, 1973). Individuals prefer the company of others who have a similar condition to themselves when experts are not available. These observations are consistent with the role played by online forums where those suffering from specific illnesses can engage with others in a similar position. Furthermore, the anonymity offered by the Internet encourages confiding to occur without immediate social repercussions. Although face-to-face support will continue to have an important part to play in provision of emotional support and counseling for some patient groups, online forums may prove to be more acceptable and helpful in the case of other groups (Davison et al., 2000).

CAN ONLINE HEALTH SERVICES
STIMULATE SELF-CARE?

Although online communications systems may have a disinhibiting effect on users that could enhance their effectiveness in the establishment of social bonds among those with serious medical conditions who seek emotional support, how effective are they in encouraging healthy people to remain healthy? Digital health services may provide hope for those who are already unwell, but in a wider context their potential is envisaged extend toward the healthy. In this case, can the healthy be helped and encouraged to stay healthy? Can those who engage in unhealthy lifestyles be encouraged to change their behaviors before ill-health sets in?

The findings so far have been mixed. There is little evidence that people with unhealthy lifestyles are more likely to seek diagnostic information via online sources with a view to changing their behavior patterns. For example, in one study of a staff health promotion Web site aimed at employees in an organization, it emerged that users were predominantly those who already exercised rather than those who were planning to change their sedentary ways (Griffin, Eves, & Cheng, 2000). This evidence is consistent with the observation that in a health information-seeking context, it is usual for people to avoid or misremember information they find threatening (Taylor, 1989). Hence, health content avoidance behavior is especially likely to occur when health information is seen as personally relevant (Sherman, Nelson, & Steele, 2000). In contrast to these observations, other writers have noted a degree of success with online mutual aid support groups in providing emotional support and even help with recovery among individuals with stigmatized health conditions (King & Moreggi, 1998).

The research on digital health services reported in this book, however, did identify some areas in which online health information and advice can have a positive impact. This point is reinforced by findings concerning the profiles of digital health content users, the stated purpose of using online health information, and the degree to which individuals use of digital health content was related to self-reports of using health information sources as an alternative to visiting the doctor (Nicholas et al., 2003a, 2003b).

Health information on interactive digital television was found to attract significant numbers of men (Nicholas et al., 2003b). This was a good sign given longer established evidence that men tend to avoid health check-ups (Davies et al., 2000). The disinhibiting effect of online technologies that has been observed elsewhere may offer one explanation for this pattern of use (Joinson, 1998, 2000). A separate investigation of cancer Web sites revealed significant traffic directed toward information about embarrassing or stigmatized cancers such as testicular or prostrate cancer in England and Wales, that matched patterns of calls to telephone helplines. Indeed, hits to testicular cancer sites were overrepresented, providing indirect evidence of more browsing of such sites by men (Joinson & Banyard, 2002).

Further evidence from U.K.-based digital health research indicated that users sought out online health content in relation to seeing their doctor. Health content on iDTV was consulted either before or after visiting the doctor (Nicholas et al., 2003a, 2003b). This suggested that iDTV provided some users with an alternative information source and that they could use this information either to double-check whatever their doctor had told them, or to inform questions they could put directly to their doctor about their condition. In the latter case, online health content provided a means to help patients get higher quality information from their own doctors. It was also clear that, in some cases, visiting health information sites on iDTV was used instead of questioning or troubling the doctor. People who had opted not to view digital health content on television indicated, conversely, that they placed more trust in health advice obtained directly from their doctor, whether by word of mouth or from printed materials given to them by the doctor (Nicholas et al., 2003a, 2003b).

CONFORMITY ONLINE

Computer-mediated communication has been found to release people from the normal constraints that govern everyday life (Jessup, Connolly, & Galegher, 1990; Sproull & Kiesler, 1986).This tendency has been manifest as uninhibited behavior online in the form of extreme verbal expressions and verbal aggressiveness or "flaming" (Kiesler & Sproull, 1992).

One view is that such extreme forms of behavior occur because individuals online may feel protected by the anonymity of the Internet and the lack of public awareness of who they are. If true, this observation suggests that the Internet is a rather impersonal environment in which people feel that normal social constraints on their behavior can be safely ignored or perhaps do not apply. As seen earlier, however, some writers have argued conversely that the Internet is not an impersonal medium. It is possible to develop serious interpersonal relationships in virtual environments and knowingly to convey positive emotions as well as unconstrained negative ones (Walther, 1994, 1996).

The idea that communication on the Internet often defies the social etiquette that governs direct social interactions has also been challenged. Indeed, there is evidence that normal rules of social conduct can be amplified in a computer-mediated setting (Postmes, Spears, & Lea, 1998). There is often a sense of greater anonymity in a computed-mediated environment because the person communicating cannot be seen or heard by others. One interesting distinction has been made between private conformity and public conformity in this context.

In the case of public conformity, the individual does not simply accept a majority point of view, but ensures that his or her adoption of this position is publicly known. In essence, this behavior is largely about keeping up appearances. With private conformity, the individual adopts a majority position more discretely because they believe it is the best position to adopt, regardless of what others may think about it. Public conformity is driven by social desirability factors. Rejecting the majority position may be bad for the individual's personal popularity. Most people like to run with the crowd and avoid being seen as deviant (Diehl & Stroebe, 1987; Nemeth, 1986).

In the presence of others, an individual will therefore think about the social consequences as well as the informational value of rejecting rather than accepting an opinion held by the majority. Where the social presence of others becomes diminished, as in CMC, when communication is conducted with others remotely, the strength of influence of what others might think over the opinions an individual displays, becomes diluted. In most instances of CMC, the communicator is isolated, sitting alone in front of a computer screen and interacting with a person who might be in the next room or thousands of miles away. The lack of nonverbal cues in CMC, as compared with face-to-face encounters, means that it is not easy to read the emotional reactions of the person at the other end anyway.

Under CMC conditions, the communicator may experience a state of *deindividuation*—a state of reduced self-awareness. Under this condition, expression of deviant opinions may be regarded as a carrying lower risk than it would in face-to-face encounters. Although the reduced social presence of CMC may lead one to expect reduced conformity to social norms, the theory of SIDE has suggested that conformity to group norms may be stronger rather than weaker in CMC (Lea & Spears, 1991; Walther, 1996, 1997). This model has argued that although self-identity is protected in the online environment, conformity to group norms is enhanced (Postmes & Spears, 1998). Under online conditions in which the individual's identity is kept hidden from those with whom he or she is interacting, stronger compliance with group attitudes occurs. In contrast, when the individuals believe their identity will be revealed or is known to group members, they are more likely to display discrepant opinions (Postmes et al., 1998; Spears, Lea, & Lee, 1990). In addition to the findings of controlled experiments, natural field observations have indicated that students who e-mailed each other as part of course developed group norms that defined the way they corresponded with each other online. Conformity to such naturally emerging group norms grew stronger over time (Postmes, Spears, & Lea, 2000).

These findings have implications for online health-related communications. The emergence of norms in relation to coping with ill-health or serious medical conditions in Internet chat rooms and other online support forums may generate greater compliance among users who feel confident that their anonymity will be maintained. For that reason it is important that the advice that is handed out in these forums is medically sound.

CONCERNS ABOUT CMC

Technological advances have opened up amazing new possibilities for the delivery of health information and diagnostic services. At the same time, a number of concerns have emerged about this form of health care provision. The major worries are linked to matters of system security and the confidentiality of patient information, the quality of service provision online, and the diminished personal nature of digital health care compared with direct contact with health professionals.

Confidentiality

As online health care develops, and more health care related traffic flows through digital systems, so concern about the security and confidentiality of patient information will grow. If patient medical details are to be transmitted electronically from one location to another and are stored online in databases that can be retrieved via computer by those who have authorized access, what are the risks of that information falling into the wrong hands? Computer systems must be secure enough to ensure that such risks are minimized. This is clearly an important issue in connection with proposal to enable iDTV systems to be adapted for the maintenance of personal medical records that individuals can maintain and interrogate from home. Although such services may be securely developed, users will need to be convinced that the security measures are water-tight.

Service Quality

There are two main aspects to this issue. The first is connected to the increased volume of health-related information to be found via the Internet. Such information is originated by many different sources and their accreditation and authority as sources must be established if patients and other users are to have confidence in the accuracy and trustworthiness of online health content. Health information sites that are backed, for instance, by organizations with vested commercial interests in particular drugs or treatments may not always provide the best advice.

The second feature relates to the provision of interactive diagnostic services online. How effectively can health professionals provide accurate diagnoses on a remote basis via electronic links? Can users always expect to obtain the advice they need and reassurance they crave via online links to physicians, nurses, and other health experts? Are health professionals confident that they can glean enough information about a patient's symptoms to provide an effective diagnosis in this way? In sum, does online health information and advice have authority?

As people become more experienced users of online health services, their cynicism about the quality of the information and advice dispensed has grown (Health on the Net Foundation, 2001). This is probably a welcome development because online health content—especially that found on the Internet—is not always clearly sourced. There is much potential for harm to be done where ill-conceived or inaccurate advice is taken seriously and acted upon by online health consumers

(Coiera, 1998). Given evidence that a majority of online health sites may contain inaccurate information (Adelhard & Obst, 1999), health consumers should take great care when entering the online world for health advice.

A number of authors have already begun to tackle the issue of accreditation of sources in respect of provision of online of health reference information (Griffiths & Christensen, 2000; Impicciatore et al., 1997; Silberg, Lundberg, & Musacchio, 1997). In this case, online technologies such as the Internet and iDTV can provide the public and patients with access to large quantities of information stored in what is, in effect, a vast electronic library. Concerns have also been raised, however, about online therapy services. These concerns may be of a more serious nature because users seek not simply reference information, but also diagnostic or treatment advice of a personal nature.

Online therapists have become established in abundance on the Internet, especially in the United States. There are Internet sites offering information about disorders, self-help sites, and psychotherapy services offering assessment, diagnosis, and intervention (Rabasca, 2000a). Many therapists have set up their own online sites. Some offer limited services free of charge and then charge fees for more detailed services. Other therapists moderate group chat lines or engage in e-mail correspondence, private instant messaging, or even video-conferencing. Online therapy via e-mail is one growing phenomenon (Alberta Alcohol and Drug Abuse Commission, 1999; Lago, 1996). Online therapists may sometimes provide instant feedback, but on other occasions delayed assessments are provided several weeks after initial contact during which the patient or client completes a clinical test that is then subsequently analyzed and interpreted (Champkin & Hughes, 1999).

Online therapy can be convenient for patient and therapist, offering greater latitude in arrangement of appointments. It is cost effective for both parties because no travel is involved or special premises needed. Online therapy may be accessible to individuals who through their geographical location cannot easily get to see a therapist in person. Therapeutically too there can be advantages in that some patients find there are better able to self-disclose online.

Problems can arise when these online health service providers may have dubious professional accreditation or qualifications (Griffiths, 2001). There may be a lack of transparency regarding not only who is providing the therapy, but also who is sponsoring the service and what is their real agenda. People seeking help online may not think to ask such searching questions and may therefore get involved in therapy services operated by unqualified therapists (Rabasca, 2000a). This issue could become even more serious if such services were to become widely available via iDTV, given the intrinsic credibility and trust with which television as a medium has traditionally been endowed by the public.

Other problematic issues relating to online therapy include legal and ethical considerations in the event of such remote crossing national boundaries where different regulations may apply concerning relationships between health professionals and their patients, the confidentiality of patient information during online consultations, and risks of commercial exploitation of patient information collated online which again would pose concerns linked to patient privacy and the confidentiality of personal medical records (Rabasca, 2000b).

Another area of concern over which there may be far less quality control is chat rooms and bulletin boards. These online activities comprise exchanges that typically occur between lay persons rather than professionals. As such, the information is often based on personal experience. This may have some value in relation to the provision of emotional support, but could be clinically suspect (Maugens, McComb, & Levy, 1998). Ordinary users, however, may lack the specialist knowledge to be able to judge when to take and when to reject such online health advice. This may be true even when using sites sourced by qualified and accredited health professionals, especially where technical language is used (Sacchetti et al., 1999).

The Personal Touch

In matters of therapeutic need, patients may seek emotional support as well as factual diagnosis. Can electronic communications systems provide for all these need requirements? Certainly, there is evidence that people can establish interpersonal relations with computers and may treat machines with which they interact as they would humans (Reeves & Nass, 1996), but in a health diagnostic context there are occasions when a stronger social presence is needed than computer-mediated communications links can provide. Engaging with automated computer programs may suffice for certain categories of general health information enquiry, but when the information need is of a more specific, personal nature a link with another person who is qualified to answer an enquiry on that basis will be expected.

In this context, it is important to establish the optimal degree of proximity between patient and health professional that is needed to achieve accurate diagnosis and effective treatment. Certain types of support may indeed be possible through digital health links, but can these be most effectively supplied (from a cost perspective and patient health benefit perspective) through particular kinds of online formats, and if so, which ones? Or are they best administered in face-to-face meetings between patients and health professionals?

UNDERSTANDING THE DIGITAL HEALTH CONSUMER

Ultimately, there is a need to understand the digital health consumer. This means knowing about their health needs, the familiarity with new technologies, and their willingness to adopt new technologies and new versions of older established technologies to access health information, advice, and diagnosis. Who are the users of an online health service? Health consumers can be defined and differentiated in terms of their demographic characteristics (e.g., age, gender, education, socioeconomic class, ethnicity). Demographics may be important in relation to technology adoption and use of different types of content. Hence, although one technology may fail to reach certain demographic groups, a different technology may plug the gaps.

Demographics may be significant determining factors of markets for specific kinds of content. Age and gender, especially, are associated with distinct content interests. It would be unwise, however, for online health service providers to stereotype health consumers. Although one might expect women within a certain age range to display the greatest interest in online content concerning pregnancy and maternity issues, such content may attract the attention and interest of male viewers too (see chap. 6, this volume).

Demographic characteristics of users may also be linked to usability issues. Age is correlated with cognitive abilities that may be important in relation to using online service interfaces. In addition to demographic factors, however, it is important to understand the psychology of online health service consumers. Demographics, however, are descriptive variables that can identify where among consumer populations, specific interests or problems lie. They do not explain why consumer interests vary or some consumers experience greater difficulty than others with online systems. Changes in perceptual, cognitive, and motor abilities can have a bearing on the ease with which new technology adopters can use online services (Mead, Lamson, & Rogers, 2002).

It is true that older adults generally report less technology experience than do younger adults. However, they nonetheless frequently voice a willingness to use new technologies and online services (Czaja, 1996). The offer of training in new technology use can further enhance the willingness of older people to go online (Rogers, Fisk, Mead, Walker, & Cabrara, 1996). Although the motivation to learn is important, age-related deterioration in perceptual and cognitive information processing abilities have significant interface design implications. Older users learn computerized tasks more slowly than younger users (Rogers et al., 1996). Declining visual and auditory functions mean that specific features in online interfaces may need to be adjusted to cater for this deterioration. Younger users can cope more readily than older users with dynamic, fast-changing modes of presentation, complex interface designs with many pop-up menus and drop lists, visual clutter, noisy backgrounds and smaller text font sizes (Echt, 2002).

It is crucial to understand the importance of consumers' information needs and service satisfaction. The degree of trust placed in online services compared with health professionals seen face-to-face represents another factor that will determine the uptake and frequency of use of such services. Beyond demographics, health information consumers vary in their dependence upon their doctors and willingness to use online information and advice services as a substitute. It may be important to know about an individual's personal health needs and health condition profiles in addition to their demographics to pinpoint those consumers for whom online health information and advice services will be used instead of visiting a health professional (Nicholas et al., 2003a).

The early signs are that information and communication technologies will be used by large numbers of people to access health information and advice. As more online health services are rolled out, however, their longer term benefits for consumers and for public health services will require a more detailed understanding of the effectiveness of specific online applications in relation to a comprehensive typology of consumer enquiries.

References

Acheson, T. (1998). *Independent inquiry into inequalities in health*. London: Her Majesty's Stationery Office.

Action Multimedia (2003). *Case studies—NHS direct*. Retrieved February 15, 2003, from www.actionmultimedia.com

Adelhard, K., & Obst, O. (1999). Evaluation of medical Internet sites. *Methods of Information in Medicine, 39,* 75–79.

Alberta Alcohol Drug Abuse Commission (1999). Counselling on the Internet. *Developments (Alberta Alcohol and Drug Abuse Commission), 10,* 3.

Allen, A. (1998/1999). Telemedicine—a global perspective. *European Telemedicine, 2,* 13–15.

Allen, J. C., & Dillman, D. A. (1994). *Against all odds: Rural community in the information age*. Boulder, CO: Westview Press.

Allen, A., Doolittle, G., & Boysen, C. D. (1999). An analysis of the suitability of home health visits for telemedicine. *Journal of Telemedicine and Telecare, 5*(2), 90–96.

Alonzo, A. A., & Reynolds, N. R. (1998). The structure of emotions during acute myocardial infarction: A model of coping. *Social Science and Medicine, 46,* 1099–1110.

American Psychological Association, Board of Professional Affairs (1996). *Task force report: Task force on on-line psychotherapy and counseling*. Washington, DC: Author.

Appleby, C. (1999). Net gain or net loss? Health care consumers become Internet savvy. *Trustee, 52*(2), 20–23.

Archer, J. L. (1980). Self-disclosure. In D. Wegner & R. Vallacher (Eds.), *Self in Social Psychology* (pp. 183–204). London: Oxford University Press.

Arthur, A. M. (1995). Written patient information: A review of the literature. *Journal of Advanced Nursing, 21,* 1081–1086.

Aspillaga, M. (1996). Perceptual foundations in the design of visual displays. *Computers in Human Behaviour, 12*(4), 587–600.

Atkin, D., & LaRose, R. (1994). An analysis of the information services adoption literature. In J. Hanson (Ed.), *Advances in telematics* (Vol. 2, pp. 91–110). New York: Ablex.

Atri, J., Falshaw, M., Livingstone, A., & Robson, J. (1996). Fair shares in health care? Ethnic and socio-economic influences on recording of preventive care in selected inner London general practices. *British Medical Journal, 312,* 614–617.

Attwell, P. (1999). Home computers and school performance. *Information Society, 1591,* 1–10.

Bader, S. S., & Braude, R. M. (1998). 'Patients informatics': Creating new partnerships in medical decision making. *Academic Medicine, 73,* 408–411.

Baer, L., Cukor, P., Jenike, M., Leahy, L., O'Loughlen, J., & Coyle, J. T. (1995). Pilot studies of telemedicine for patients with obsessive-compulsive disorder. *American Journal of Psychiatry, 152,* 1383–1385.

Baer, W. (1995). Telecommunications Infrastructure Competition: The costs of delay. *Telecommunications Policy, 19,* 351–363.

Bagozzi, R. P., Davis, F. D., & Warshaw, P. R. (1992). Development and test of a theory of technological learning and usage. *Human Relations, 45*(7), 659–686.

Baker, L., Wagner, T. H., Singer, S., Bundorf, M., & Jama, M. K. (2003). Use of the Internet and e-mail for health care information: Results from a national survey. *Journal of the American Medical Association, 289,* 18, 2400.

Baldwin, J. R., & Hunt, S. K. (2002). Information seeking behaviour in intercultural and intergroup communication. *Human Communication Research, 28*(2), 272–286.

Bailey, B. P., Gurak, L. J., & Konstan, J. A. (2003). Trust in cyberspace. In J. Ratner (Ed.), *Human Factors and Web Development* (2nd ed., pp. 311–321), Mahwah, NJ: Lawrence Erlbaum Associates.

Ball, C. J., Scott, N., McLaren, P. M., & Watson, J. P. (1993). Preliminary evaluation of a low-cost videoconferencing system for remote cognitive testing of adult psychiatric patients. *British Journal of Clinical Psychology, 32,* 303–307.

Bandura, A. (1986). *Social foundations of thought and action.* Englewood Cliffs, NJ: Prentice-Hall.

Barak, A. (1999). Psychological applications on the Internet: A discipline on the threshold of a new millennium. *Applied and Preventive Psychology, 18,* 231–246.

Bashur, R. (1997). Critical issues in telemedicine. *Telemedicine Journal, 3,* 113–126.

BBC Online (2002, February 20). Waiting lists top public concern. Retrieved February 24, 2002, from http://www.news.bbc.co.uk?1/hi/health/1829708.stm

Beiseeker, A. E. (1990). Patient power in doctor-patient communication: What do we know? *Health Communication, 2,* 105–122.

Bekkers, V., Koops, B-J., & Nouwt, S. (1996). *Emerging electronic pathways: New challenges for politics and law.* London: Kluwer Law International.

Bellamy, C., & Taylor, J. A. (1998). *Governing in the Information age.* Buckingham, UK: Open University Press.

Bellon, E., Van Cleynenbreugel, J., Delaere, D., et al. (1995). Experimental teleradiology and remote cooperation to improve image-based medical decision-making. *Journal of Telemedicine and Telecare, 1,* 100–110.

Beresford, B. (1999). *The information needs of chronically old or physically disabled children and adolescents.* York, UK: York University Social Policy Research Unit.

Berthold, H. (Ed.). (1997). *Users needs and priorities. Project Deliverable for ACTION, DE 3001.* Unpublished report, European Commission DG XIII telematics application programme, disabled and elderly sector.

Beyene, Y. (1992). Medical disclosure and refugees: Telling bad news to Ethiopian patients. *Eastern Journal of Medicine, 157,* 328–332.

Biner, P. M., Dean, R. S., & Mellinger, A. E. (1994). Factors underlying distance learner satisfaction with televised college-level courses. *American Journal of Distance Education, 8*(1), 60–71.

Binik, Y. M., Cantor, J., Ochs, F., & Meana, M. (1997). From the couch to the keyboard: Psychotherapy in cyberspace. In S. Kiesler (Ed.), *Culture of the Internet* (pp. 71–100). Mahwah, NJ: Lawrence Erlbaum Associates.

Blackmon, L. A., Kaak, H. O., & Ranseen, J. (1997). Consumer satisfaction with telemedicine child psychiatry consultation in rural Kentucky. *Psychiatric Services, 48,* 1464–1466.

Blumler, J. G. (1980). Information overload: Is there a problem? In E. White (Ed.), *Human aspects of telecommunication.* New York: Springer-Verlag.

Bogardus, S. T., Jr., Holmboe, E., & Jekel, J. F. (1999). Perils, pitfalls, and possibilities in talking about medical risk. *Journal of the American Medical Association, 281,* 1037–1041.

Borzekowski, D. L. G., & Rickert, V. (2001). Adolescent cybersurfing for health information: A new resource that crosses barriers. *Archives of Pediatrics and Adolescent Medicine, 155,* 813–817.

Boston Consulting Group (2001). Most European e-health ventures are failing because they rely on typical retail e-commerce business models. Retrieved April 4, 2002, from http://www.bcg.commediacenter/mediapressreleasesugpage36

Bosworth, K., & Gustafson, D. H. (1991). CHESS: Providing decision support for reducing health risk behaviour and improving access to health services. *Interfaces, 21,* 93–104.

Boudioni, M. (2003). Availability and use of information touch-screen kiosks (to facilitate social inclusion). *Aslib Proceedings, 55,* (5/6), 320–333.

Bower, H. (1996). Internet sees growth of unverified health claims. *British Medical Journal, 313,* 381.

Bowseley, S. (1999, December 16). *Web life: Health,* p. 5.

Braithwaite, D. O., Waldron, V. R., & Finn, J. (1999). Communication of social support in computer-mediated groups for persons with disabilities. *Health Communication, 11,* 123–151.

Branger, P. J., & Duisterhout, J. S. (1995). Communication on health care. *Methods of Information in Medicine, 34,* 244–252.

Brashers, D. E. (2001). Communication and uncertainty management. *Journal of Communication, 51,* 477–497.

Brashers, D. E., Neidig, J. L., Haas, S. M., Dobbs, L. K., Cardillo, L. W., & Russell, J. A. (2000). Communication in the management of uncertainty: The case of persons living with HIV or AIDS. *Communication Monographs, 67,* 63–84.

Bray, J., Lovelock, R., & Philp, I. L. (1995). Using a softer approach: Techniques for interviewing older people. *Professional Nurse, 4,* 350–353.

Brennan, P. F. (1996). The future of clinical communication in an electronic environment. *Holistic Nursing Practice, 11,* 97–104.

Brennan, L. K., Kreuter, M. W., Caburnay, C. A., & Wilshire, B. L. (1998, March). *Linking smokers to smoking cessation programs: Does perceived importance of specific program characteristics predict cessation?* Paper presented at the 1962 Society of Behavioral Medicine annual meeting, New Orleans, LA.

Brennan, P. F., & Fink, S. V. (1997). Health promotion social support and computer networks. In R. L. Street, Jr., W. R. Gold, & T. Manning (Eds.), *Applications and future directions* (pp. 151–169). Mahwah, NJ: Lawrence Erlbaum Associates.

Brennan, P. F., Moore, S. M., & Smythe, K. A. (1995). The effects of a special computer network on care givers of persons with Alzheimer's disease. *Nursing Research, 44,* 166–172.

Brennan, P. F., & Ripich, S. (1996). Use of a home-care computer network by persons with AIDS. *International Journal of Technology Assessment in Health Care, 10,* 258–272.

Brown, J., & Smith, D. (2003). A website a day keeps the doctor away: Will the Internet bring a new doctor-patient paradigm? Paper presented at ESOMAR: Global Healthcare 3 Conference. Produced by CitigateDVL, London, UK. Retrieved July 22, 2003, from: www.citigatedvl.co.uk

Brown, J., & Williams, D. (2003). A Web site a day keeps the doctor away: Will the Internet bring a new doctor-patient paradigm? Paper presented to ESOMAR Global Health Care 3 Conference, Citigate DVL Smith, London. Available at: www.citigatedvl.co.uk

Brown, R., Pain, K., Berwald, C., Hirschi, P., Delahanty, R., & Miller, H. (1999). Distance education and caregiver support groups: Comparison of traditional and telephone groups. *Journal of Head Trauma Rehabilitation, 163,* 257–268.

Brownsell, S. J. (2000). Pre-assistive technologies: An enhancement to the present health, care and support mechanisms. Unpublished doctoral dissertation, University of Abertay, Dundee, UK.

Brug, J., Campbell, M., & van Assema, P. (1999). The application and impact of computer-generated personalized nutrition education: A review of the literature. *Patient Education and Counseling, 36,* 145–156.

Brug, J., Steenhaus, I., van Assema, P., & de Vries, H. (1996). The impact of computer-tailored nutrition information. *Preventive Medicine, 25,* 236–262.

Budman, S. H. (2000). Behavioural health care dot-com and beyond: Computer-mediated communications in mental health and substance abuse treatment. *American Psychologist, 55,* 1290–1300.

Brenk, D. (2002). Telemedicine is effective in reaching rural elderly. *Family Practice News, 30,* 1, 32–35.

Bull, F. C., Kreuter, M. W., & Scharff, D. P. (1999). Effects of tailored, personalised, and general materials on physical activity. *Patient Education and Counseling, 36,* 181–192.

Bull, S. S., McFarlane, M., & King, D. (2001). Barriers to STD/HIV prevention on the Internet. *Health Education Research, 16*(6), 661–670.

Buntic, R. F., Siko, P. P., Buncke, G. M., Ruebeck, D., Kind, G. M., & Buncke, H. J. (1997). Using the Internet for rapid exchange of photographs and X-ray images to evaluate potential extremity replantation candidates. *Journal of Trauma, 43,* 342–344.

Burleson, B. R., & Goldsmith, D. J. (1998). How the comforting process works: Emotional distress through conversationally induced reappraisals. In P. A. Andersen & L. K. Guerrero (Eds.), *Handbook of Communication and emotion: Research, theory, applications, and contexts* (pp. 246–281). San Diego, CA: Academic Press.

Burrows, R., Nettleton, S., Pleare, N., Loader, B., & Munce, S. (2000). Virtual community care? Social policy and the convergence of computer mediated social support. *Information, Communication and Society, 3,* 45–121.

Buxton, J., White, M., & Osoba, D. (1999). Patients' experiences using a computerised program with a touch-sensitive video monitor for the assessment of health-related quality of life. *Quality of Life Research, 7*(6), 513–519.

Byers, D. L., Hilgenberg, C., & Rhodes, D. M. (1996). Evaluation of interactive television continuing education programs for health care professionals. *Journal of Educational Technology Systems, 24*(3), 259–270.

Byers, D. L., Hilgenberg, C., & Rhodes, D. M. (1999). Telemedicine for patient education. *American Journal of Distance Education, 13*(3), 52–61.

Callahan, E., Hilty, D., & Nesbitt, T. (1998). Patients satisfaction with telemedicine consultation in primary care: Comparison of ratings of medical and mental health applications. *Telemedicine Journal, 4,* 363–369.

Campbell, A. K., & Birkhead, G. S. (1976). Municipal reform revisited: The 1970s compared with the 1920s. In A. K. Campbell & R. W. Bahl (Eds.), *State and local government: The political economy of reform*. New York: Free Press.

CareDirect (2001). Retrieved October 1, 2001, from http://www.caredirect.gov.uk

Carrigan, T. (2001, May). Positive interaction. *eBusiness, 1,* p. 50.

Carter, R. F., & Greenberg, B. S. (1965). Newspapers or television: Which do you believe? *Journalism Quarterly, 42,* 28–34.

Cawson, A., Haddon, L., & Miles, I. (1995). *The shape of things to consume*. Aldershot, UK: Avebury.

Champkin, J., & Hughes, J. (1999, October 7). Online neurotics take problems to the e-shrink. *The Independent on Sunday*, p.5.

Charnock, D., & Shepperd, S. (1997). *The DISCERN instrument*. Retrieved April 26, 2001, from www.discern.org.uk

Charnock, D., Shepperd, S., Gann, B., & Needham, G. (1999). DISCERN—an instrument for judging the quality of consumer health information on treatment choices. *Journal of Epidemiology and Community Health, 53,* 105–111.

Chen, W., Turner, J., & Crawford, C. (1996). The process of elimination: Video compression in telemedicine. *Telemedicine Journal, 2*(1), 37–41.

Chisholm, J., Carey, J., & Hernandez, A. (1999). Access and utilisation of computer technology by minority university students. SITE 99: Society for Information Technology and Teacher Education.

Clark, B., Knupfer, N., Mahoney, J., Kramer, K. Ghazali, H., & Al-Ari, N. (1997). Creating web pages: Is anyone considering visual literacy? In R. E. Griffin, J. M. Hunter, C. B. Schiffman, & W. J. Gibbs (Eds.), *VisionQuest: Journeys toward visual literacy* (pp. 355–362). (ERIC Document Reproduction Service No. ED 408 940)

Clarke, P. H. (1997). A referrer and patient evaluation of a telepsychiatry consultation-liaison service in South Australia. *Journal of Telemedicine and Telecare, 3*(1), 12–14.

Cline, R. J. W. (1999). Communication in social support groups. In L. Frey, D. Gouran, & S. Poole (Eds.), *Handbook of small group communication* (pp. 516–538). Thousand Oaks, CA: Sage.

Cline, R. J. W., & Haynes, R. M. (2001). Consumer health information seeking on the Internet: The state of the art. *Health Education Research, 16,* 671–692.

Coieru, E. (1998). Information epidemics, economics and community on the Internet: We still know so little about the effects of information on public health. *British Medical Journal, 317,* 1469–1470.

Coile, R. C., Jr., & Howe, R. C. (1999). The Internet: Changing the way consumers receive health care. *Russ Coiles Health Trends, 11*(9), 9–12.

Coleman, S. (2000). The new media and democratic politics. *New Media & Society, 1*(1), 67–74.

Coleman, S., Griffiths, B., & Simmons, E. (2002). *Digital jury—the final verdict*. London: Broadcasting Standards Commission and Hansard Society.

Collinge, A., Gray, S., & Hall, N. (2003). *The pension service's interactive digital television project: A qualitative evaluation*. Research study conducted for Department for Work and Pensions. London: Her Majesty's Stationery Office.

Collins, M. (1986). The perception of bias in television news. In *BBC Broadcasting Research Findings, 10*, London: BBC Data Publications, pp. 100–115.

Collins-Jarvis, L. (1992, May 24–28). *Gender representation in an electronic city hall*. Paper presented at the International Communication Association meeting, Miami, FL.

Comptroller and Auditor General (2002). *NHS Direct in England*. London: Her Majesty's Stationery Office.

Coulter, A., Entwistle, V., & Gilbert, D. (1999a). *Informing patients: An assessment of the quality of patient information materials*. London: The King's Fund.

Coulter, A., Entwistle, V., & Gilbert, D. (1999b). Sharing decisions with patients: Is the information good enough? *British Medical Journal, 318,* 318–322.

Crispell, D. (1994, February). Computers at home. *American Demographics*, p. 59.

Cross, D. (1989, February 28). Salmonella in eggs scare. *The Times*, p. 3.

Curry, S. J., Warner, E. H., & Grothaus, L. C. (1990). Intrinsic and extrinsic motivation for smoking cessation. *Journal of Consulting and Clinical Psychology, 58,* 310–316.

Cutrona, C., & Russell, D. (1990). Type of social support and specific stress: Toward a theory of optimal matching. In B. Sarason & G. Pierce (Eds.), *Social support: An international view* (pp. 319–366). New York: Wiley.

Cyber Dialogue (2000). *Cyber Dialogue Releases Cybercitizen Health 2000*. Retrieved April 24, 2000, from www.cyberdialogue.com/news/release/2000/08-22-cch-launch.html

Cyberatlas.com (2000). *The mess known as online healthcare*. Darien, CT: internet.com Corp. Retrieved October 24, 2000, from http://cyberatlas.internet.com/markets/professional/article/0,1323,5971_379231,00html

Czaja, S. J. (1996). Aging and the acquisition of computer skills. In W. A. Rogers, A. D. Fisk, & N. Walker (Eds.), *Aging and Skilled performance* (pp. 201–220). Mahwah, NJ: Lawrence Erlbaum Associates.

Czaja, S. J., & Lee, C. C. (2003). Designing computer systems for older adults. In J. Jacko & A. Sears (Eds.), *The Human–computer interaction handbook* (pp. 413–428). Mahwah, NJ: Lawrence Erlbaum Associates.

Daft, R. L., & Lengel, R. H. (1984). Information richness: A new approach to managerial behaviour and organisation design. In B. M. Staw & L. L. Cummings (Eds.), *Research in Organizational Behavior* (pp. 191–233). Greenwich, CT: JAI Press.

Dakins, D. R. (1997, May 2). Universities and transdisciplinary: The role of universities in modern society. In *Le congres de Locarno, Annexes au document de synthese*. Paris: Centre International de Recherches et Etudes Transdisciplines. Retrieved January 5, 2000, from http://perso.club-internet.fr/nicol/ciret/rechnom/rech.htm

Dakof, G. A., & Taylor, S. E. (1990). Victims' perceptions of social support: What is helpful from whom? *Journal of Personality and Social Psychology, 58,* 80–89.

Davies, J., McCrae, B. P., Frank, I., Dochnahl, A., Pickering, T., Harrison, B., Zakrzewski, M., & Wilson, K. (2000). Identifying male college students' perceived health needs, barriers to seeking help and recommendations to help men adopt healthier lifestyles. *Journal of American College Health, 48*(6), 259–267.

Davison, K. P., & Pennebaker, J. W. (1997). Virtual narratives; Illness representations in online support groups. In K. J. Petrie & J. Weinman (Eds.), *Perceptions of health and illness: Current research and applications* (pp. 463–486), London: Harwood Academic Press.

Davison, K. P., Pennebaker, J. W., & Dickerson, S. S. (2000). Who talks? The social psychology of illness support groups. *American Psychologist, 55,* 205–217.

Delamothe, T. (2000). Quality of websites: Kitemarking the west wind. *British Medical Journal, 321,* 843–844.

Delamothe, T. (2002). Three new initiatives involving BMJ.com. *British Medical Journal, 324,* 559–560.

Della Mea, V. (1999). Internet electronic mail: A tool for low-cost telemedicine. *Journal of Telemedicine and Telecare, 5,* 84–89.

Department of Health (1992). *Long-term care for elderly people: Purchasing, providing and quality.* London, UK: HMSO.
Department of Health (1997). *The new NHS: Modern, dependable.* London: HMSO.
Department of Health (2000a). *Raising standards for patients: New partnerships in out-of-hours care.* London: Her Majesty's Stationery Office.
Department of Health (2000b). *The NHS plan.* Cm 4818-1, London: HMSO.
Department of Health (2001a, January). *Building the information core—implementing the NHS plan.* London: Author.
Department of Health (2001b, May). *National service framework for older people.* Wetherby, UK: Author.
Department of Health (2002). *Information strategy for older people in England.* London: Author.
Department of Health (2003). *health information to be available through TV sets.* Press release. Retrieved December 20, 2003, from www.info.doh.gov.uk
Dervin, B., Harpring, J., & Foreman-Wernet, L. (1999). In moments of concern; A sense-making study of pregnant, drug-addicted women and their information needs. *The Electronic Journal of Communication, 9*(2–4). Private access URL available from Jayne Harpring at partners@nettally.com
Des Jarlais, D. C., Paone, D., Milliken, J., Turner, C. F., Miller, H., Gribble, J., Shi, Q., Hagan, H., & Friedman, S. R. (1999). Audio-computer interviewing to measure risk behaviour for HIV among injecting drug users: A quasi-randomised trial. *Lancet, 353,* 1657–1661.
De Vries, H., & Brug, J. (1999). Computer-tailored interventions motivating people to adopt health promoting behaviours: Introduction to a new approach. *Patient Medicine, 28,* 203–211.
Dickerson, M. D., & Gentry, J. W. (1983). Characteristics of adopters and non-adopters of home computers. *Journal of Consumer Research, 10,* 225–235.
Dickerson, S. S., Flaig, D. M., & Kennedy, M. C. (2000). Therapeutic connection: Help seeking on the Internet for persons with implantable cardioverter defibrillators. *Heart and Lung, 29,* 248–255.
Diehl, M., & Stroebe, W. (1987). Productivity loss in brainstorming groups: Towards the solution of a riddle. *Journal of Personality and Social Psychology, 53,* 497–509.
Doctor, S., & Dutton, W. H. (1998). The First Amendment on-line: Santa Monica's public electronic network. In R. Tsagarousianou, D. Tambini, & C. Bryan (Eds.), *Cyberdemocracy: Technology, cities, and civic networks* (pp. 125–151). London: Routledge.
Douglas, F., Jones, R., & Navin, L. (1995). Schoolchildren's use of, and ideas for, a computer-based health information system. In B. Richards (Ed.), *Healthcare Computing 1995: Conference Proceedings* (pp. 139–144). Weybridge, UK: BJHC Books.
Duffy, M., Wimbush, E., Reece, J., & Eadie, D. (2003). Net profits? Web site development and health improvement. *Health Education, 103*(5), 278–285.
Dutton, W. H. (1993). Electronic service delivery and the inner city: The risk of benign neglect. In Berleur, J., Beardon, C., & Laufer, R. (Eds.), *Facing the challenge of risk and vulnerability in an information society* (pp. 209–228). Amsterdam: North-Holland.
Dutton, W. H. (1996). Network rules of order: Regulating speech in public electronic fora. *Media, Culture and Society, 18*(2), 269–290.
Dutton, W. H. (1999). *Society on the line: Information politics in the digital age.* Oxford, UK: Oxford University Press.

Dutton, W., Rogers, E., & Jun, U. H. (1987). Diffusion and social impacts of personal computers. *Communication Research, 14,* 219–250.

Dutton, W. H., Taylor, J., Bellamy, C., & Peltu, M. (1994). *Electronic service delivery: Themes and issues in the public sector.* (PICT Policy Research paper No. 28) Uxbridge, UK, Brunel University.

Dyer, R., Green, R., Pitts, M., & Millward, G. (1995). What's the flaming problem? CMC—deindividuating or disinhibiting? In M. A. R. Kirby, A. J. Dix, & J. E. Finley (Eds.), *People and computers.* Cambridge, UK: Cambridge University Press.

Echt, K. V. (2002). Designing web-based health information for older adults: Visual considerations and design directives. In R. Morrell (Ed.), *Older adults, health information, and the World Wide Web* (pp. 61–87). Mahwah, NJ: Lawrence Erlbaum Associates.

Echt, K. V., & Pollack, R. H. (1998, April). *The effect of illumination, contrast, and age on text comprehension performance.* Poster session presented at the Cognitive Aging Conference, Atlanta, GA.

Edmonds, G. (2003). *The good Web site guide 2003.* London: Orion.

e-Health Ethics Initiative (2000). E-Health code of ethics. *Journal of Medical Internet Research, 9.* Retrieved November 1, 2001, from http://www.jmir.org/2002/2/e9/

Emery, D. (2001). Telecare in practice: A telecare initiative focusing on carers of older people based on ACTION. *Health Informatics Journal, 7*(1), 41–48.

Emery, D., Heyes, B. J., & Cowan, A. M. (2002). Telecare delivery of health and social care information. *Health Informatics Journal, 8,* 29–33.

Emery, D., Cowan, A., Eaglestone, B., Heyes, B., Proctor, P., & Willis, T. (2002, June). *Care plus.* Final Report to National Health Service, Sheffield, UK, University of Sheffield.

Eng, T. R., & Gustafson, D. H. (Eds.). (1999). *Wired for health and well-being: The emergence of interactive health communication.* Science panel on Interactive Communication and Health, US Department of Health and Human Services, Office of Disease Prevention and Health Promotion, Washington, DC.

Eng, T. R., Maxfield, A., Patrick, K., Deering, M. J., Ratzan, S. L., & Gustafson, D. H. (1998). Access to health information and support: A public highway or a private road? *Journal of the American Medical Association, 280,* 1371–1375.

Ettema, J. S. (1984). Three phases in the creation of information inequities: An empirical assessment of a prototype videotext system. *Journal of Broadcasting, 28,* 383–395.

Eurobarometer (2000). *Measuring information society 2000.* Brussels, INRA for the European Commission.

Eysenbach, G., & Diepgen, T. L. (1998). Towards quality management of medical information on the Internet: Evaluation, labelling and filtering of information. *British Medical Journal, 317,* 1496–1502.

Eysenbach, G., & Diepgen, T. (1999). Shopping around the Internet today and tomorrow: Towards the millennium of cybermedicine. *British Medical Journal, 319,* 1294.

Eysenbach, G., Sen, E. A., & Diepgen, T. L.(1999). Shopping around the Internet today and tomorrow: Toward the millennium of cybermedicine. *British Medicine Journal, 319,* 1294.

Ferguson, T. (1996). *Health online.* Reading, MA: Addison-Wesley.

Ferguson, T. (1997). Health care in cyberspace: Patients lead a revolution. *Futurist, 31*(6), 29–34.

Ferguson, T. (2000). Online patient-helpers and physicians working together: A new partnership for high quality healthcare. *British Medical Journal, 324,* 1129–1132.

Ferguson, T. (2002). From patients to end users. *British Medical Journal, 324,* 555–556.

Ferriter, M. (1993). Computer-aided interviewing and the psychiatric social history. *Social Work and Social Sciences Review, 4,* 255–263.

Field, M. J. (Ed.). (1996). *Telemedicine: A guide to assessing telecommunications in health care.* Washington, DC: National Academy Press.

Finn, J. (1999). An exploration of helping processes in an online self-help group focusing on issues of disability. *Health and Social Work, 2493,* 220–231.

Fishman, C. (1997, August). Inside to 1-800 factory. *Los Angeles Times Magazine, 3,* 14–29.

Fishman, D. J. (1997). Telemedicine: Bringing the specialist to the patient. *Nursing Management, 28*(7), 30–32.

Flanagin, A. J., & Metzger, M. J. (2000). Perceptions of Internet information credibility. *Journalism & Mass Communication Quarterly, 77*(3), 515–540.

Flavell, J. H. (1977). *Cognitive development.* Englewood Cliffs, NJ: Prentice-Hall.

Fleming, P. J. (1990). Software and sympathy: Therapeutic interaction with the computer. In G. Gumpert & S. L. Fish (Eds.), *Talking to strangers: Mediated therapeutic communication* (pp. 176–183). Norwood, NJ: Ablex.

Foulger, D. A. (1990, June). *Medium as process.* Unpublished dissertation, Philadelphia, PA, Temple University.

Fox, S., & Rainie, L. (2000). *The online health care revolution: How the Web helps Americans take better care of themselves.* Washington, DC: The Pew Internet & American Life Project. Retrieved September 3, 2002, from http://www.pewinternet.org

Foxall, G. R., & Bahte, S. (1991). Psychology of computer use: XIX. Extent of computer use; relationship with adaptive-innovative cognitive style and personal involvement in computing. *Perceptual and Motor Skills, 72,* 195–202.

Fredriksen, P. R., Pettersen, S., & Pedersen, S. (1997). Store and forward multimedia in primary health-care. In T. N. Arvanitis & D. Watson (Eds.), *Cognitive science research papers* (p. 58). Brighton, UK: University of Sussex.

French, K. S., & Larrabee, J. H. (1999). Relationships among educational material readability, client literacy, perceived beneficence, and perceived quality. *Journal of Nursing Care Quality, 13*(6), 68–82.

Friedman, C., & Wyatt, J. (1997). *Evaluation methods in medical information,* New York: Springer-Verlag.

Fuchs, R. (1996). Causal models of physical exercise participation: Testing the predictive power of the construct "pressure to change." *Journal of Applied Social Psychology, 26,* 1931–1960.

Gagliardi, A., & Jadad, A. R. (2002). Examination of instruments used to rate quality of health information on the Internet: Chronicle of a voyage with an unclear destination. *British Medical Journal, 324,* 569–573.

Gale Group (2003, March 26). Most people do also seek health information online. *Mental Health Weekly, 13,* 127.

Gann, R. (1998). Empowering the patient and public through information technology. In J. Lenaghan (Ed.), *Rethinking IT and health* (pp. 000–000). London: Institute for Public Policy Research.

Gann, R., & Sadler, M. (2001, February 2). Letter: Quality of information on NHS Direct Online. *British Medical Journal, 322,* 175.

Garramone, G. M., Harris, A. C., & Anderson, R. (1986). Use of political computer bulletin boards. *Journal of Broadcasting & Electronic Media, 30*(3), 325–339.

Garvin, B. J., Huston, G. P., & Baker , C. F. (1992). Information used by nurses to prepare patients for a stressful event. *Applied Nursing Research, 5,* 158–163.

Gask, L. (1998). Small group interactive techniques utilizing video feedback. *International Journal of Psychiatry in Medicine, 28,* 97–113.

Gates, B. (1995). *The road ahead.* London: Viking.

Geist, P., & Hardesty, M. (1990). Reliable, silent, hysterical, or assured: Physicians assess patient cues in their medical decision-making. *Health Communication, 2,* 69–90.

George, S. (2002). NHS Direct audited: Customer satisfaction, but at what price? *British Medical Journal, 324,* 558–559.

Gleason, N. A. (1995). A new approach to disordered eating—using an electronic bulletin board to confront social pressure on body image. *Journal of American College Health, 44,* 78–80.

Goddard, J., & Cornford, J. (1994, May–June). Superhighway Britain: Eliminating the divide between the haves and have-nots. *Parliamentary Brief,* 48–50.

GoDigital (2003, April). *Key findings.* London: GoDigital.

Goldsmith, D. J. (2000). Soliciting advice: The role of sequential placement in mitigating face threat. *Communication Monographs, 67,* 1–19.

Goldsmith, D. J. (2001). A normative approach to the study of uncertainty and communication. *Journal of Communication, 51,* 514–533.

Goodwin, R., & Plaza, S. H. (2000). Perceived and received social support in two cultures: Collectivism and support among British and Spanish students. *Journal of Social & Personal Relationships, 17,* 282–291.

Graber, M., Roller, C., & Kaeble, B. (1999). Readability levels of patient education material on the World Wide Web. *Journal of Family Practice, 48*(1), 58–61.

Graham, W., Smith, P., Karnal, A., Fitzmaurice, A., Smith, N., & Hamilton, N. (2000). Randomised controlled trial comparing effectiveness of touch-screen system and leaflet for providing women with information on prenatal tests. *British Medical Journal, 320,* 155–160.

Grandinetti, D. A. (2000, April). Doctors and the Web: Help your patients surf the Web safely. *Medical Economics,* 28–36.

Greef, P., & de Ijsselsteijn, W. A. (2001). Social presence in a home tele-application. *CyberPsychology and Behaviour, 492,* 307–315.

Greener, M. (2002, September). Screen test. *Community Pharmacy,* pp. 38–39.

Greenfield, S., Kaplan, S., & Ware, J. E. (1985). Expanding patient involvement in care: Effects on patient outcomes. *Annals of Internal Medicine, 102*(4), 520–528.

Gregory-Head, B. (1999). Patients and the Internet: Guidance for evidence-based chores. *Journal of the American College of Dentists, 66*(2), 46–50.

Greist, J. H., & Klein, M. H. (1980). Computer programs for patients, clinicians and researchers in psychiatry. In J. D. Didowsky, J. H. Johnson, T. A. Williams (Eds.), *Technology in Mental Health Care Delivery Systems* (pp. 161–182). Norwood, NJ: Ablex.

Greist, J. H., Klein, M. H., & van Cura, L. J. (1973). A computer interview by psychiatric patient target symptoms. *Archives of General Psychiatry, 29,* 247–253.

Griffin, C., Eves, F., & Cheng, K. K. (2000, December 20). Issues in promoting exercise using the World Wide Web. Paper presented to the British Psychological Society London Conference, Institute of Education.

Griffiths, K. M., & Christensen, H. (2000). Quality of web based information on treatment of depression: cross sectional survey. *British Medical Journal, 321,* 1511–1515.

Griffiths, M. (2001). Online therapy: A cause for concern? *The Psychologist, 14*(5), 244–248.

Grohol, J. M. (1998). Future clinical directions: Professional development, pathology, and psychotherapy on-line. In J. Gackenbach (Ed.), *Psychology and the Internet: Intra-*

personal, interpersonal and transpersonal implications (pp. 111–140). San Diego, CA: Academic Press.

Gronmark, S. (2001). The future of interactive TV. *UsableiTV, 1,* 20–23.

Grossman, L. K. (1995). *The electronic republic: Reshaping democracy in the information age.* New York: Viking.

Grossman, L. K. (1999). An outbreak of Internet problems. *Columbia Journalism Review, 38*(3), 15–16.

Gunter, B. (1987). *Poor reception: Misunderstanding and forgetting broadcast news.* Hillsdale, NJ: Lawrence Erlbaum Associates.

Gunter, B. (2003a). *News and the Net.* Mahwah, NJ: Lawrence Erlbaum Associates

Gunter, B. (2003b). Digital information provision via interactive television: Understanding the digital consumer. *Aslib Proceedings, 55*(½), 43–51.

Gunter, B., Furnham, A., & Lineton, Z. (1995). Watching people watching television. *Journal of Educational Television, 21*(3), 165–191.

Gunter, B., Sancho-Aldridge, J., & Winstone, P. (1994). *Television: The public's view—1993.* London: John Libbey.

Gunter, B., & Winstone, P. (1993). *Television: The public's view—1992.* London: John Libbey.

Gunter, B., Nicholas, D., Huntington, P., & Williams, P. (2003). Digital interactive television: Health information platforms of the future? *Aslib Proceedings, 55*(5/6), 346–356.

Gunter, B., Nicholas, D., Williams, P., & Huntington, P. (2001). Is TV good for you? *Library and Information Update, 103*(9), 528–559.

Guttman, N. (1993). Patient-practitioner information exchange as an asymmetrical social encounter: Do patients actually know what their practitioners think they know? In J. R. Schement & B. D. Ruben (Eds.), *Between communication and information* (pp.293–318). New Brunswick, NJ: Transaction.

GVU (1998). 8th WWW user study. Retrieved from http://www.cc.gatech.edu/gvu/user.surveys/survey-1998

Hale, M. L. (1997). *California cities and the World Wide Web.* Unpublished master's thesis. Los Angeles: The Graduate School, University of Southern California.

Harris Interactive (2000). *Sharp Rise in Internet users Seeing Health Information.* Retrieved November 14, 2001, from www.ada.org/prof/pubs/daily/netnews/stories/health.html

Harrison, J. (2003). e-Public services and interactive television: Re-evaluating the remit and scope of public service broadcasting (PSB) in the digital age. *Journal of Communications Law, 7*(5), 145–151.

Harrison, J., & Cooke, M. (2000). Study of early warning of accident and emergency departments by ambulance services. *Journal of Accident and Emergency Medicine, 16*(5), 339–341.

Hartley, J. (1999). What does it say? Text design, medical information, and older readers. In D. C. park, R. W. Morrell, & K. Sifren (Eds.), *Processing of medical information* (pp. 233–248). New York: Wiley.

Hawkins, R. P., Pingree, S., Gustafson, D. H., Boberg, E. W., Bricker, E., McTavish, F., et al. (1997). Aiding those facing health crises: The experience of one CHESS project. In R. L. Street, Jr., W. A. Gold, & T. Manning (Eds.), *Health promotion and interactive technology: Theoretical applications and future directions.* Mahwah, NJ: Lawrence Erlbaum Associates.

Health on the Net Foundation (2001). *Evolution of Internet use for health purposes—Feb/Mar 2001.* retrieved January 17, 2002, from www.hon.ch/survey/FebMar2001/survey.html

Heathfield, H., Pitty, D., & Hanka, R. (1998). Evaluating information technology in health care: Barriers and challenges. *British Medical Journal, 316,* 1959–1961.

Hellerstein, L. (1990). Electronic advice columns: Humanizing the machine. In G. Gumpert & S. L. Fish (Eds.), *Talking to strangers: Mediated therapeutic communication* (pp. 112–127). Norwood, NJ: Ablex.

Hernandez-Borges, A. A., Macias-Cervi, P., Gaspar-Guardado, M. A., Torres-Alvarez De Arcousa, M. L., Ruiz-Rabaza, A., & Jimenez-Sosa, A. (1999). Can examination of WWW usage statistics and other indirect quality indicators help to distinguish the relative quality of medical websites? *Journal of Medical Internet Research, 1*(1), 1.

Hiltz, S. R., & Turoff, M. (1978). *The network nation: Human communication via computer.* Reading, MA: Addison-Wesley.

Hines, S. C., Babrow, A. S., Badzek, L., & Moss, A. H. (2001). From coping with life to coping with death: Problematic integration for the seriously ill elderly. *Health Communication, 13,* 327–342.

Hirschman, E. C. (1980). Innovativeness, novelty seeking, and consumer creativity. *Journal of Consumer Research, 7*(3), 283–295.

Health on the Net Foundation [HONF] (1999). *HONF's Fourth Survey on the use of the Internet for medical and health purposes.* Retrieved April 17, 2001, from www.hon.ch/survey/

Hoot, J. L., & Hayslip, B. (1983). Microcomputers and the elderly: New directions for self sufficiency and lifelong learning. *Educational Gerontology, 9,* 5–6.

Hopkins, N. (1995, May 10–12). *Doing business with government electronically.* Paper presented at the PICT International Conference on the Social and economic Implications of Information and Communication Technologies, Queen Elizabeth II Conference Centre, Westminster.

Houston, J. D., & Fiore, D. C. (1995). Online medical surveys: Using the Internet as a research tool. *MD Computing, 15,* 116–120.

Howard, P., Rainie, L., & Jones, S. (2001). Days and nights on the Internet: The impact of a diffusing technology. *American Behavioral Scientist, 45*(3), 383–404.

Hufford, R. J., Gleuckauf, R. L., & Webb, P. M. (1999). Home-based interactive video-conferencing for adolescents with epilepsy and their families. *Rehabilitation Psychology, 44*(2), 1–18.

Hunt, R. (1999, May 8). *Living in the digital wild west.* Lecture presented at City University, London.

Huntington, P., Williams, P., & Nicholas, D. (2002a). Age and gender user differences of a touch-screen kiosk: A study of kiosk transaction log files. *Informatics in Primary Care, 10,* 3–9.

Huntington, P., Williams, P., Nicholas, D., & Gunter, B. (2002b). Characterising the health information consumer: An examination of the health information sources used by digital television users. *Libri, 52*(1), 16–27.

Huntington, P., Nicholas, D., Williams, P., & Gunter, B. (2003). An evaluation of a health video on demand search available to the public via interactive digital television. *Libri, 53*(6), 266–281.

Huntington, P., Nicholas, D., & Williams, P. (2003a). Comparing the use of two DiTV transmission services: Same service, different outcomes. *Aslib Proceedings, 55*(½), 52–63.

Huntington, P., Nicholas, D., & Williams, P. (2003b). Characterising and profiling health web user and site types: Going beyond "hits." *Aslib Proceedings, 55*(5/6), 277–289.

Hutchison, D., Eastman, C., & Tirrito, T. (1997). Designing user interfaces for older adults. *Educational Gerontology, 23,* 497–513.

Impicciatore, P., Pandolfini, C., Casella, N., & Bonati, M. (1997). Reliability of health information for the public on the world wide web: Systematic survey of advice on managing fever in children at home. *British Medical Journal, 314,* 1875–1979.

InTouch with Health (2002). *About Us.* Retrieved January 10, 2003, from www.Intouchwithhealth.co.uk

Jadad, A. R. (1999). Promoting partnerships: Challenges for the Internet age. *British Medical Journal, 319,* 761–764.

Jadad, A. R., & Gagliardi, A. (1998). Rating health information on the internet. *Journal of the American Medical Association, 279,* 611–614.

Jakobi, P. (1999). Using the World Wide Web as a teaching tool: Analysing images of aging and the visual needs of an aging society. *Educational Gerontology, 25*(6), 581–593.

James, M. L., Wotring, C. E., & Forrest, E. J. (1995). An exploratory study of the perceived benefits of electronic bulletin board use and their impact on other communication activities. *Journal of Broadcasting & Electronic Media, 39,* 30–50.

James, C., James, N., Davies, D., Harvey, P., & Tweedle, S. (1999). Preferences for different sources of information about cancer. *Patient Education and Counseling, 37*(3), 273–282.

Jeffres, L., & Atkin, D. (1996). Predicting use of technologies for consumer and communication needs. *Journal of Broadcasting & Electronic Media, 40,* 318–330.

Jerome, L. (1999). Telehealth: Clinical tool for psychology. *National Psychologist, 9*(5), 7–8.

Jerome, L. W., DeLeon, P. H., James, L. C., Folen, R., Earles, J., & Gedney, J. J. (2000). The coming age of telecommunications in psychological research and practice. *American Psychologist, 55*(4), 407–421.

Jessup, L. M., Connolly, T., & Galegher, J. (1990). The effects of anonymity on group process in automated group problem solving. *S Quarterly, 14,* 87–105.

Johnson, B. (2004, March 22). E-democracy in action. *The Guardian: New Media,* p. 38.

Johnson, J. D. (1997). *Cancer-related information seeking.* Cresskill, NJ: Hampton Press.

Johnson, M. M. S. (1990). Age differences in decision making: A process methodology for examining strategic information processing. *Journal of Gerontology: Psychological Sciences, 45*(2), 75–78.

Joinson, A. N. (1998). Causes and implications of disinhibited behaviour on the Internet. In J. Gackenbach (Ed.), *Psychology and the Internet: Intrapersonal, interpersonal and transpersonal implications* (pp. 43–60). San Diego, CA: Academic Press.

Joinson, A. N. (2000). Information seeking on the Internet: A study of soccer fans on the WWW. *CyberPsychology and Behaviour, 392,* 185–191.

Joinson, A. N. (2001). Self-disclosure in computer-mediated communication: The role of self-awareness and visual anonymity. *European Journal of Social Psychology, 31,* 177–192.

Joinson, A. N., & Banyard, P. (2003). Seeking alcohol information on the Internet. *Aslib Proceedings, 55*(5/6), 313–319.

Jones, N. (1997). Getting wired to telemedicine. *International Nursing Review, 4492,* 57–58.

Jones, R. (2003). Making health information accessible to patients. *Aslib Proceedings, 55*(5/6), 534–538.

Jones, R., McLachlan, K., & Bell, G. (1990). HEALTHPOINT: A public-access health information system. In H. Deglanville & H. Roberts (Eds.), *Current perspectives in health computing* (pp. 65–69). Weybridge, UK: BJHC Books.

Jones, R., Navin, L., & Murray, K. (1993). Use of a community based touch-screen public-access health information system. *Health Bulletin, 51,* 34–42.

Jones, R., Labajo, R., Soler Lopez, M., Sanz, J. J., Alonso, P., & Clavena, L. E. (2000). Evaluation of a Scottish touch-screen health information system in rural Spain. In J. Bryant (Ed.), *Healthcare computing 2000* (pp. 45–54). Weybridge, UK: BJHC Books.

Jones, R., Pearson, J., Cawsey, A., & Barrett, A. (1996). Information for patients with cancer: Does personalisation make a difference? Pilot study results and randomised trial in progress. *Journal of the American Medical Informatics Association Symposium Supplement,* 423–427.

Jones, R., Pearson, J., McGregor, S., Cawsey, A. J., Barrett, A., Gray, N., Atkinson, J. M., Gilmour, W. H., & McEwen, J. (1999). Randomised trial of personal computer-based information for cancer patients. *British medical Journal, 319,* 1241–1247.

Kahn, G. (1997). Digital interactive media and the health care balance of power. . In R. L. Street, Jr., W. R. Gold, & T. Manning (Eds.), *Health promotion and interactive technology: Theoretical applications and future directions* (pp. 187–208). Mahwah, NJ: Lawrence Erlbaum Associates.

Kai, J. (1996). Parents' difficulties and information needs in coping with acute illness in their pre-school children: A qualitative study. *British Medical Journal, 313,* 987–990.

Kalichman, S. C., Benotsch, E. G., Weinhardt, L., Austin, J., Luke, W., & Cherry, C. (2003). Health-related Internet use, coping, social support and health indicators in people living with HIV/AIDS: Preliminary results from a community survey. *Health Psychology, 22*(1), 111–116.

Kaufert, J. M., & Putsch, R. W. (1997). Communication through interpreters in healthcare: Ethical dilemmas arising from differences in class, culture language and power. *Journal of Clinical Ethics, 8,* 71–87.

Kaufert, J. M., Putsch, R. W., & Lavallee, M. (1999). End-of-life decision making among aboriginal Canadians: Interpretation, mediation, and discord in the communication of "bad news." *Journal of Palliative Care, 15,* 31–38.

Keighron, P. (2003, April 25). Tony's television. *Broadcast,* p.13.

Kennedy, A. J. (2002). *The rough guide to the Internet.* London: Penguin.

Kennedy, I. (2000, May 10). *Learning from Bristol: The report of the public enquiry into heart surgery at the Bristol Royal Infirmary 1984–1999.* Retrieved May 12, 2000, from http://www.bristol-inquiry.org.uk/final_report

Kessler, R. C., Mickelson, K. D., & Zhao, S. (1997). Patterns and correlates of self-help group membership in the United States. *Social Policy, 27*(3), 27–47.

Kiesler, S., & Sproull, L. (1992). Group decision making and communication technology. *Organisational Behaviour and Human Decision Processes, 52,* 96–123.

Kiesler, R. C., Siegal, J., & McGuire, T. W. (1984). Social psychological aspects of computer-mediated communication. *American Psychologist, 39,* 1123–1134.

Kiley, R. (2000). Finding health information on the Internet: Health consumers. *Hospital Medicine, 61*(11), 799–801.

Kim, P., Eng, T. R., Deering, M. J., & Maxfield, A. (1999). Published criteria for evaluating health related websites: review. *British Medical Journal, 318,* 647–649.

King, S. A. (1994). Analysis of electronic support groups for recovering addicts. *Interpersonal Computing and Technology: An Electronic Journal for the 21st Century, 2,* 47–56. Retrieved July 2, 2003 from http://www.helsinki.fi/science/optek/1994/n3/king.txt

King, S. A. (1995). *Effects of mood states on social judgments in cyberspace: Self-focused sad people as the source of flame wars.* Retrieved July 2, 2003 from www.grohol.com/storm1.htm

King, S. A., & Moreggi, D. (1998). Internet therapy and self-help groups—The pros and cons. In J. Gackenbach (Ed.), *Psychology and the Internet: Intrapersonal, interpersonal and transpersonal implications* (pp. 77–109). San Diego, CA: Academic Press.

Kings Fund (2000). *What do Londoners think of healthcare?* Retrieved November 11, 2002, from http://www.kingsfund.org.uk/eKingsFund/assets/applets/Healthcare.pdf

Kissinger, P., Rice, J., Farley, T., Trim, S., Jewitt, K., Margavio, V., & Martin, D. H. (1999). Application of computer-assisted interviews to sexual behaviour research. *American Journal of Epidemiology, 149,* 950–954.

Klein, J. Karger, S., & Sinclair, K. (2003, September). *Digital television for all: A report on usability and accessible design.* Cambridge, UK: The Generics Group and London, UK: Department of Trade and Industry.

Klein, J., Karger, S., & Sinclair, K. (2004, January). *Attitudes on digital television: Preliminary findings on consumer adoption of digital television.* Cambridge, UK: The Generics Group and London, UK: Department of Trade and Industry.

Klemm, P., & Nolan, M. T. (1998). Internet cancer support groups: Legal and ethical issues for nurse researchers. *Oncology Nursing Forum, 25,* 673–676.

Kline, D. W. (1994). Optimising the visibility of displays for older observers. *Experimental Aging Research, 20,* 11–23.

Kraut, R., Mukhopadhyuy, T. Szczypuda, J., Kiesler, S., & Scherlis, B. (1999). Information and communication: Alternative uses of the Internet in households. *Information Systems Research, 10,* 287–303.

Kreuter, M., Farrell, D., Olevitch, K., & Brennan, L. (2000). *Tailoring health messages: Customizing communication with computer technology.* Mahwah, NJ: Lawrence Erlbaum Associates.

Kreuter, M., Oswald, D. L., Bull, F. C., & Clark, E. M. (2000). Are tailored health education materials always more effective than non-tailored materials? *Health Education Research, 15,* 305–315.

Kunst, H., Groot, D., Latthe, P. M., & Khan, K. S. (2002). Accuracy of information on apparently credible websites: Survey of five common health topics. *British Medical Journal, 324,* 581–582.

Labour Party (1997). *New Labour: Because Britain deserves better.* London: Author.

Lago, C. (1996). Computer therapeutics. *Counselling, 7,* 287–289.

Lamp, J. M., & Howard, P. A. (1999). Guiding parents' use of the Internet for newborn education. *MCN, American Journal of Maternal Child Nursing, 24*(1), 33–36.

LaRose, R., & Atkin, D. (1988). Satisfaction, demographic and media environment predictors of cable subscription. *Journal of Broadcasting & Electronic Media, 32,* 403–413.

LaRose, R., & Atkin, D. (1992). Audiotext and the re-invention of the telephone as a mass medium. *Journalism Quarterly, 69,* 413–421.

LaRose, R., & Mettler, J. (1989). Who uses information technologies in rural America? *Journal of Communication, 39*(3), 48–60.

Latour, B., & Woolgar, S. (1979). *Laboratory life: The construction of scientific facts.* Princeton, NJ: Princeton University Press.

Lea, M., O'Shea, T., Fung, P., & Spears, R. (1992). "Flaming" in computer-mediated communication: Observations, explanations, implications. In M. Lea (Ed.), *Contexts of computer-mediated communication* (pp. 89–112). Hertfordshire, UK: Harvester Wheatsheaf.

Lea, M., & Spears, R. (1991). Computer-mediated communication, de-individuation, and group decision-making. *International Journal of Man-Machine Studies, 34,* 283–301.

Lea, M., & Spears, R. (1992). Paralanguage and social perception in computer-mediated communication. *Journal of Organisational Computing, 2,* 321–341.

Lea, M., & Spears, R. (1995). Love at first byte? Building personal relationships over computer networks. In J. T. Wood & S. Duck (Eds.), *Under-studied relationships: Off the beaten track* (pp. 197–233). Thousand Oaks, CA: Sage.

Leake, J. (2000, April 9). Scientists fear thousands may have CJD. *The Times,* p. 6.

Lee, R. (1975). Credibility of newspaper and TV news. *Journalism Quarterly, 55,* 282–287.

Lee, E.-J., & Nass, C. (2002). Experimental tests of normative group influence and representation effects in computer-mediated communication: When interacting via computers differs from interacting with computers. *Human Communication Research, 28*(3), 349–381.

Ley, P. (1982). Satisfaction, compliance and communication. *British Journal of Clinical Psychology, 21,* 241–254.

Leydon, G., Boulton, M., Moynihan, C., Jones, A., Mossman, J., Boudioni, M., & McPherson, K. (2000). Cancer patients' information needs and information seeking behaviour: In depth interview study. *British Medical Journal, 320,* 913.

Lieberman, D. A. (1995). *Three studies of an asthma education video game.* Report to the National Institute of Allergy and Infectious Diseases. National Institutes of Health, Bethesda, MD.

Lieberman, D. A., & Brown, S. J. (1995). Designing interactive video games for children's health education. In K. Morgan, R. M. Satava, H. B. Sieborg, R. Matthews, & J. P. Unristenger (Eds.), *Interactive technology and the new paradigm for health care* (pp. 210–210). Amsterdam: IOS Press.

Lieberman, D. A. (1997). Interactive video games for health promotion: Effects on knowledge, self-efficacy, social support, and health. In R. L. Street, Jr., W. R. Gold, & T. Manning (Eds.), *Health promotion and interactive technology: Theoretical applications and future directions* (pp. 103–120). Mahwah, NJ: Lawrence Erlbaum Associates.

Lin, C. (1994). Exploring potential factors for home videotext adoption. *Advances in telematics, 2,* 111–121.

Lin, C. (1997, August). *Exploring potential predictors of personal computer adoption.* Paper presented at the annual conference of the Association for Education in Journalism & Mass Communication, Chicago.

Lin, C. (1998). Exploring personal computer adoption dynamics. *Journal of Broadcasting & Electronic Media, 42,* 95–112.

Lincoln, T. C., & Builder, C. (1999). Global health care and the flux of technology. *International Journal of Medical Informatics, 53,* 213–224.

Lindberg, D. A. B. (2002). Older Americans, health information, and the Internet. In R. W. Morrell (Ed.), *Older adults, health information, and the World Wide Web* (pp 13–19). Mahwah, NJ: Lawrence Erlbaum Associates,

Locke, S. E., Kawaloff, H. B., Hoff, R. G., Safran, C., & Popovsky, M. A. Cotton, D. J., Finkelstein, D. M., Page, P. L. & Slack, W. V. (1992). Computer interview for screening blood donors for risk of HIV transmission. *Journal of the American Medical Association, 268,* 1301–1305.

London, J. (1999). Lay public use of healthcare Web sites. In P. Donaldson (Ed.), *Healthcare information systems.* New York: Auerbach.

Lucas, R. W., Mullins, P. J., Luria, C. B., & McInray, D. L. (1977). Psychiatrists and a computer as interrogators of patients with alcohol-related illness: A comparison. *British Journal of Psychiatry, 131,* 160–167.

Luck, D. D., & Hunter, J. M. (1997). Visual design principles applied to World Wide Web construction. In R. E. Griffin, J. M. Hunter, C. B. Schiffman, & W. J. Gibbs (Eds.), *VisionQuest: Journeys towards visual literacy* (pp. 319–324). International Visual Literacy Association. (ERIC Document Reproduction Service No. ED 408 940)

Lyons, C. M., MacBrayne, P., & Johnson, J. L. (1994). Interactive television as a vehicle for the delivery of higher education to rural areas. *Journal of Educational Technology Systems, 22*(3), 205–211.

M2Presswire (2000). UK-specific health web site aims to capture a fifth of online health market. *M2 Presswire news release* (Lexis-Nexis Universe UK news database). Available online, password access only: http://www.lexis-nexis.com/universe

Madara, E. J. (1997). The mutual-aid self help online revolution. *Social Policy, 27,* 20–26.

Madara, E. J., & White, B. J. (1997). On-line mutual support: The experience of a self-help cleaning house. *Information & Referral, 19,* 91–108.

Madden, D. J., & Allen, P. A. (1991). Adult age differences in the rate of information extraction during visual search. *Journal of Gerontology, 4693,* 124–126.

Mair, F., & Whitten, P. (2000). Systematic review of studies of patient satisfaction with telemedicine. *British Medical Journal, 320,* 1517–1520.

Manning, T. (1997). Interactive environments for promoting health. In R. L. Street, Jr., W. R. Gold, & T. Manning (Eds.), *Health promotion and interactive technology: Theoretical applications and future directions* (pp. 67–78). Mahwah, NJ: Lawrence Erlbaum Associates.

Manton, K., Corder, L., & Stallard, E. (1997). Chronic disability trends in elderly United States populations: 1892–1994. *Proceedings of the National Academy of Sciences: Medical Sciences, 94,* 2593–2598.

Marks, W., & Dulaney, C. (1998). Visual information processing and the World Wide Web. In C. Forsythe, E. Grose, & J. Ratner (Eds.), *Human factors and Web development* (pp. 25–43). Mahwah, NJ: Lawrence Erlbaum Associates.

Marwick, C. (1999). Cyberinformation for seniors. *Journal of American Medical Association, 281,* 16.

Maugens, T. A., McComb, J. G., & Levy, M. L. (1998). The Internet as a pediatric neurosurgery information resource. *Pediatric Neurosurgery, 28,* 186–190.

Mayer, R. E. (1997). Multimedia learning: Are we asking the right questions. *Educational Psychologist, 32*(1), 1–19.

Mazzuca, S. A. (1982). Does patient education in chronic disease have therapeutic value? *Journal of Chronic Disease, 35,* 521–529.

McClung, H. J., Murray, R. D., & Heitlinger, L. A. (1998). The Internet as a source for current patient information. *Pediatrics, 101,* 1–4.

McDowd, J., & Shaw, R. (2000). Attention and aging: A functional perspective. In F. I. M. Craik & T. A. Salthouse (Eds.), *The Handbook of aging and cognition* (2nd ed., pp. 222–292). Mahwah, NJ: Lawrence Erlbaum Associates.

McKenna, K., & Bargh, J. (1998). Coming out in the age of the Internet: Identity participation. *Journal of Personality & Social Psychology, 75,* 681–694.

McMillan, S. J. (1999). Health communication and the Internet: Relations between interactive characteristics of the medium and site creators, content and purpose. *Health Communication, 11,* 375–390.

McNeilis, K. S. (2001). Analysing communication competence in medical consultations. *Health Communication, 13,* 5–18.

McWhirter, G. (2003). The potential for using hospital bedside TV services in England to provide patients with access to health information. *Aslib Proceedings, 55*(5/6), 339–345.

Mead, S. E., Lamson, N., & Rogers, W. A. (2002). Human factors guidelines for Web site usability: Health-oriented Web sites for older adults. In R. W. Morrell (Ed.), *Older adults, health information, and the World Wide Web* (pp. 89–107). Mahwah, NJ: Lawrence Erlbaum Associates.

Meric, F., Bernstam, F. V., Mirza, N. Q., Hunt, K. K., Ames, F. C., Ross, M. I., et al (2002). Breast cancer on the World Wide Web: Cross sectional survey of quality of information and popularity of Websites. *British Medical Journal, 324,* 577–581.

Metcalf, M. P., Tanner, T. B., & Coulehan, M. B. (2001). Using the Internet for healthcare information—and beyond. *Caring, 20*(5), 42–44.

Meyer, B. J. F., & Poon, L. W. (1997). Age differences in efficiency of reading comprehension from printed versus computer-displayed text. *Educational Gerontology, 23,* 789–807.

Mickelson, K. (1997). Seeking social support: Patients in electronic support groups. In S. Kiesler (Ed.), *Culture of the Internet* (pp. 157–178). Mahwah, NJ: Lawrence Erlbaum Associates.

Mickelson, K. (1998). Seeking social support: Parents in electronic support groups. In S. Kiesler (Ed.), *Culture of the Internet* (pp. 157–178). Mahwah, NJ: Lawrence Erlbaum Associates.

Midgely, D. F., & Dowling, G. R. (1978). Innovativeness: The concept and its measurement. *Journal of Consumer Research, 4,* 229–242.

Miles, I (1988). *Home informatics: Information technology and the transformation of everyday life.* London: Pinter Publishers.

Mitchell, S. (1994, February). Technology's best friends. *American Demographics,* p. 38.

MORI (2002). *Internet access statistics.* Available at: www.mori.com/emori/tracker.shtml

Morrell, R. W. (2002). *Older adults, health information, and the World Wide Web.* Mahwah, NJ: Lawrence Erlbaum Associates.

Morrell, R. W., & Echt, K. V. (1997). Designing written instructions for older adults: Learning to use computers. In A. D. Fisk & W. A. Rogers (Eds.), *Handbook of human factors and the older adult* (pp. 335–361). San Diego: Academic Press,

Morrell, R. W., Mayhorn, C. B., & Bennett, J. (2000). A survey of World Wide Web use in middle-aged and older adults. *Human Factors, 62,* 175–182.

Morrell, R. W., Mayhorn, C. B., & Bennett, J. (2002). Older adults online in the Internet century. In R. W. Morrell (Ed.), *Older adults, health information, and the World Wide Web.* Mahwah, NJ: Lawrence Erlbaum Associates.

Moursand, J. (1997). Sanctuary: Social support on the Internet. In J. E. Behar (Ed.), *Mapping cyberspace: Social research on the electronic frontier* (pp. 53–78). New York: Dowling College Press.

Mulligan, J. (2000, Winter). Policy comment: What do the public think? *Healthcare UK.* Retrieved November 11, 2002, from http://www.kingsfund.org/eHealthSystems/assets.applets/public.pdf

Mun, S. K., & Turner, J. W. (1999). Telemedicine: Emerging e-medicine. *Annual Review of Biomedical Engineering, 1,* 589–610.

Munro, J., Nichol, A., O'Cathain, A., & Knowles, E. (2000). *Evaluation of NHS Direct first wave sites. First interim report to the Department of Health (1999).* Retrieved May 12, 2001, from www.shef.ac.uk/uni/academic/R-Z/scharr/mcru/reports/nhsd1.pdf

Munro, J., Nichol, J., O'Cathain, A., Knowles, E., & Morgan, A. (2001). Evaluation of NHS Direct first wave sites: Final report of the phase 1 research. Sheffield: Sheffield University Medical Care Research Unit.

Naisbitt, J., & Aburdene, P. (1990). *Megatrends 2000: Ten new directions for the 1990s.* New York: William Morrow.

Nass, C., Moon, Y., Fogg, B. J., Reeves, B., & Dryer, C. (1995). Can computer personalities be human personalities? *International Journal of Human-Computer Studies, 43,* 223–239.

Nass, C., Reeves, B., & Leshner, G. (1996). Technology and roles: A tale of two TVs. *Journal of Communication, 46*(2), 121–128.

Navaline, H. A., Snider, E. C., Petro, C. J., Tobin, D., Metzger, D., Alterman, A. I., & Woody, G. E. (1994). An automated version of the Risk Assessment battery (RAB): Enhancing the assessment of risk behaviours. *AIDS Research and Human Retroviruses,* 10 (2), S281–S283.

Navin, L., Jones, R., Kohil, H., & Crawford, J. (1996). How should we evaluate a public-access health information system. In B. Richards (Ed.), *Healthcare computing, 96* (pp. 557–562). Weybridge, UK: BJHC Books.

Neff, J. (1999). Internet could see more web site sponsorship. *Advertising Age, 70*(11), 6–7.

Nemeth, C. J. (1986). Differential contributions of majority and minority influence. *Psychological Review,* 93, 23–32.

NetValue (2002, March 28). *Silver Surfers continue to join the Internet revolution.* Press release, London. Retrieved May 21, 2002, from: http://uk.netvalue.com/press/cp0084.htm

NHS Direct (2001). Retrieved October 1, 2001, from http://www.nhs.direct.nhs.uk

NHS Executive (1996). *Patients partnership: Building a collaborative strategy.* London: Her Majesty's Stationery Office.

NHS Executive (1998). *Information for health: Information strategy for the modern NHS: 1998–2005.* London: Her Majesty's Stationery Office.

NHS Information Authority (1998). *Information for health.* London: National Health Service.

Nicholas, D. (1996). An assessment of the online searching behaviour of practitioner end-users. *Journal of Documentation, 52*(3), 227–251.

Nicholas, D. (2000). *Assessing information needs: Tools, techniques and concepts for the Internet age* (2nd ed.) London: Aslib.

Nicholas, D., & Huntington, P. (1999, July). Who uses Web newspapers, how much and for what? In *netmedia99: The Internet conference for journalists.* London: City University.

Nicholas, D., Huntington, P., Gunter, B., Russell, C., & Withey, R. (2003). The British and their use of the Web for health information and advice: A survey. *Aslib Proceedings, 55*(5/6), 261–276.

Nicholas, D., Huntington, P., & Williams, P. (2000). Digital health information provision for the consumer: Analysis of Web kiosks as a means of delivering health information. *He@lth on the Net, 17,* 9–11.

Nicholas, D., Huntington, P., & Williams, P. (2001a). Comparing Web and touch screen transaction log files. *Journal of Medical Internet Research, 3*(2). Retrieved January 22, 2002, from www.jmir.org/2001/2/e18/

Nicholas, D., Huntington, P., & Williams, P. (2001b). Establishing metrics for the evaluation of touch screen kiosks. *Journal of Information Science, 27*(2), 61–72.

Nicholas, D., Huntington, P., & Williams, P. (2001c). Health kiosk use: A national comparative study. *Aslib Proceedings, 5394,* 130–140.

Nicholas, D., Huntington, P., & Williams, P. (2001d). When titans clash: Digital health information providers and the health service square up to each other. *Managing Information, 893,* 5057.

Nicholas, D., Huntington, P., & Williams, P. (2002a). Evaluating metrics for comparing the use of Web sites: A case study of two consumer health Web sites. *Journal of Information Science, 2891,* 63–75.

Nicholas, D., Huntington, P., & Williams, P. (2002b). The impact of location on the use of information systems: Case study—health information kiosks. *Journal of Documentation, 58*(3), 284–301.

Nicholas, D., Huntington, P., & Williams, P. (2003). Three years of digital consumer health information: A longitudinal study. *Information Processing and Management, 39*, 479–502.

Nicholas, D., Huntington, P., & Williams, P. (2004). The characteristics of users and non-users of a kiosk information system. *Aslib Proceedings, 56*(1), 48–61.

Nicholas, D., Huntington, P., Williams, P., & Blackburn, P. (2001). Digital health information and health outcomes. *Journal of Information Science, 27*, 265–276.

Nicholas, D., Huntington, P., Williams, P., & Chahal, P. (2001). Determinant of health kiosk use and usefulness: case study of kiosk which serves a multi-cultural population. *Libri, 51*, 102–113.

Nicholas, D., Huntington, P., Williams, P., & Gunter, B. (2001). Delivering consumer health information digitally: Platform comparisons. *International Online Conference, Olympia December 2001*. Oxford, UK: Learned Information Limited, pp. 145–153.

Nicholas, D., Huntington, P., Williams, P. & Gunter, B. (2002a). *First steps towards providing the nation with health care, advice and information via their television sets*. Report to the Department of Health, Centre for Information Behaviour and Evaluation of Research (CIBER), City University, London, UK.

Nicholas, D., Huntington, P., Williams, P., & Gunter, B. (2002b, September). Health information and health benefits: A case study of digital interactive television information users. *Proceedings of the Information Seeking in Context Conference*, Lisbon, Portugal.

Nicholas, D., Huntington, P., Williams, P., & Gunter, B. (2002c). Digital visibility: Menu prominence and its impact on use. Case study: The NHS Direct Digital channel on Kingston Interactive Television. *Aslib Proceedings, 54*(4), 213–221.

Nicholas, D., Williams, P., Huntington, P., & Gunter, B. (2003a). Broadband nursing: A multi-method evaluation of a one-way video-conferencing health information and advice service: "In-Vision." *Journal of Documentation, 59*(3), 341–358.

Nicholas. D., Huntington, P., Williams, P., & Gunter, B. (2003b). First steps towards providing the UK with health care information and advice via their television sets: an evaluation of four department of health sponsored pilot services. *Aslib Proceedings, 55*(3), 138–154.

Nicholas, D., Huntington, P., Williams, P., Gunter, B., & Monopoli, M. (2002). The characteristics of users and non-users of a digital interactive television health service. Case study—the Living Health channel. *Journal of Informatics in Primary Care, 10*(2), 73–84.

Nicholas, D., Huntington, P., Williams, P., & Jordan, M. (2002). NHS Direct Online: Its users and their concerns. *Journal of Information Science, 28*(4), 305–319.

Nicholas, D., Huntington, P., Williams, P., & Vickery, P. (2001). Health information: An evaluation of the use of health science kiosks in two hospitals. *health Information and Library Journal, 18*, 213–219.

Nicholas, D., Williams, P., & Huntington, P. (2000). Digital health information: Case study of the information kiosk. *Aslib Proceedings, 52*(9), 315–330.

Nicholas, D., Williams, P., & Huntington, P. (2001). Health information kiosk use in health organisations: The view of one health professional. *Aslib Proceedings, 53*(9), 368–386.

Nickelson, D. W. (1998). Telehealth and the evolving health care system: Strategic opportunities for professional psychology. *Professional Psychology: Research and Practice, 29*, 527–535.

Nickerson, R. S. (1994). Electronic bulletin boards: A case study of computer-mediated communication. *Interacting with Computers, 6,* 117–134.

Nielsen, J. (1998, September). *Web usability: Why and how.* Retrieved April 10, 2002 from http://www.zdnet.com/d...es/articles/0,4413,2137433,00.html

Nielsen, J. (1999, July). *Web research: Believe the data.* Retrieved April 10, 2002 from http://www.zdnet. com/devhead/alertbox/990711.html

Nielsen, J., & Morkes, J. (1997, October). *Alert box: How users read on the Web.* Retrieved April 10, 2002 from http://www.useit.com/alertbox/9710a.html

Niiranen, S., Lamminen, H., Mattila, H., Niemi, K., & Kalli, S. (2002). Personal health care services through digital television *Computer methods and Programs in Biomedicine, 68,* 249–259.

Nolan, M., Grant, G., Caldock, K., & Keady, J. (1994). *A framework for assessing the needs of family carers: A multidisciplinary guide.* Guildford, UK: BASE Publication in association with Rapport Productions.

National Opinion Poll [NOP] (2001). *Web access through TV becoming reality for boy surfers.* Retrieved April 4, 2002, from http://www.nop.co.uk/news/news_survey_web_access.html

Norris, P. (2001). *Digital divide.* New York: Cambridge University Press.

National Telecommunications and Information Administration [NTIA] (1996). *Lessons learned from the telecommunications and information infrastructure assistance program.* Washington, DC: Author.

Nuttall, N. (1999, December 2). GM crop toxins are leaking into soil. *The Times,* p. 3.

O'Cathain, A., Munro, J., Nicholls, J., & Knowles, E. (2000). How helpful is NHS Direct? Postal survey of callers. *British Medical Journal, 320,* 1035.

Oenema, A., Brug, J., & Lechner, L. (2001). Web-based tailored nutrition education: Results of a randomized controlled trial. *Health Education Research, 1696,* 647–660.

Office of the e-Envoy (2002). E-government: What's the big idea? *Library and Information Update, 1*(3), p. 39.

OFTEL (2001, August). *Digital television—Consumers' use and perceptions.* A Report on a Research Study. Counterpoint Research for Oftel. London: Office of Telecommunications.

O'Mahoney, B. (1999). Irish health care Web sites: A review. *Irish Medical Journal, 92,* 334–337.

OPSS (1994). *The civil service: Continuity and change.* White Paper, Cmd 2627. London: Her Majesty's Stationery office.

Oravec, J. A. (2000). On-line medical information and service delivery: Implications for health education. *Journal of Health Education, 31,* 105–110.

Owens, B. H., & Robbins, K. C. (1996). CHESS: Comprehensive health enhancement system for women with breast cancer. *Plastic Surgical Nursing, 16,* 172–175, 182.

Pallen, M. (1995). Guide to the Internet: The World Wide Web. *British Medical Journal, 311,* 1552–1556.

Pandolfini, C., & Bonati, M. (2002). Follow up of quality of public oriented health information on the world wide web: Systematic re-evaluation. *British Medical Journal, 324,* 582–583.

Park, D. (1992). Applied cognitive aging research. In F. I. M. Craik & T. A. Salthouse (Eds.), *The handbook of aging and cognition* (pp. 44–49). Hillsdale, NJ: Lawrence Erlbaum Associates.

Parks, M. R., & Floyd, K. (1996). Making friends in cyberspace. *Journal of Communication, 46,* 80–97.

Patyk, M., Gaynor, S., Kelly, J., & Ott, V. (1998). Touch-screen computerised education for patients with brain damage. *Rehabilitation Nursing, 23*(2), 84–87.

Payne, S., Large, S., Jarrett, N., & Turner, P. (2000). Written information given to patients and families by palliative care units: A national survey. *Lancet, 355,* 1792.

Pearson, J., Jones, R., & Cawsey, A., et al. (1999). The accessibility of information systems for patients: Use of touch-screen information systems by 345 patients with cancer in Scotland. *American Medical Informatics Association Annual Symposium 1999: Session 66— Consumer Health Informatics II.* Retrieved June 4, 2002 from www.amia.org/pubs.symposia/ D005289.htm

Pereira, J., & Bower, E. (1998). The Internet as a resource for palliative care and hospice: A review and proposals. *Journal of Pain and Symptom Management, 16*(1), 59–68.

Perse, E. M., & Courtright, J. A. (1993). Normative images of communication media: Mass and interpersonal channels in the new media environment. *Human Communication Research, 19,* 485–503.

Peterson, C., & Stunkard, A. J. (1989). Personal control and health promotion. *Social Science and Medicine, 28,* 819–828.

Petty, R. E., & Cacioppo, J. T. (1979). Issue involvement can increase or decrease persuasion by enhancing message-relevant cognitive responses. *Journal of Personality and Social Psychology, 37,* 1915–1926.

Pew Internet and American Life Project (2003, February). Internet visits soaring. *Health Management Technology, 24,* 2.

Pew Institute (2000). *The online healthcare revolution: How the Web helps Americans take better care of themselves.* The Pew Internet and American Life Project. Retrieved August 30, 2001, from www.pewinternet.org/reports.toc.asp?report=26

Pew Research Center (2000, January). *The Internet news audience goes ordinary.* Retrieved August 30, 2001, from http://www.people-press.org/tech98sum.htm

Pinder, R. (1990). *The Management of chronic illness.* Basingstoke, UK: Macmillan.

Poensgen, A., & Larsen, S. (2001). *Parents, physicians and the Internet: Myth, reality, and implications.* Boston: Boston Consulting Group.

Postmes, T., & Spears, R. (1998). Deindividuation and anti-normative behavior: A meta-analysis. *Psychological Bulletin, 123,* 238–259.

Postmes, T., Spears, R., & Lea, M. (1998). Breaching or building social boundaries? SIDE-effects of computer-mediated communication. *Communication Research, 25,* 689–715.

Postmes, T., Spears, R., & Lea, M. (2000). The formation of group norms in computer-mediated communication. *Human Communication Research, 26,* 341–371.

Prochaska, J. O., DiClemente, C. C., Velicer, W. F., & Rossi, J. S. (1993). Standardized, individualized, interactive and personalized self-help programs for smoking cessation. *Health Psychology, 12*(5), 399–405.

Provost, N., Kopf, A. W., Rabinovitz, H. S., et al. (1998). Comparison of conventional photographs and telephonically transmitted compressed digitized images of melanomas and dysplastic nevi. *Dermatology, 196,* 299–304.

Purcell, G. P., Wilson, P., & Delamothe, T. (2002). The quality of health information on the Internet. *British Medical Journal, 324,* 557–558.

Quick, B. G. (1999). *The role of support groups on the Internet for those suffering from chronic kidney disease.* Unpublished doctoral dissertation, University of the Pacific, Honolulu, Hawaii. *Dissertation Abstracts International, 3705,* p. 1522.

Raab, C., Bellamy, C., Taylor, J., Dutton, W. H., & Peltu, M. (1996). The information polity: Electronic democracy, privacy, and surveillance. In W. H. Dutton (Ed.), *Information and communication technologies: Vision and realities* (pp. 283–299). Oxford, UK: Oxford University Press.

Rabasca, L. (2000a). Self-help sites: A blessing or a bane? *APA Monitor on Psychology, 31*(4), 28–30.

Rabasca, L. (2000b). Confidentiality not guaranteed by most health Web sites, report finds. *APA Monitor on Psychology, 31*(4), 13.

Rafaeli, S. (1986). The electronic bulletin board: A computer-driven mass medium. *Computers in the Social Sciences, 2,* 123–136.

Ratner, J. (Ed.). (2003). *Human factors and Web development* (2nd ed.). Mahwah, NJ: Lawrence Erlbaum Associates.

Reagan, J. (1995). Classifying adopters and non-adopters for technologies using political activity, media use and demographic variables. *Telematics and Informatics, 4,* 3–16.

Redfern, M. (2001). *The Royal Liverpool Children's Hospital Enquiry Report.* London: Her Majesty's Stationery Office.

Reese, S. D., Shoemaker, P. J., & Danielson, W. A. (1987). Social correlates of public attitudes toward new communication technologies. *Journalism Quarterly, 64,* 675–682, 692.

Reeves, B., & Nass, C. (1996). *The media equation: How people treat computers, televisions and new media like real people and places.* Stanford, CA: Cambridge University Press.

Reeves, P. M. (2001). How individuals coping with HIV/AIDS use the Internet. *Health Education Research, 16*(6), 709–719.

Reicher, S. D., Spears, R., & Postmes, T. (1995). A social identity model of deindividuation phenomena. In W. Stroebe & M. Hewstone (Eds.), *European review of social psychology* (pp. 161–198). Chichester, UK: Wiley.

Reuters (2003, May). Reuters consumer-targeted Internet investment: Online strategies to improve patient care and product positioning. *Reuters Business Insight.*

Rheingold, H. (1993). *The virtual community: Homesteading on the electronic frontier.* New York: HarperCollins.

Rice, R. E. (1993). Media appropriateness: Using social presence theory to compare traditional and new organisational media. *Human Communication Research, 19*(4), 415–484.

Rice, R. E., & Katz, T. E. (Eds.). (2001). *The Internet and health communication: experiences and expectations.* Thousand Oaks, CA: Sage.

Rice, R. E., & Love, G. (1987). Electronic emotion: Socio-emotional content in a computer-mediated communication network. *Communication Research, 14,* 85–108.

Rigby, M., Forstrom, J., Roberts, R., & Wyatt, J. (2001). Verifying quality and safety in health informatics services. *British Medical Journal, 323,* 552–556.

Rimal, R. N. (2001). Perceived risk and self-efficacy as motivators: Understanding individuals' long-term use of health information. *Journal of Communication, 51,* 633–654.

Rimal, R. N., & Adkins, A. D. (2003). Using computers to narrowcast health messages: The role of audience segmentation, targeting, and tailoring in health promotion. In T. L. Thompson, A. M. Dorsey, K. I. Miller, & R. Parrott (Eds.), *Handbook of health communication* (pp. 497–514). Mahwah, NJ: Lawrence Erlbaum Associates.

Rimal, R. N., & Flora, J. A. (1998). Bidirectional familial influences in dietary behavior: Test of a model of campaign influences. *Human Communication Research, 24,* 610–637.

Rimmer, T., & Weaver, D. (1987). Different questions, different answers? Media use and credibility. *Journalism Quarterly, 64,* 28–36.

Robinson, R., & West, R. (1992). A comparison of computer and questionnaire methods of history-taking in a genito-urinary clinic. *Psychology and Health, 6,* 77–84.

Robinson, T. N., Patrick, K., Eng, T. R., & Gustafson, D. (1998). An evidence-based approach to interactive health communication: A challenge to medicine in the information age. *Journal of the American Medical Association, 280,* 1264–1269.

Rogers, E. M. (1962). *Diffusion of innovations.* New York: Free Press.

Rogers, E. M. (1995). *Diffusion of innovations* (5th ed.). New York: Free Press.

Rogers, E. M., & Storey, J. D. (1987). Communication campaigns. In C. R. Berger & S. H. Chaffee (Eds.), *Handbook of communication science* (pp. 817–846). Beverly Hills, CA: Sage.

Rogers, W., & Fisk, A. (2000). Human factors, applied cognition, and aging. In F. I. M. Craik & T. A. Salthouse (Eds.), *The handbook of aging and cognition*. Mahwah, NJ: Lawrence Erlbaum Associates.

Rogers, W. A., Fisk, A. D., Mead, S. E., Walker, N., & Cabrera, E. F. (1996). Training older adults to use automatic teller machines. *Human Factors, 38,* 425–433.

Rolnick, S. J., Owens, B., Botta, R., Sathe, L., Hawkins, R., Cooper, L., Kelley, M., & Gustafson, D. (1999). Computerized information and support for patients with breast cancer or HIV infection. *Nursing Outlook, 47*(2), 78–82.

Rosen, C. S. (2000). Integrating stage and continuum models to explain processing of exercise messages and exercise initiation among sedentary college students. *Health Psychology, 19,* 172–180.

Rubin, A. (1983). Television uses and gratifications: The interactions of viewing patterns and motivations. *Journal of Broadcasting, 27,* 37–51.

Rumbelow, H. (1999, November 6). Doctors usurped by the Internet. *The Times,* p. 7.

Sacchetti, P, Zvara, P., & Plank, M. K. (1999). The Internet and patient education—resources and reliability: Focus on a selected urologic topic. *Urology, 53,* 1117–1120.

Salem, D. A., Bogat, G. A., & Reid, C. (1997). Mutual help goes on-line. *Journal of Community Psychology, 25,* 189–201.

Salmon, C., & Atkin, C. (2003). Using media campaigns for health promotion. In T. L. Thompson, A. M. Dorsey, K. I. Miller, & R. Parrott (Eds.), *Handbook of health communication* (pp. 449–472). Mahwah, NJ: Lawrence Erlbaum Associates.

Scott, D. (1993). Status conspicuity, peripheral vision, and text editing. *Behaviour and Information Technology, 12*(1), 23–31.

Schachter, S. (1959). *The psychology of affiliation.* Stanford, CA: Stanford University Press.

Scheerhorn, D., Warisse, J., & McNeilis, K. (1995). Computer-based telecommunication among are illness-related community: Design, delivery, early use and the functions of the HIGH net. *Health Communication, 7*(4), 301–325.

Schoenberg, R., & Safran, C. (2000). Internet based repository of medical records that retains patient confidentiality. *British Medical Journal, 321,* 1199–1203.

Sears, A. (2003). Universal usability and the WWW. In J. Ratner (Ed.), *Human factors and Web development* (2nd ed., pp. 21–45). Mahwah, NJ: Lawrence Erlbaum Associates.

Sellen, A. (1995). Remote conversations: The effects of mediating talk with technology. *Human-Computer Interaction, 10,* 401–444.

Sharf, B. F. (1997). Communicating breast cancer on-line: Support and empowerment on the Internet. *Woman and Health, 26*(1), 65–84.

Shaw, B. R., McTavish, F., Hawkins, R., Gustafson, D. H., & Pingree, S. (2000). Experiences of women with breast cancer: Exchanging social support over the CHESS computer network. *Journal of Health Communication, 5,* 135–159.

Shepperd, S., & Charnock, D. (2002). Against internet exceptionalism. *British Medical Journal, 324,* 556–557.

Sherer, C. W. (1989). The videocassette recorder and information inequality. *Journal of Communication, 3993,* 94–109.

Sherman, D. A. K., Nelson, L. D., & Steele, C. M. (2000). Do messages about health risks threaten the self? Increasing the acceptance of threatening health messages via self-affirmation. *Personality and Social Psychology Bulletin, 26*(9), 1046–1058.

Shon, J., Marshall, J., & Mussen, M. A. (1999). The impact of displayed awards on the credibility and retention of Web site information. *Proceedings of the American Medical Association Symposium, 794–798.*

Short, J., Williams, E., & Christie, B. (1976). *The social psychology of telecommunications.* London: Wiley.

Siegel, D. (1999). *Futurize your enterprise: Business strategy in the age of the e-customer.* New York: Wiley.

Sieving, P. C. (1999). Factors driving the increase in medical information on the Web—one American perspective. *Journal of Medical Internet Research, 1*(1), e3. Retrieved May 14, 2001, from www.symposium.com/jmir/1999/1/e3/index.htm

Silberg, W. M., Lundberg, G. D., & Musacchio, R. A. (1997). Assessing, controlling and assuring the quality of medical information on the Internet: Caveat lector et viewor—Let the reader and viewer beware. *Journal of the American Medical Association, 277*(15), 1244–1245.

Silverstone, R., & Haddon, E. (1996). Television, cable and AB households: A report for Telewest. Falmer, Sussex: University of Sussex.

Simon, P (2001). The strange online death and possible rebirth of brand theory and practice. *Aslib Proceedings, 53,* 245–249.

Singhal, A., & Rogers, E. (1999). *Entertainment-education: A communication strategy for social change.* Mahwah, NJ: Lawrence Erlbaum Associates.

Skinner, C. S., & Kreuter, M. W. (1997). Using theories in planning interactive computer programs. In R. L. Street, W. R. Gold, & T. Manning (Eds.), *Health promotion and interactive technology: Theoretical applications and future direction* (pp. 39–65). Mahwah, NJ: Lawrence Erlbaum Associates.

Skinner, C. S., Siegfried, J. C., Kegeler, M. C., & Strecher, V. J. (1993). The potential of computers in patient education. *Patient Education and Counseling, 22*(1), 27–36.

Slaytor, E. K., & Ward, J. E. (1998). How risks of breast cancer and benefits of screening are communicated to women: Analysis of 58 pamphlets. *British Medical Journal, 347,* 263–264.

Smith, N. W., Sharit, J., & Czaja, S. J. (1999). Aging, motor control and performance of computer mouse tasks. *Human Factors, 41*(3), 389–396

Soot, L. C., Moneta, G. L., & Edwards, J. M. (1999). Vascular surgery and the Internet: A poor source of patient-oriented information. *Journal of Vascular Surgery, 30,* 84–91.

Spears, R., Lea, M., & Lee, S. (1990). De-individuation and group polarisation in computer-mediated communication. In M. Lea (Ed.), *Context of computer-mediated communication* (pp. 31–65). New York: Harvester Wheatsheaf.

Spears, R., & Lea, M. (1992). Social influence and the influence of one "sound" in computer-mediated communication. In M. Lea (Ed.), *Contexts of computer-mediated communication* (pp. 30–69). London: Harvester Wheatsheaf.

Spears, R., & Lea, M. (1994). Panacea or perception? The hidden power in computer-mediated communication. *Communication Research, 21,* 627–659.

Spielberg, A. R. (1998). On call and online: Sociohistorical, legal, ethical implications of e-mail for the physician–patient relationship. *Journal of the American Medical Association, 280,* 1353–1359.

Sproull, L., & Kiesler, S. (1984). Encountering an alien culture. *Journal of Social Issues, 40,* 31–48.

Sproull, L., & Kiesler, S. (1986). Reducing social context cues: Electronic mail in organisational communication. *Management Science, 32,* 1492–1512.

Sproull, L., & Kiesler, S. (1991). *Connections: New ways of working in the networked organization.* Cambridge, MA: MIT Press.

Sproull, L., & Kiesler, S. (1995). Computers, networks and work. *Scientific American: The Computer in the 21st century* (Special issues), *6*(1), 128–139.

Stamm, B. H. (1998). Clinical applications of telehealth in mental health care. *Professional Psychology: Research and Practice, 29,* 536–542.

Stanley, H., & Niemi, R. (1990). *Vital statistics on American politics* (2nd ed.). Washington, DC: Congressional Quarterly.

Steinfeld, C. W., Dutton, W. H., & Kovaric, P. (1989). A framework and agenda for research on computing in the home. In J. L. Salvaggio & J. Bryant (Eds.), *Media use in the information age* (pp. 61–86). Hillsdale, NJ: Lawrence Erlbaum Associates.

Stirling, A. (2001, January). Computer to take over GPs' gatekeeper role by 2020. *Pulse News, 27,* 18.

Street, R. L. (1991). Information-giving in medical consultations: The influence of patients' communicative styles and personal characteristics. *Social Science and Medicine, 32,* 541–548.

Street, R. L. Jr. (Ed.). (1996). *Health and multimedia.* Mahwah, NJ: Lawrence Erlbaum Associates.

Street, R. L., Jr., Gold, W. R., & Mannings, T. (Eds.). (1997). *Health promotion and interactive technology: Theoretical applications and future directions.* Mahwah, NJ: Lawrence Erlbaum Associates.

Street, R. L., Jr., & Manning, T. (1997). Information environments for breast cancer education. In R. L. Street, Jr., W. R. Gold, & T. Manning (Eds.), *Health promotion and interactive technology: Theoretical applications and future directions* (pp. 121–139). Mahwah, NJ: Lawrence Erlbaum Associates.

Street, R. L., Jr., & Rimal, R. N. (1997). Health promotion and interactive technology; A conceptual foundation. In R. L. Street, Jr., W. R. Gold, & T. Manning (Eds.), *Health promotion and interactive technology: Theoretical applications and future directions* (pp. 1–18). Mahwah, NJ: Lawrence Erlbaum Associates.

Stout, R. (1997). *Web site stats: Tracking hits and analysing traffic.* New York: Osborne McGraw-Hill.

Suler, J. (1996). *Why is this thing eating my life? Computer and cyberspace addiction at the "Palace."* Retrieved from http: www1.rider.edu/~suler.psycyber/eatlife.html

Swindell, R., & Mayhew, L. (1996). Educating the isolated aging: Improving the quality of life of the homebound elderly through educational tele-learning. *International Journal of Lifelong Education, 15*(2), 89–93.

Taylor, H. (2000). Explosive growth of 'cyberchondriacs' continues. The Harris Poll, August Harris Interactive. New York. Available at www.harrisinteractive.com/harris_poll

Taylor, S. (1989). *Positive illusions: Creative self deception and the healthy mind.* New York: Basic Books.

Taylor, J., Bellamy, C., Raab, C., Dutton, W. H., & Peltu, M. (1996). Innovation in public service delivery. In W. H. Dutton (Ed.), *Information and communication technologies: Visions and realities* (pp. 265–282). Oxford, UK: Oxford University Press.

Teichmann, Y. (1973). Emotional comparison and affiliation. *Journal of Experimental Social Psychology, 9,* 591–605.

Thomas, L. (1998). The arrival of the Internet. *Nursing Standard, 12*(21), 1.

Thomas, F., & Mante, E. (2001). Internet haves and have nots in Europe. In *Proceedings of the International Conference on Uses and Services in Telecommunications.* Amsterdam, Holland: ICUST.

Thompson, D., Williams, P., Nicholas, D., & Huntington, P. (2002). Accessibility and usability of a digital TV health information database. *Aslib Proceedings, 56*(5), 296–308.

Thompson, L. A., & Ogden, W. C. (1995). Visible speech improves human language understanding: Implications for speech processing systems. *Artificial Intelligence Review, 9,* 347–358.

Tidwell, L. C., & Walther, J. B. (2002). Computer-mediated communication effects on disclosure, impressions, and interpersonal evaluations: Getting to know one another a bit at a time. *Human Communication Research, 28*(3), 317–348.

Towler, R. (2002). *The public's view 2001.* London: Independent Television Commission.

Towler, R. (2003). *The public's view 2002.* London: Independent Television Commission.

Trevino, L. K., Lengel, R. H., & Daft, R. L. (1987). Media symbolism, media richness and media choice in organisations: A symbolic interactionist perspective. *Human Communication Research, 14,* 553–575.

Trott, P. (1996). The Queensland Northern Regional Health Authority telemental health project. *Journal of Telemedicine and Telecare, 2,* 98–104.

Trott, P., & Blignault, I. (1998). Cost evaluation of a telepsychiatry service in northern Queensland. *Journal of Telemedicine and Telecare, 4,* 66–68.

Tseng, S., & Fogg, B. J. (1999, May). Credibility and computing technology. *Communications of the ACM, 42*(5), 39–44.

Turkle, S. (1996). Virtuality and its discontents: Searching for community in cyberspace. *The American Prospect, 24,* 50–57.

Turner, C. F., Ku, L., Rogers, S. M., Lindberg, L. D., Pleck, J. H., & Sonenstein, F. L. (1998, May 8). Adolescent sexual behaviour, drug user, and violence: Increased reporting with computer survey technology. *Science, 280,* 867–873.

Turner, J. W. (2003). Telemedicine: Expanding health care into virtual environments. In T. L. Thompson, A. M. Dorsey, K. J. Miller, & R. Parrott (Eds.), *Handbook of health communication* (pp. 515–535). Mahwah, NJ: Lawrence Erlbaum Associates.

Turner, J. W., Grube, J. A., & Meyers, J. (2001). Developing an optimal match within online communities: An exploration of CMC support communities and traditional support. *Journal of Communication, 51*(2), 231–251.

Vastag, B. (2001). Easing the elderly online in search of health information. *Journal of American Medical Association, 285*(12), 1563–1564.

Velikova, G., Wright, E. P., Smith, A. B., Cull, A., Gould, A., Forman, D., Perren, T., Stead, M., Brown, J., & Selby, P. J. (1999). Automated collection of quality of life data: A comparison on paper and computer touch-screen questionnaires. *Journal of Clinical Oncology, 1793,* 998–1007.

Vickery, P. (2000). *The information kiosk project report.* Truro, UK: Royal Cornish Hospitals, Internal unpublished report.

Vitalari, N. P., Venkatesh, A., & Gronhaug, K. (1985). Computing in the home: Shifts in the time allocation patterns of households. *Communications of the ACM, 28,* 512–522.

Vora, P. (1998). Human factors methodology for designing web sites. In C. Forsythe, E. Grose, & J. Ratner (Eds.), *Human factors and Web development* (pp. 153–172). Mahwah, NJ: Lawrence Erlbaum Associates,

Waitzkin, H. (1985). Information giving in medical care. *Journal of Health and Social Behaviour, 26,* 81–105.

Walker, A. (2002). Growing Older: An ESRC research programme. *Quality in Aging, 391,* 4–12.

Walther, J. B. (1992). Interpersonal effects in computer-mediated interaction: A relational perspective. *Communication Research, 19,* 52–90.

Walther, J. B. (1994). Anticipated ongoing interaction versus channel effects on relational communication in computer-mediated interaction. *Human Communication Research, 20,* 473–501.

Walther, J. B. (1995). Relational aspects of computer-mediated communication; Experimental observations over time. *Organization Science, 6,* 186–203.

Walther, J. B. (1996). Computer-mediated communication: Impersonal, interpersonal, and hyperpersonal interaction. *Human Communication Research, 23,* 3–43.

Walther, J. B. (1997). Group and interpersonal effects in international computer-mediated collaboration. *Human Communication Research, 23,* 342–369.

Walther, J. B., & Boyd, S. (1997, May). *Attraction to computer-mediated social support.* Paper presented at the annual meeting of the International Communication Association, Montreal, Canada.

Walther, J. B., & Burgoon, J. K. (1992). Relational communication in computer-mediated interaction. *Human Communication Research, 19,* 50–88.

Walther, J. B., Slovacek, C., & Tidwell, L. C. (1999). Is a picture worth a thousand words? Photographic images in long term and short term virtual teams. *Communication Research, 28,* 105–134.

Walther, J. B., & Tidwell, L. C. (1995). Nonverbal cues in computer-mediated communication, and the effect of chronemics on relational communication. *Journal of Organizational Computing, 5,* 355–378.

Wanless, D. (2002). *Securing our future health: Taking a long-term view: Final report.* London: Her Majesty's Stationery Office.

Wei, R. (2001). From luxury to utility: A longitudinal analysis of cell phone laggards. *Journalism & Mass Communication Quarterly, 78*(4), 702–719.

Wellman, B. (1996). An electronic group is virtually a social network. In S. Kiesler (Ed.), *Culture of the Internet* (pp. 179–205). Mahwah, NJ: Lawrence Erlbaum Associates.

Wetle, T. (2002). The use of new information technologies in an aging population. In. R. Morrell (Ed.), *Older adults, health information, and the World Wide Web* (pp. 3–11). Mahwah, NJ: Lawrence Erlbaum Associates.

White, H., Gould, D., Mills, W., & Brendish, L. (1999). The Cornwall dermatology electronic referral and image-transfer project. *Journal of Telemedicine and Telecare, 5*(1), 85–86.

White, M., & Dorman, S. M. (2001). Receiving social support online: Implications for health education. *Health Education, 16*(6), 693–707.

Whittaker, S. (1995). Rethinking video as a technology for interpersonal communications: Theory and design implications. *International Journal of Human-Computer Studies, 42,* 510–529.

Wilkins, A. S. (1999). Expanding Internet access for health care consumers. *Health Care Management Review, 26,* 30–61.

Williams, B. (1999a). Provider profiles on-line—making care choices easier for consumers. *Tennessee Medicine, 337,* 1483.

Williams, D. (1999b). *Data plays a key role in net success.* Retrieved October 17, 1999, from www.adage.com/interactive/articles/19990802/article3.html

Williams, E., Parker, A., Stoddard, J., Bomken, S., & Prabhu, V. (2000). Assessment of informed decision making. *British Medical Journal*. [Electronic letter] Retrieved from www.bmj.com/cgi/letters/320/7228/155

Williams, P., Huntington, P., & Nicholas, D. (2000a). Remote health information for the patient: A touch-screen kiosk in action. *Managing Information, 7*(9), 72–75.

Williams, P., Huntington, P., & Nicholas, D. (2000b). Women on the Web: Why the Internet may still be a male dominated information system. *Online and CD Notes 13*(9), 5–9.

Williams, P., Huntington, P., & Nicholas, D. (2003). Health information on the Internet: A qualitative study of NHS Direct Online users. *Aslib Proceedings, 55*(5/6), 304–312.

Williams, P., Nicholas, D., & Huntington, P. (2001). Walk in to (digital) health information: The introduction of an digital health information system at an NHS walk-in centre. *CD & Online Notes, 14*(2), 4–7.

Williams, P., Nicholas, D., & Huntington, P. (2003). Home electronic health information for the consumer: user evaluation of a DiTV video-on-demand service. *Aslib Proceedings, 55*(½), 64–74.

Williams, P., Nicholas, D., Huntington, P., & McClean, F. (2002). Surfing for health: User evaluation of a health information Web site part 1. *Health Information and Libraries Journal, 19*(2), 98–108.

Williams, P., Nicholas, D., Huntington, P., & Gunter, B. (2002). Doc dot com: Reviewing the literature in digital health information. *Aslib Proceedings, 54*(1), 127–141.

Withey, R. (2003). (Mis)understanding the digital media revolution. *Aslib Proceedings, 55*(½), 18–22.

Yankee group (2001). *Yankee Group reports find growing consumer demand in Europe, coupled with fast growth of digital TV, will create TV-based 'Internet for the masses'* new release. Retrieved March 16, 2001, from www.yankeegroup.com/webfolder/yg21a.nsf/press/17CCFD73A796194085256A110049AFE7?OpenDocument

Yokley, J. M., Coleman, D. J., & Yates, B. T. (1990). Cost effectiveness of three child mental health assessment methods: Computer-assisted assessment is effective and inexpensive. *Journal of Mental Health Administration, 17,* 99–107.

Young, K. S., & Rogers, R. C. (1998). The relationship between depression and Internet addiction. *CyberPsychology and Behaviour, 1,* 25–28.

Zarate, C. A., Weinstock, L., Cukor, P., Morabito, C., Leahy, L., Burns, C., & Baer, L. (1997). Applicability of telemedicine for assessing patients with schizophrenia: Acceptance and reliability. *Journal of Clinical Psychiatry, 58,* 22–25.

Zawitz, W. M. (1999). *Web statistics—Measuring user activity, 1998.* Retrieved May 19, 2000, from www.ojp.usdoj.giv/bjs/pub.ascii.wsmua.tx

Author Index

Note: *t* indicates table.

A

Abelhard, K., 181
Aburdene, P., 22
Acheson, T., 62
Adkins, A. D., 136, 137
Al-Ari, N., 130
Allen, A., 22, 44
Allen, J. C., 14
Allen, P. A., 130
Alonso, P., 29
Alonzo, A. A., 30
Alterman, A. I., 148
Ames, F. C., 57
Anderson, R., 4
Appleby, C., 167
Archer, J. L., 171
Arthur, A. M., 38, 51, 115, 138
Aspillaga, M., 130
Atkin, C., 134
Atkin, D., 4, 92, 93
Atkinson, J. M., 78, 83
Atri, J., 62
Attwell, P., 63

B

Babrow, A. S., 34
Bader, S. S., 167

Badzek, L., 34
Baer, L., 49
Baer, W.,
Bagozzi, R. P., 92
Bahte, S., 4, 91
Bailey, B. P., 13, 158
Baker, C. F., 31
Baker, L., 61
Baldwin, J. R., 35
Ball, C. J., 47
Bandura, A., 137
Banyard, P., 178
Barak, A., 169
Bargh, J., 148, 173
Barrett, A., 77, 83, 85
Bashur, R., 44
Beiseeker, A. E., 34
Bekkers, V., 9
Bell, G., 73, 76
Bellamy, C., 2, 7, 15, 17
Bellon, E., 33
Bennett, J., 20, 28, 113
Benotsch, E. G.,
Beresford, B., 26
Bernstam, F. V., 57
Berthold, H., 22
Berwald, C., 147
Beyene, Y., 35
Biner, P. M., 91

Binik, Y. M., 172, 173
Birkhead, G. S., 2
Blackburn, P., 61, 66, 67, 138, 144
Blackmon, L. A., 49
Blignault, I., 49
Blumler, J. G., 92
Boberg, E. W., 42
Bogardus, S. T., Jr., 34
Bogat, G. A., 141
Bomken, S., 75
Bonati, M., 9, 37, 55, 57, 115, 156, 181
Borzekowski, D. L. G., 31
Bosworth, K.,
Botta, R., 139
Boudioni, M., 29, 75
Boulton, M., 29
Bower, E., 169
Bower, H., 37, 52
Bowseley, S., 26, 52, 59
Boyd, S., 46
Boysen, C. D., 22
Braithwaite, D. O., 174, 176
Branger, P. J., 33
Brashers, D. E., 30
Braude, R. M., 167
Bray, J., 28
Brendish, L., 33
Brenk, D., 147
Brennan, L. K., viii, 40, 41, 90, 136
Brennan, P. F., 41, 141
Bricker, E., 42
Brown, J., 21, 30, 60, 62, 70, 78
Brown, R., 147
Brown, S. J., 43
Brownsell, S. J., 22
Brug, J., 41, 136, 137, 139
Budman, S. H., 149, 169
Builder, C., 167
Bull, F. C., 41, 136, 137
Bull, S. S., 139
Buncke, G. M., 33
Buncke, H. J., 33
Bundorf, M., 61
Buntic, R. F., 33
Burgoon, J. K., 124
Burleson, B. R., 31
Burns, C., 49
Burrows, R., 140
Buxton, J., 74
Byers, D. L., 90, 142, 152

C

Cabrera, E. F., 183
Cacciopo, J. T., 137
Caldock, K., 20, 22
Callahan, E., 147
Campbell, A. K., 2
Campbell, M., 136
Cantor, J., 172, 173
Cardillo, L. W., 30
Carey, J., 63
Carrigan, T., 104
Carter, R. F., 161
Casella, N., 9, 37, 55, 57, 115, 156, 181
Cawson, A., 133
Cawsey, A., 74, 77, 83, 85, 88
Chahal, P., 6, 80, 83
Champkin, J., 181
Charnock, D., 53, 54, 58
Chen, W., 44
Cheng, K. K., 177
Cherry, C., 61
Chisholm, J., 63
Christensen, H., 55, 56, 70, 156, 181
Christie, B., 123
Clark, B., 130
Clark, E. M., 41, 136
Clarke, P. H., 49, 147
Clavena, L. E., 29
Cline, R. J. W., 3, 29, 38, 52, 59, 140
Caburnay, C. A., 41
Coile, R. C., Jr., 52
Coiera, 181
Coleman, D. J., 149
Coleman, S., 3, 155
Collinge, A., 15
Collins, M., 160
Collins-Jarvis, L., 13
Connelly, T., 178
Cooke, M., 63
Cooper, L., 139
Corder, L., 20
Cornford, J., 14
Cotton, D. J., 152
Coulehan, M. B., 27
Coulter, A., 25, 55, 156
Courtright, J. A., 93, 123
Cowan, A. M., 22, 69, 71, 176
Coyle, J. T., 49
Crawford, C., 44

Crawford, J., 76, 83
Crispell, D., 4, 92
Cross, D., 20
Cukor, P., 49
Cull, A., 78
Curry, S. J., 40
Cutrona, C., 175
Czaja, S. J., 28, 183

D

Daft, R. L., 123
Dakins, D. R., 48
Dakof, G. A., 31
Danielson, W. A., 118
Davies, D., 25, 29
Davies, J., 177
Davis, F. D., 92
Davison, K. P., 31, 33, 55, 140, 176, 177
Dean, R. S., 91
Deering, M. J., 58, 70, 72, 152, 156
De Ijsselsteijn, W. A., 129
Delaere, D., 33
Delahanty, R., 147
Delamothe T., 50, 53, 54
DeLeon, P. H., 45
Della Mea, V., 33
Dervin, B., 29
Des Jarlais, D. C., 148
de Vries, H., 137
Dickerson, M. D., 92
Dickerson, S. S., 31, 33, 140, 176, 177
DiClemente, C. C., 40
Diehl, M., 179
Diepgen, T. L., 27, 34, 52, 59
Dillman, D. A., 14
Dobbs, L. K., 30
Dochnahl, A., 177
Doctor, S., 10, 13
Doolittle, G., 22
Dorman, S. M., 139, 140, 141
Douglas, F., 77, 83, 88
Dowling, G. R., 4, 91
Dryer, C., 158
Duffy, M., 51
Duisterhout, J. S., 33
Dulaney, C., 130
Dutton, W. H., vii, 4, 7, 10, 11, 13, 14, 15,
    17, 92, 133
Dyer, R., 12, 12

E

Eadie, D., 51
Eaglestone, B., 69, 176
Earles, J., 45
Eastman, C., 130
Echt, K. V., 130, 131, 183
Edmonds, G., 50
Edwards, J. M., 55
Emery, D., 22, 69, 71, 176
Eng, T. R., 24, 34, 58, 70, 72, 152, 156,
    166, 167
Entwistle, V., 25, 55, 156
Ettema, J. S., 92
Eves, F., 177
Eysenbach, G., 27, 34, 52, 59

F

Falshaw, M., 62
Farley, T., 148
Farrell, D., viii, 40, 90, 136
Ferguson, T., 46, 47, 48, 61, 70, 115, 140
Ferriter, M., 172
Fink, S. V., 41
Finkelstein, D. M., 152
Finn, J., 33, 139, 140, 141, 174, 176
Fiore, D. C., 33
Fishman, C., 8
Fishman, D. J., 142
Fisk, A., 28, 183
Fitzmaurice, A., 74, 77, 88
Flaig, D. M., 140
Flanagan, A. J., 161, 164
Flavell, J. H., 91
Fleming, P. J., 172
Flora, J. A., vii
Floyd, K., 123, 171
Fogg, B. J., 158
Folen, R., 45
Forman, D., 78
Foreman-Wernet, L., 29
Forrest, E. J., 93
Forstrom, J., 59
Foulger, D. A., 13
Fox, S., vii, 1, 5, 31, 32, 35, 36, 60, 62, 169
Foxall, G. R., 4, 91
Frank, I., 177
Fredriksen, P. R., 33
French, K. S., 152

Friedman, C., 38
Friedman, S. R., 148
Fuchs, R., 137
Fung, P., 12
Furnham, A., 135

G

Gagliardi, A., 9, 55, 56, 58, 70, 156
Galegher, J., 178
Gann, B., 53, 58
Gann, R., 27, 60, 64, 140
Garramone, G. M., 4
Garvin, B. J., 31
Gask, L., 137
Gaspar-Guardado, M. A., 58, 156
Gates, B., 12
Gaynor, S., 79, 88
Gedney, J. J., 45
Geist, P., 34
Gentry, J. W., 92
George, S., 38, 39
Ghazali, H., 130
Gilbert, D., 25, 55, 156
Gilmour, W. H., 78, 83
Gleason, N. A., 139
Gleuckauf, R. L., 47
Goddard, J., 14
Gold, W. R., 40
Goldsmith, D. J., 31, 32, 35
Goodwin, R., 35
Gould, A., 78
Gould, D., 33
Graber, M., 63
Graham, W., 74, 77, 88
Grandinetti, D. A., 167
Grant, G., 20, 22
Gray, N., 77, 83
Gray, S., 15
Greef, P., 129
Green, R., 12, 13
Greenberg, B. S., 161
Greener, M., 73
Greenfield, S., 38, 115, 138
Gregory-Head, B., 167
Greist, J. H., 172
Gribble, J., 148
Griffin, C., 177
Griffiths, B., 155
Griffiths, K. M., 55, 56, 70, 156, 181
Grohol, J. M., 10, 46, 47

Gronhaug, K., 93
Gronmark, S., 104
Groot, D., 57, 70
Grossman, L. K., 52
Grothaus, L. C., 40
Grube, J. A., 176
Gunter, B., ix, 7, 8, 9, 13, 14, 16, 49, 51,
    53, 95, 98, 100, 102, 103t, 105,
    106, 107, 108, 109, 110, 118,
    119, 120, 124, 125, 126, 127,
    129, 135, 141, 143, 144, 145,
    146, 148, 149, 150, 151, 152,
    155, 156, 159, 160, 161, 163,
    164, 165, 171, 172, 174, 175,
    177, 178, 183
Gurak, L. J., 12, 158
Gustafson, D. H., 24, 34, 42, 72, 139, 140,
    141, 166, 167
Guttman, N., 34

H

Haas, S. M., 30
Haddon, E., 113
Haddon, L., 133
Hagan, H., 148
Hale, M. L., 10
Hall, N., 15
Hamilton, N., 74, 77, 88
Hanka, R., 28
Hardesty, M., 34
Harpring, J., 29
Harris, A. C., 4
Harrison, B., 177
Harrison, J., 17
Hartley, J., 130
Harvey, P., 25, 29
Hawkins, R. P., 42, 139, 140
Haynes, R. M., 3, 29, 38, 52, 59
Hayslip, B., 62
Healthfield, H., 28
Heitlinger, L. A., 55
Hellerstein, L., 172
Hernandez, A., 63
Hernandez-Borges, A. A., 58, 156
Heyes, B, J., 22, 69, 71, 176
Hilgenberg, C., 90, 142, 152
Hilty, D., 147
Hiltz, S. R., 12
Hines, S. C., 34
Hirschi, P., 147

Hirschman, E. C., 4, 91
Hoff, R. G., 152
Holmboe, E., 34
Hoot, J. L., 62
Hopkins, N., 2
Houston, J. D., 33
Howard, P., 34, 51, 167
Howe, R. C., 52
Hufford, R. J., 47
Hughes, J., 181
Hunt, K. K., 57
Hunt, R., 155, 164
Hunt, S. K., 35
Hunter, J. M., 130
Huntington, P., 6, 7, 8, 9, 26, 27, 29, 49,
    51, 53, 61, 64, 65, 66, 67, 68, 71,
    73, 75, 76, 77, 80, 81, 82, 83, 84,
    85, 86, 87, 88, 95, 98, 100, 102,
    103*t*, 105, 106, 107, 108, 109,
    110, 118, 119, 120, 124, 125,
    126, 127, 129, 131, 138, 142,
    143, 144, 145, 146, 148, 149,
    150, 151, 152, 155, 156, 158,
    161, 162, 163, 164, 165, 171,
    174, 175, 177, 178, 183
Huston, G. P., 31
Hutchison, D., 130

I, J

Impicciatore, P., 9, 37, 55, 57, 115, 156,
    181
Jadad, A. R., 9, 53, 55, 56, 58, 70, 141,
    156
Jakobi, P., 130
Jama, M. K., 61
James, C., 25, 29
James, L. C., 45
James, M. L., 93
James, N., 25, 29
Jarrett, N., 54
Jeffres, L., 4, 93
Jekel, J. F., 34
Jenike, M., 49
Jerome, L., 45, 47
Jessup, L. M., 178
Jewitt, K., 148
Jimenez-Sosa, A., 58, 156
Johnson, B., 5
Johnson, J. D., 31
Johnson, J. L., 91

Johnson, M. M. S., 130
Joinson, A. N., 12, 47, 123, 148, 170, 173,
    178
Jones, A., 29
Jones, N., 8, 142
Jones, R., 29, 72, 73, 74, 76, 77, 78, 80, 83,
    85, 88
Jones, S., 51
Jordan, M., 67, 68, 71
Jun, U. H., 4, 92

K

Kaak, H. O., 49
Kaeble, B., 63
Kahn, G., 53, 70
Kai, J., 25
Kalichman, S. C., 61
Kalli, S., 9, 168
Kaplan, S., 38, 115, 138
Karger, S., 19, 28, 36, 91, 93, 104, 114,
    171, 172
Karnal, A., 74, 77, 88
Katz, T. E., 50
Kaufert, J. M., 35
Kawaloff, H. B., 152
Keady, J., 20, 22
Kegeler, M. C., 40, 140
Keighron, P., 9, 166, 168
Kelley, M., 139
Kelly, J., 79, 88
Kennedy, A. J., 50
Kennedy, I., 157
Kennedy, M. C., 140
Kessler, R. C., 46
Khan, K. S., 57
Kiesler, S., 12, 13, 46, 47, 149, 170, 173,
    178
Kiley, R., 55
Kim, P., 58, 70, 154, 156
Kind, G. M., 33
King, D., 139
King, S. A., viii, 10, 33, 46, 47, 177
Kissinger, P., 148
Klein, J., 19, 28, 36, 91, 93, 104, 114, 171,
    172
Klein, M. H., 172
Klemm, P., 140, 141
Kline, D. W., 130
Kohil, H., 76, 83
Knowles, E., 24, 39

Knupfer, N., 130
Konstan, J. A., 13, 158
Koops, B.-J., 9
Kopf, A. W., 33
Kovaric, P., 4, 92
Kramer, K., 130
Kraut, R., 170
Kreuter, M. W., viii, 12, 40, 41, 90, 136, 137
Ku, L., 148, 152
Kunst, H., 57, 70

L

Labajo, R., 29
Lago, C., 181
Lamminen, H., 9, 168
Lamp, J. M., 34, 167
Lamson, N., 28, 62, 183
Large, S., 54
LaRose, R., 4, 92
Larrabee, J. H, 152
Larsen, S., 27, 61
Latour, B., 113
Latthe, P. M., 57, 70
Lavallee, M., 35
Lea, M., 12, 124, 173, 178, 179
Leahy, L., 49
Leake, J., 20
Lechner, L., 139
Lee, C. C., 28
Lee, E. -J., 123
Lee, R., 160
Lee, S., 179
Lengel, R. H., 123
Leshner, G., 158
Levy, M. L., 182
Ley, P., 38, 115, 138
Leydon, G., 29
Lieberman, D. A., 43
Lin, C., 4, 92
Lincoln, T. C., 167
Lindberg, D. A. B., 20, 37, 51
Lindberg, L. D., 148, 152
Lineton, Z., 135
Livingstone, A., 62
Loader, B., 140
Locke, S. E., 152
London, J., 27
Love, G., 170
Lovelock, R., 28

Lucas, R. W., 172
Luck, D. D., 130
Luke, W., 61
Lundberg, G. D., 55, 56, 70, 156, 181
Luria, C. B., 172
Lyons, C. M., 91

M

MacBrayne, P., 91
Macias-Cervi, P., 58, 156
Madara, E. J., 46, 140
Madden, D. J., 130
Mahoney, J., 130
Mair, F., 147
Manning, T., 40, 41, 42
Mante, E., 113
Manton, K., 20
Margavio, V., 148
Marks, W., 130
Marshall, J. N., 55
Martin, D. H., 148
Marwick, C.,
Mattila, H., 9, 168
Maugens, T. A., 182
Maxfield, A., 58, 70, 72, 154, 156
Mayer, R. E., 128
Mayhew, L., 147
Mayhorn, C. B., 20, 28, 113
Mazzuca, S. A., 38, 115, 138
McClean, F., 53, 68, 71
McClung, H. J., 55
McComb, J. G., 182
McCrae, B. P., 177
McDowd, J., 130
McEwen, J., 78, 83
McFarlane, M., 139
McGregor, S., 78, 83
McGuire, T. W., 12, 13, 149, 170, 173
McInray, D. L., 172
McKenna, K., 148, 173
McLachlan, K., 73, 76
McLaren, P. M., 47
McMillan, S. J., 169
McNeilis, K., 139, 176
McNeilis, K. S., 34
McPherson, K., 29
McTavish, F., 42, 139, 140
McWhirter, G., 111
Meana, M., 172, 173
Mead, S. E., 28, 62, 183

Mellinger, A. E., 91
Meric, F., 57
Metcalf, M. P., 27
Mettler, J., 92
Metzger, D., 148, 161, 164
Meyer, B. J. F., 130
Meyers, J., 176
Mickelson, K. D., 46, 173
Midgely, D. F., 4, 91
Miles, I., 133
Miller, H., 147, 148
Milliken, J., 148
Millward, G., 12, 13
Mills, W., 33
Mirza, N. Q., 57
Mitchell, S., 4
Moneta, G. L., 55
Monopoli, M., 105, 106, 107, 108
Moon, Y., 158
Moore, S. M., 41
Morabito, C., 49
Moreggi, D., viii, 10, 33, 46, 177
Morgan, A., 23
Morkes, J., 130
Morrell, R. W., 20, 28, 40, 90, 113, 130
Moss, A. H., 34
Mossman, J., 29
Moursand, J., 46
Moynihan, C., 29
Mukhopadhyuy, T., 170
Mulligan, J., 157, 165
Mullins, P. J., 172
Mun, S. K., 33
Munce, S., 140
Munro, J., 23, 24, 39
Murray, K., 73, 85
Murray, R. D., 55
Musacchio, R. A., 55, 56, 70, 156, 181
Mussen, M. A., 55

N

Naisbitt, J., 22
Nass, C., 123, 137, 158, 182
Navaline, H. A., 148
Navin, L., 77, 83, 88
Navin, L., 73, 83, 85
Needham, G., 53, 58
Neff, J., 167
Neidig, J. L., 30
Nelson, L. D., 177

Nemeth, C. J., 179
Nesbitt, T., 147
Nettleton, S., 140
Nichol, A., 24, 39
Nicholas, D., 6, 7, 8, 9, 26, 27, 29, 49, 51,
    53, 61, 64, 65, 66, 67, 68, 71, 73,
    75, 76, 77, 80, 81, 82, 83, 84, 85,
    86, 87, 88, 95, 98, 100, 102,
    103t, 105, 106, 107, 108, 109,
    110, 118, 119, 120, 124, 125,
    126, 127, 129, 131, 138, 142,
    143, 144, 145, 146, 148, 149,
    150, 151, 152, 155, 156, 158,
    161, 162, 163, 164, 165, 171,
    174, 175, 177, 178, 183
Nicholl, J., 23, 39
Nickelson, D. W., 44
Nickerson, R. S., 47
Nielsen, J., 130
Niemi, K., 9, 168
Niemi, R., 159, 160
Niiranen, S., 8, 168
Nolan, M. T., 20, 22, 140, 141
Norris, P., vii, 2, 3, 7, 10, 11, 14, 49, 133,
    166
Nouwt, S., 9
Nuttall, N., 20

O

Obst, O., 181
O'Cathain, A., 23, 24, 39
Ochs, F., 172, 173
Oenema, A., 139
Ogden, W. C., 128
Olevitch, K., viii, 40, 90, 136
O'Loughlen, J., 49
O'Mahoney, B., 55
Oravec, J. A., 167
O'Shea, T., 12
Osoba, D., 74
Oswald, D. L., 41, 136
Ott, V., 79, 88
Owens, B. H., 139, 141

P

Page, P. L., 152
Pain, K., 147
Pallen, M., 38
Pandolfini, C., 9, 37, 55, 57, 115, 156, 181

Paone, D., 148
Park, D., 28
Parker, A., 75
Parks, M. R., 123, 171
Patrick, K., 24, 72, 166
Patyk, M., 79, 88
Payne, S., 54
Pearson, J., 74, 78, 83, 85
Pedersen, S., 33
Peltu, M., 7, 15, 17
Pennebaker, J. W., 31, 33, 55, 140, 176, 177
Pereira, J., 169
Perren, T., 78
Perse, E. M, 93, 123
Peterson, C., 43
Petro, C. J., 148
Pettersen, S., 33
Petty, R. E., 137
Philp, I. L., 28
Pickering, T., 177
Pinder, R., 29
Pingree, S., 42, 139, 140
Pitts, M., 12, 13
Pitty, D., 28
Plank, M. K., 182
Plaza, S. H., 35
Pleare, N., 140
Pleck, J. H., 148, 152
Poensgen, A., 27, 61
Pollack, R. H., 131
Poon, L. W., 130
Popovsky, M. A., 152
Postmes, T., 178, 179
Prabhu, V., 75
Prochaska, J. O., 40
Proctor, P., 69, 176
Provost, N., 33
Purcell, G. P., 54
Putsch, R. W., 35

Q, R

Quick, B. G., 141
Raab, C., 7, 15, 17
Rabasca, L., 181, 182
Rabinovitz, H. S., 33
Rafaeli, S., 4
Rainie L., vii, 1, 5, 31, 32, 35, 36, 51, 60, 62, 169
Ranseen, J., 49
Ratner, J., 16, 40

Ratzan, S. L., 72
Reagan, J., 92
Redfern, M., 157
Reece, J., 51
Reese, S. 118
Reeves, B., 123, 137, 141, 158, 182
Reid, C., 141
Reynolds, N. R., 30
Rheingold, H., 170, 174
Rhodes, D. M., 90, 142, 152
Rice, J., 148
Rice, R. E., 50, 123, 170
Rickert, V., 31
Rigby, M., 59
Rimal, R. N., vii, 53, 136, 137
Rimmer, T., 161
Ripich, S., 141
Robbins, K. C., 141
Roberts, R., 59
Robinson, R., 172
Robinson, T. N., 24, 166
Robson, J., 62
Rogers, E. M., 4, 91, 92, 113, 118, 135, 136
Rogers, R. C., 47
Rogers, S. M., 148, 152
Rogers, W. A., 28, 62, 183
Roller, C., 63
Rolnick, S. J., 139
Rosen, C. S., 136
Ross, M. I., 57
Rossi, J. S., 40
Rubin, A., 160
Ruebeck, D., 33
Ruiz-Rabaza, A., 58, 156
Rumbelow, H., 51, 115, 141
Russell, C., 51
Russell, D., 175
Russell, J. A., 30

S

Sacchetti, P., 182
Sadler, M., 64
Safran, C., 152
Salem, D. A., 141
Salmon, C., 134
Sancho-Aldridge, J., 159, 160
Sanz, J. J., 29
Sathe, L., 139
Schacter, S., 176
Scharff, D. P., 136, 137

Scheerhorn, D., 139
Scherlis, B., 170
Scott, D., 130
Scott, N., 47
Sears, A., 29
Selby, P. J., 78
Sellen, A., 129
Sen, E. A., 52
Sharf, B. F., 139
Sharit, J., 28
Shaw, B. R., 139, 140
Shaw, R., 130
Shepperd, S., 53, 54, 58
Sherer, C. W.,
Sherman, D. A. K., 177
Shi, Q., 148
Shoemaker, P. J., 118
Shon, J., 55
Short, J., 123
Siegal, J., 12, 13, 149, 170, 173
Siegel, D., 3
Siegfried, J. C., 40
Sieving, P. C., 19
Siko, P. P, 33
Silberg, W. M., 55, 56, 70, 156, 181
Silverstone, R., 113
Simmons, E., 155
Simon, M., 159
Sinclair, K., 19, 28, 36, 91, 93, 104, 114,
      171, 172
Singer, S., 61
Singhal, A., 135
Skinner, C. S., 12, 40
Slack, W. V., 152
Slaytor, E. K., 54
Slovacek, C., 173
Smith, A. B., 78
Smith, D., 60, 62, 70
Smith, N. W., 28, 74, 77, 88
Smith, P., 74, 77, 88
Smythe, K. A., 41
Snider, E. C., 148
Soler Lopez, M., 29
Sonenstein, F. L., 148, 152
Soot, L. C., 55
Spears, R., 12, 124, 173, 178, 179
Spielberg, A. R., 32
Sproull, L., 12, 47, 178
Stallard, E., 20
Stamm, B. H., 47
Stanley, H., 159, 160
Stead, M., 78

Steehnaus, I., 137
Steele, C. M., 177
Steinfeld, C. W., 4, 92
Stirling, A., 51
Stoddard, J., 75
Storey, J. D., 136
Stout, R., 76
Strecher, V. J., 40
Street, R. L., 34
Street, R. L., Jr., 40, 41, 42, 53
Stroebe, W., 179
Stunkard, A. J., 43
Suler, J., 47
Swindell, R., 147
Szczypuda, J., 170

T

Tanner, T. B., 27
Taylor, H., 26
Taylor, J. A., 2, 7, 15, 17
Taylor, S. E., 31, 177
Teichman, Y., 176
Thomas, F., 113
Thomas, L., 167
Thompson, D., 131
Thompson, L. A., 128
Tidwell, L. C., 124, 173
Tirrito, T., 130
Tobin, D., 148
Torres-Alvarez De Arcousa, M. L., 58, 156
Towler, R., ix, 11, 15, 18, 93, 104, 113,
      115, 117, 122, 159, 171
Trevino, L. K., 123
Trim, S., 148
Trott, P., 49
Tseng, S., 158
Turkle, S., 140
Turner, C. F., 148, 152
Turner, J. W., 33, 44, 176
Turner, P., 54
Turoff, M., 12
Tweedle, S., 25, 29

V

van Assema, P., 136, 137
Van Cleynenbreugel, J., 33
van Cura, L. J., 172
Vastag, B., 28
Velicer, W. F., 40
Velikova, G., 78

Venkatesh, A., 93
Vickery, P., 24, 86
Vitalari, N. P., 93
Vora, P., 130

W

Wagner, T. H., 61
Waitzkin, H., 34
Waldron, V. R., 174, 176
Walker, A., 19, 20
Walker, N., 183
Walther, J. B., 30, 49, 123, 124, 170, 173, 174, 175, 178, 179
Wanless, D., 21, 114, 148, 169
Ward, J. E., 54
Ware, J. E., 38, 115, 138
Warisse, J., 139
Warner, E. H., 40
Warshaw, P. R., 92
Watson, J. P., 47
Weaver, D., 161
Webb, P. M., 47
Wei, R., 92
Weinhardt, L., 61
Weinstock, L., 49
Wellman, B., 47
West, R., 172
Wetle, T., vii, 20, 53
White, B. J., 46
White, H., 33
White, M., 74, 139, 140, 141
Whittaker, S., 128
Whitten, P., 147
Wilkins, A. S., 167
Williams, B., 52, 76
Williams, D., 21, 30
Williams, E., 75, 123

Williams, P., 6, 7, 8, 9, 26, 27, 29, 49, 53, 61, 64, 65, 66, 67, 68, 71, 73, 75, 76, 77, 80, 81, 82, 83, 84, 85, 86, 87, 88, 95, 98, 100, 102, 103t, 105, 106, 107, 108, 109, 110, 118, 119, 120, 124, 125, 126, 127, 129, 131, 138, 142, 143, 144, 145, 146, 149, 150, 151, 152, 155, 156, 158, 161, 162, 163, 164, 165, 171, 174, 175, 177, 178, 183
Willis, T., 69, 176
Wilshire, B. L., 41
Wilson, K., 177
Wilson, P., 54
Wimbush, E., 51
Winstone, P., 159, 160
Withey, R., 28, 51
Woody, G. E., 148
Woolgar, S., 113
Wotring, C. E., 93
Wright, E. P., 78
Wyatt, J., 38, 59

Y

Yates, B. T., 149
Yokley, J. M., 149
Young, K. S., 47

Z

Zakrzewski, M., 177
Zarate, C. A., 49
Zawitz, W. M., 65
Zhao, S., 46
Zvara, P., 182

Subject Index

Note: *t* indicates table.

A

Accessing information, 9–11
Accountability, 56
ACTION (Assisting Carers Using
    Telematic Interventions), 22
Age
    and Internet use, 47–48, 62
    and kiosk use, 81
Aging population, vii, 20–21
Age-related difficulties, 28
AIDS, 140–141
Alcoholism, 42
Anonymity, 173, 178
Anxiety over using information
    technology, 69
Application effectiveness, 117, 122–123
Ask Congress, 6
Asynchronous two-way links, 10
Authority, 155–156, 159–161, 164

B

Brain Injury Resource Center (BIRC), 79
Breast cancer education, 41–42
British Health Care Internet Association
    (BHIA), 58
British Medical Journal, 50
Bush Babies, 100

C

Caching, 98
CAREdirect, 23, 54
CarePlus Project, The, 68
Channel Health, 99, 101, 105, 126, 151
Chat rooms, 31
Claim filing, 31
Clinical Assessment System (CAS),
    126–127, 143
Communicopia, 99, 101–105, 126, 143
Comprehensive Health Enhancement Sup-
    port System, The, (CHESS), 42
Computer
    literacy, vii, 1
    technology (interactive nature of), 40
Computer Link, 141
Computer-mediated applications and
    health, 39–43
Computer-mediated communication
    (CMC), 123–124, 134, 148–149,
    167, 170, 179
    concerns about, 180
    hyperpersonal, 174–175
    impersonal, 174
    interpersonal, 174
Computers
    perception as complicated, 28
Confidence, 19

Confidentiality, 180
Conformity online, 178–179
Consumer
    needs of, 60–61
    options, 59–60
Content retrieval services, 10
Credibility, 154, 161, 164, 181
    perceived, 160

D

Databases, 37
Deindividuation, 179
Demographics, 4, 19
    of *i*DTV users, 111
    of Internet access, 62–63
    of kiosk users, 83–85
Developing Emerging Services in the Community, 24
Digital divide, vii, 3, 133
    closing, 4–5
Digital health services, viii, 1
    versus paper sources, 77–79
Digital logs, 120
Digital television (*see also* Interactive digital television [iDTV])
    consumers, 118–119
Directgov, 5
DISCERN, 58
DKTV, 99, 101, 142–143
Doctor-patient relationships, 34–35, 38, 144–145
Domestication of innovation, 113

E

e-democracy, 2
Elderly and online health care, 68–69
Electronic program guide (EPG), 118
Electronic public forums
    establishing, 13–14
Electronic service delivery, vii, 1
e-mail, 33, 37, 48, 176
Emotional support, 33
Emotionality, 174–177
Etiology of a disease, 30

F

Face-to-face communication, 12–13, 31, 33, 123–124, 141, 174
Fear
    over using information technology, 69

Feedback, viii, 40, 123, 137, 175
First amendment rights, 13
Flaming, 12, 170, 178

G

Government
    online, 2
    provision of health and medical services in, vii
    services, 2–3
        electronic, 28, 54, 133
    sponsored initiatives in Britain, 63–68, 80–83
    web sites, 3, 7–8
Group interaction, 45–47, 172, 175

H

Health campaigning, 134–137
Health care costs, 20
Health and computer-mediated applications, 39–43
Health consumer, 182–183
Health information (online), vii, 4, 22–23
    dissemination of, 10
    impact of, 143–144
    needs, 23–26
    reliability of, 70
    seeking groups, 107–108
    and self-care
Health professionals
    communicating with, 47–48
    use of Internet by, 61
Health promotion, 40
Health Information Service, 23–24
Health on the Net Foundation (HONF), 58
HIV, 42, 140–141
Human capital, 3

I

Info/California, 6
INFOCID, 6
Information
    and the appeal of the Internet, 35
    gathering online, 34
Information and communication technologies (ICTs), vii, 2–4, 11, 64, 168–169
    constraints on, 14
    costs, 1

governmental applications of, vii, 1
Information for Health, 23
Informed
    choices, 19
    patient, 166
Interactive digital television (iDTV),
    vii–ix, 1, 4–5, 8–9, 13, 15, 32,
    64, 117, 133, 164–165, 170
    early adopters of, 104–105
    finding information on, 119–122
    health services, 100–102
    perceived benefits of, 145–146
    perceptions of health on, 162–163
    pilot projects (in Britain), 94–95, 96*t*,
    97
    potential as a health platform, 93–94
    real time user measurement of, 97–98
    repeat use of, 101
    self-report data on, 98–99
    service access, 118–119
    as substitute for doctor's visit, 146–147
    television audience measurement of,
    99–100
    video nurse on, 149–150
Interactive video (ITV)
    mediated psychiatry, 44
Interactivity
    complexity of, 111
    use of , 117–118
Internet, 7–8
    and health information, 11–12
    health websites on, 26
    nonusers of, 28–29
    perceptions of health on, 162
    searching the, 26–27
    unregulated sites on, 156
    users, 173
Interpersonal communication, 12
InVision, 126–128

K

Kiosks, 1, 3, 6–7, 24–25, 88–89, 165
    age of users, 81
    automatic office, 6
    children's use of, 77
    health professional's use of, 79–80
    history of, 73–75
    laypeoples use of, 79–80
    location of, 85–87
    methodological issues of, 75–77
    pages viewed per session, 80–81

    public access to, 72–74
    use over time, 87–88

L

Language
    and Internet use, 63
Living Health service, 98–103, 103*t*,
    106–108, 124, 126, 129,
    142–143, 151, 162–163
    nonuse of, 109–110
    reasons for using, 108–109
Lurking, 140

M

Mass communication systems, viii
Media richness theory, 123
Mediated information sources, 31
Medical records
    online, 35
MEDLINE, 51
Message tailoring, 137
Minorities, 62–63
Mobile phone, 5, 47
Mutual aid groups, 46

N

National Health Service (NHS), viii, 1,
    23–24, 38, 54, 105, 108, 143,
    162–163
National Library of Medicine (NLM),
    50–51
NHS Direct Online Web site, 17, 24,
    38–39, 63–65, 80–81, 126, 161,
    164–165
    customer satisfaction with, 39
    user opinion about, 66–67, 126
National Service Framework (NSF), 20, 22
National Telecommunications and Infor-
    mation Administration (NTIA),
    2
New NHS: Modern, Dependable, The, 24
Newspapers, 160
Netiquette, 14, 124

O

Older Web users, 47–48, 113, 129
Online consultations, 47

Online diagnostics, 33–35
Online health services, (*see also* Public
　　service online) 1, 45
　booking appointments, 129
　emergence of, 167–168
　and health status of the public, 150–151
　promise of, 22–23
　and the public, 157–159
　satisfaction with, 29–31
　usability of, ix, 114–115
　user opinions about, 66–68
Online information
　impact of, 137–139, 167
Online networks
　potential impact of, 12–13
Online publications, 50–51
Online support networks
　disadvantages associated with, 140
　impact of, 139–141

P

Patient Partnership, 24
Patients helping other patients, 45–47
Patient's Charter, The, 24
PC-based internet, 1, 5, 9, 18, 24, 117
　regulatory control of, 13
Performance data, 51–52
Political dialogue, 11
Prescriptions
　filling, 31
Printed material, 40
Prognosis, 30–31
Project Vereda, 6
Public Electronic Network (PEN), 10–11
Public service(s)
　agencies, vii
　barriers to innovation in, 15–18
　delivery, 1–3
　online, 5–11
　potential of, 11–12

Q

Quality
　assessment, 57–58, 180–182
　control, 52–54, 155–156
　　addressing concerns of, 55–56
　　improving, 56–57

R

Radio, 160
Rationality, 174–177
Reception of new ideas, 4
Risk
　awareness, 30–31
　of exploitation of patient information,
　　181–182
　perceived, 137

S

Satisfaction, 28
　online, 29–31, 49
　with online health on TV, 141–143
Self-care, 177–178
Self-disclosure, 172–174
Self-efficacy, 137
Self-help
　booklet, 40
　online, 32–33, 169
Setting Priorities for Retirement Years
　　(SPRY), 50–51
Site characteristics, 56
Smokers, 40–41
Social identification and deindividuation
　　model (SIDE), 124, 175
Social information processing theory
　　(SIPT), 124
Social presence, 123–124
Socioeconomic status, 4, 90
　and Internet access, 49
Software accreditation, 59
Source credibility, 57
Specialist information transfer, 48
Subscriber, 98
SurgeryDoor, 64–66, 161
Symptoms, 33

T

Tailor-made materials, 40–41
Technology (*see also* Touch-screen tech-
　　nology)
　adoption of, 91–93, 113
　diffusion of, 4
　importance of, 170–172
　interactive nature of, 137
　and online health care, 22–23

roll out, 14–15
Telehealth, 43–44
Telemedicine, 37, 43–44, 127
Telephone, 1, 3, 23–24, 37, 126
Television, (*see also* Digital television) ix, 14–15, 18, 90, 159–160
Therapists, 181
Touch-screen technology, 6–7
Transactional services, 37, 126–129
Trust, 13, 19–20, 154–155, 159–161, 164, 181
    and older people, 70
Tulare Touch Welfare Advisory, 6

U

U.K. Online, 5
United States Telecommunications and Information Infrastructure Assistance Program(TIIAP), 2
Usability, 117, 129–131
USENET, 11

User, 98
    access, 115–116
    opinions, 66–68
    psychology, 116–117
    remarks, 128
    research, 64–65

V

Video
    diagnosis, 126–129, 147–149
    games, 42–43
    links, 37
    nurse, 149–150
    versus text, 125–126
Visual elements, 126

W

Walled gardens, 118–119
Women seeking information online, 47–48
Written information, 38